ON THE GROUND

On the Ground

TERRESTRIAL THEOPOETICS AND PLANETARY POLITICS

O'neil Van Horn

FORDHAM UNIVERSITY PRESS   NEW YORK   2024

Copyright © 2024 Fordham University Press

All rights reserved. No part of this publication may be reproduced, stored in a retrieval system, or transmitted in any form or by any means—electronic, mechanical, photocopy, recording, or any other—except for brief quotations in printed reviews, without the prior permission of the publisher.

Wendell Berry, excerpt from "The Body and the Earth" from *The Art of the Commonplace: The Agrarian Essays*. Copyright © 2002 by Wendell Berry. Reprinted with the permission of The Permissions Com pany, LLC on behalf of Counterpoint Press, counterpointpress.com.

Tess Taylor, excerpt from "Apocalypto for a Small Planet" from *Work & Days*. Copyright © 2016 by Tess Taylor. Reprinted with the permission of Tess Taylor.

Jenny O'Dell, excerpt from *How to Do Nothing: Resisting the Attention Economy*. Copyright © 2018 by Jenny O'Dell. Reprinted with the permission of Melville House Publishing.

Fordham University Press has no responsibility for the persistence or accuracy of URLs for external or third-party Internet websites referred to in this publication and does not guarantee that any content on such websites is, or will remain, accurate or appropriate.

Fordham University Press also publishes its books in a variety of electronic formats. Some content that appears in print may not be available in electronic books.

Visit us online at www.fordhampress.com.

Library of Congress Cataloging-in-Publication Data available online at https://catalog.loc.gov.

Printed in the United States of America

26 25 24   5 4 3 2 1

First edition

Contents

Introduction 1

Interlude: *The Differences of Our Soils, the Soils of Our Differences* 15

1. *Planting*: Ground Is Not Foundation 18

   Interlude: *Poetics at the Edge* 42

2. *Rooting*: Terrestrial Theopoetics of and for the Planetary 44

   Interlude: *Mountaintop Removal and the Impossibility of Hope* 62

3. *Sprouting*: Dark Hope in Undecidable Times 67

   Interlude: *Seeds and the Subversive Act of Sowing* 96

4. *Blooming*: (De)Compositional Planetary Politics 101

   Conclusion 125

ACKNOWLEDGMENTS 129

NOTES 131

BIBLIOGRAPHY 167

INDEX 179

But digging now I feel an otherness—
Life, a great inhuman freedom—
Here I work a plot that also grounds—
—TESS TAYLOR

Introduction

The soil is the great connector of lives, the source and destination of all. It is the healer and restorer and resurrector, by which disease passes into health, age into youth, death into life. Without proper care for it we can have no community, because without proper care for it we can have no life.

— WENDELL BERRY

A Beginning, On Beginnings

How does one begin something that's already in process, already begun? How does one mark a beginning in such a way as to not erase what makes that beginning *even possible*? If beginnings emerge *not* from nowhere, not *ex nihilo*, but from particular places, from contextual matrices, then is it feasible to open a beginning without erasing past grounds?

Perhaps there is no other way than by invitation, by welcoming one into open-ended becomings, even as one attempts to mark their particularities. This may be the point of an invitation: the invocation of a ritual and the making of space for gathering in a world that is ever in flux.

To tune in to but not force, open but not pry—*that* is the task of any good beginning. But this opening must extend, perhaps paradoxically, in both directions, uncovering both that which enabled such a beginning *and* the possibilities that might sprout forth from those grounds. Beginnings, unthinkably, open forward and backward. What's more, embedded in any beginning is not only what "was" but also what "was not"—foreclosed potentialities, unrealized opportunities, unmaterialized matters.[1] Ritual, in this way, carves space for study and meditation; in a word, it contemplates.[2]

And so, I begin this project as an invitation to the space made here: a study of the concept of "ground" and its philosophical, theological, ethical, and ecological consequences. Beginning by means of invitation foregrounds that this work emerges, like all others, from an entanglement of matrices—scholarly, religious, communal, geographical, cultural, and beyond. The particularities of these webs will manifest throughout and find at least a preliminary explication in this introduction. What's crucial to note here, though, concerns the dipolar space made by and in beginnings: opening the present to *both* the past and future. That is, this beginning uncovers the milieu whence this work germinates *as well as* the trajectories this study aims to take. To mobilize what will become an operative metaphor in this work, I intend to limn here the soils giving life to this work, all the while envisioning the budding aims of this project. To be addressed here—here in the beginning—are the traditions, manners, and concerns that this project inherits and the measures it hopes to add thereto; in other words, this beginning intends to trace the bounds of this toil and its hopeful contribution not just to critical theory or philosophical theology but to environmental justice.

The Anthropocene and the Desire for Ground

The Anthropocene poses grave threats to ecosystemic flourishing. Anthropogenic climate change portends to rupture a vast majority of this planet's functions. And yet, these threats, though they're shared planetarily, are disproportionate and differential in both their causes and consequences—namely, those who contribute most to greenhouse gas emissions, chemical contamination, and so on are often the least susceptible to their ravaging effects, insulated by capital and privilege from the consequences of their toxic actions.[3] To review the scientific literature on the present and pending violences of anthropogenic climate change here would belabor a reality that's already known—indeed, already felt. This project presumes that global climate change and its disastrous effects are caused primarily by human activity and are a reality we are already facing. The volume of research on this reality is immense and speaks for itself.

If not an investigation of the grave futures posed by anthropogenic climate change, what, then, does this project purport to explore? It explores a set of questions around what it means to experience and respond to the Anthropocene in such a way as to account for the paradoxical tensions between planetarity and particularity. In this project, I will argue for the notion of "ground" as a fecund possibility for theorizing the paradoxical co-constitution of connectivity and contextuality, entanglement and exclusion. I contend that ground—when read as the metonymic materialization of ground *as earth-ground, as soil*—carves space for the conceptualization of shared terrain that, paradoxically, remains particular. That is, this project experiments with the idea of *ground as earth-ground* as a way of conceiving of the effects of climate change as collective and yet located, as shared and yet placed. *On the Ground* will thus take on the philosophical notion of "ground" itself, harnessing insights from poststructuralist, "new" materialist, process, and other traditions to reimagine this notion of ground as a liminal, mattering space fissuring the dichotomy of "absolutism" and "relativism," transgressing the polemics of "foundationalism" and "groundlessness." "Ground" does not aim to transcend these binaries in some Hegelian *Aufhebung* but rather seeks something else entirely—subverting or, perhaps better, decomposing these tired binaries. Instead, drawing inspiration from farmers, gardeners, soil scientists, poets, and others, the proposed ground will be modeled after the cycling, shifting assemblage of soil. This earth-ground is never selfsame, certain, or guaranteed, though these represent caricatured qualities projected onto a stereotype of ground as a static entity. In this way, this project does not set out to be genealogical but instead commits itself to constructive imagination, to creative composition. A contribution made by this notion of ground concerns its transdisciplinary vitality: uncovering transversal links between process metaphysics, agricultural wisdom, theopoetic sensibilities, social ethics, and political theory.

The risk of this argument is that the multiplicitous tensions I aim to hold at once will unintentionally slip into one of two familiar categories: that of "common ground" or that of "identitarian essentialisms." The ground argued for in this project seeks a third way—neither content with the erasures of social location that so often come from those who seek "common ground" nor with the siloed and disconnected towers erected by those who wrongly essentialize facets of identity into unshakeable molds. Could the Anthropocene catalyze a different understanding of ground—one that embraces the heterogeneity of difference, ecologically *and* socially, all the while proffering the possibility of *the terrestrial* as a grounding network? In these uncertain times when the future of the planetary is at stake, I argue that it is high time we reclaim the notion of "ground"—a shared plane that supports not only differential becomings but *the very possibility of* becoming. There persists a deeply vital political need for "ground," a material milieu that allows one to grasp the simultaneous paradoxical interconnection and critical difference that constitutes planetary life. In a "post-truth" world marked by "fake news" and "alternative facts" (often manufactured by fascist governments, fossil fuel corporations, and the like), the need for "ground" is paramount—not an abstract foundation that neglects Earth as a "backdrop" but instead a soily plane by which one is constituted and suffused. Ground as soil, soil as ground, will signify a reinvigoration of contextually and perspectivally minded methods, all the while drawing connections between those contexts, those eco-social locations. That is to say, ground thus read recaptures the need for transgressive solidarity across lines of critical difference, thereby rupturing identitarian essentialisms and other siloed approaches of engagement while still directing one's attention to the particular contextual needs of a community—human and beyond. Ground will serve here as a connective commons, yet it refrains from recapitulating the gross indifferences of "common ground," a staple of misguided white liberal approaches to activism, that can easily serve to cheapen vital differences in an effort to achieve some sort of glamorous "unity."[4] Instead, what's sought in this project is a lens and symbol that maintains the need for heterogeneous relations between diverse subjects without sliding into the traps of foundational "Harmony"; ground, as a fragmented-yet-connected phenomenon, does not seek any sort of naïve or "innocent" holism so much as a patchwork web of intersecting and intersectional transversals, in relation but irreducible to any "One-ness" or "Accord." Such a rejection of any method that homogenizes, whitewashes, or otherwise imposes coercive control not only destabilizes classical and modern assumptions of philosophy and theology but further disrupts any ethical mode of activity that does the same.

Experimental Grounds

As is perhaps becoming quickly apparent, this project is an experiment in many ways and in multiple senses.

First, as already noted, this work transgresses the boundaries and borders of disciplines. The transdisciplinarity of this investigation endeavors to embody the interconnected, coalitional solidarity that is necessary to the work of environmental justice. The impending and already-here planetary crises of the Anthropocene require the formation of unthinkable collectives and impossible relations, and it is my goal here, in some minute way, to incarnate these principles by working both within and across disciplinary borders for the sake of more robust eco-ethical possibilities.

Second, *On the Ground* experiments with the *types* of questions it investigates: This project concerns itself *not* with the question of "What?" so much as the queries of "What processes make possible?" or "What relations catalyze creativity?" The question "What?" implies attention to things, substances, objects. While this project makes a case for tending to critical materiality, it does so with attention to *processes, becomings, relations*. If ground is not a "thing in itself" so much as an entangled milieu of forces, matters, energies, animacies, and so forth, one becomes concerned less with "What?" and more with "What lends possibility?" Put differently, the grounding queries of this project involve minding that which enables possibility, that which makes room for novelty, that which carves space for way-making. For this reason, as will become apparent in the outline below, this project primarily aims to cultivate one's consideration of *that which prefigures*—whether ecological, theological, political, and so forth. Additionally, this will mean that this project is concerned with the theorization of what is implied by contextuality, but it does not limit its exploration to any one particular context. This work to conceptualize particularity and planetarity, though, indeed emerges from *nowhere other than* the material grounds of this here author: This work weaves together my experiences as a Californian concerned with the ravages of droughts and wildfires, as an apprentice of organic farming in New Jersey and on land long-stewarded by the Lenape peoples, as a witness to the resilience of Appalachians resisting strip mining operations, and beyond.

Finally, this project plays with language in experimental ways. Informed by the fecund practice of theopoetics, I intend for the contentions of this work to materialize in a performative fashion. That is, I hope to enact and not merely "state" the arguments.[5] My theopoetic commitments are not simply "stylistic"[6] but instead gesture at that which cannot be uttered, either as a consequence of mystery, apophasis, or wonder.[7] *On the Ground* is also something of an experiment in organization, design, and even genre. Drawing on Gilles Deleuze, it is possible to understand this work as an unfolding of rhizomatic questions, a multiplication of lines of flight that still bears some semblance of organization—always at the edge of chaos.

On the Ground intends to explore the following four sets of queries:

1. In the face of planetary climate catastrophe, how might one theorize this calamitous experience as shared yet particular, as interconnected yet contextual? Might there be a way to conceptualize transversal interconnections of experience without erasing the critical constitutive differences, particularly of social and ecological location, therein? What might be the consequences of this theorization when applied to matters of race and pluralistic, anti-racist coalition-building amid the Anthropocene?
2. If a concept or symbol of this nature were possible, what effects might it have on practices of knowledge production—especially in theological registers? In other words, how might this concept more

robustly reorient one's perspective toward the terrestrial, and what would its effects be on theological ethics?
3. Could such a terrestrially attuned conceptual framework offer novel modes for reimagining the possibility of "hope" in such times? If so, how might one imagine this terrestrial hope as different from other, often escapist, iterations of hope? And how might this hope catalyze the possibilities for the crucial work of solidarity in efforts to generate multiracial, pluralistic collectives aimed at environmental justice?
4. And, finally, in what ways might this theoretical framework shape new possibilities for socio-political coalition-building across critical difference for the sake of environmental justice?

These four sets of questions organize the four chapters of this work. Between these main chapters dwell brief interludes, functioning as transitions between, contemplations on, and narrativizations of the contentions of the main chapters. The interludes experiment with storying the arguments of the four chapters, whether through narrative or theopoetic meditation.

Mapping Trails on the Ground

The first task of *On the Ground* is something of a conceptual intervention: I will contend that "ground" is fundamentally distinct from "foundation." Taking cues from Catherine Keller's "Talking Dirty: Ground Is Not Foundation" (2007), Chapter One will parse the distinctions between these two terms that have long been assumed to be synonymous but could hardly, I will argue, be further apart—both in their definitional qualities as well as their promise for critical theory and critical activism. Foundation concretizes the processual into the static, the inspired into the dogmatic, the fecund into the stagnant; ground bears the promise of relational wholesomeness, ongoingness, fertility, and catalyzing emergence. While foundation is a universalizing, homogeneous plane that flattens, at least architecturally, all meaningful difference, the earth-ground, the grounding principle proffered here, is a shifting assemblage, a cycling of relations. Indeed "ground" is irreducible to any one principle, matter, relationship, force, or even species. This relational assemblage called "ground" will emerge not only through continental critical theory, primarily in the works of Jacques Derrida and Gilles Deleuze, but, crucially, the assemblage of ground will materialize as I engage ecologically and agriculturally minded writers like William Bryant Logan, Wendell Berry, Nyle C. Brady, and Raymond R. Weil. This chapter will explore ground as thus liminal in the sense that it is neither some Modern foundation nor some (caricatured) postmodern groundlessness.

Ground is amply material, but it is not reducible to substance—physically or metaphysically. It is better figured as a processual matrix—or, as Berry puts it, as "the great connector of lives, the source and destination of all." My hypothesis, to be investigated in the first chapter, is as follows: Whereas foundations form absolutisms, ground may yet cultivate processual possibilities; put differently, earth-ground enables, while foundations incapacitate. That is not to say that there is some sort of *ur-ground* below or beneath top-soil that enables or sustains, but, rather, the earthy matrix, which is nothing but a web of entangled relations, sponsors the very possibility of life itself—at least for a whole host of land-based subjects.

The subsequent sections of the project will mobilize this conceptual optic across the registers of critical theory, theology, and ethics; that is, I intend to exercise ground as a theoretical principle to uncover more just modes of theologizing, philosophizing, gathering, resisting, and so forth. Ground's messiness, its heterogeneity, its nonlinearity, its decomposing composition, its emergent, even fractal, qualities—all of these matters bear the promise of breaking open present strategies and, vitally, contemporary conceptual lenses for the sake of creating coalitions among and across critical difference.

The second chapter of *On the Ground* will argue that this proposed ground recreates and reinvigorates philosophical and theological imaginations, reorienting one's perspective of the terrestrial and the divine. By re-centering ground as earth-ground, I hope to lay out a plane, a geography, to be navigated. Such a plane may be something of a terrain—not topological, not "from above," but sensed, touched—onto which we're thrown, feet tenderly treading. In short, philosophizing and theologizing must take place with attention to place. To return philosophizing and theologizing to the face of the earth-ground is to reemphasize the complexity of decisions and responsibilities, which are necessary in the horizontal but inessential if one pretends to take on some sort of "from above" approach. To return philosophizing and theologizing to the face of the earth-ground is to render these concerns immanent and material—indeed, to make them matter. To return decisions to the "horizontal" is to reintroduce surprise, imperfection, and novelty. This will require a poetic imagination of sorts. No longer can that purported "bird's-eye view" of the Enlightenment dictate, much less predict, mechanistic one-to-one cause-effect relations; instead, the work of re-grounding one's perspective offers a landscape for encounter that might hopefully reject the abstractions and externalizations that neoliberal capitalism, much like modern philosophical theologies, generate—all at the expense of the planetary.[8] The second chapter takes up the query of a thoroughly terrestrial perspectivalism that requires *poietic* way-making.

It is a terrestrially theopoietic imagination, through the rupture of language itself in the face of divine mystery, that might begin to give expression to, which is not to say, "explain," another *way*—unfolding, unfinished. Here, Édouard Glissant, Mayra Rivera, and Mary-Jane Rubenstein, among others, will guide my work. Reorienting the perspective of the philosophical as well as the theological requires a novelty that may not be possible outside of the poetic, the aesthetic, the affective. These registers, long eschewed by the logo-centric dogmatisms of modernity, carve space for creative discernment, alluring mystery, on-the-way world-making, and cloudy unknowing.[9] To be on the ground is to reintroduce the phenomenon of the horizon, to refigure the unknown as intimately constitutive of the very experience of having a perspective. The mysterious, the unsayable, challenges the predestinies projected onto any such subject or world, as both static projections onto geological systems and fixed conceptions of the divine pretend; instead, the apophatic unspeakable obliges—or, better, invites—an open-ended ongoingness, characteristic of contextually connected, immanently minded, processual theopoetics. In short, then, a grounded philosophical theology materializes in the apophatic rift left by the incapacities of language when faced with impossibility—of the divine and of the disastrous. These matters will animate Chapter Two.

The third task of this project is twofold: (1) the germination of a concept of hope that is sufficiently robust for dwelling amid the ruins of a contaminated planet and (2) the emergence of a model of ethical action and social activism predicated on the concept and symbol of "ground." The former develops a conceptual grammar that pursues the existential and spiritual resonances sparking ethico-political action; the latter illustrates the grounds for contextual coalition-building that may yet be possible when motivated by this resonant, terrestrial hope. These pursuits will materialize in Chapters Three and Four, respectively.

Building on the arguments made in Chapter Two concerning the value and necessity of theopoetic apophasis in the face of the Anthropocene, *On the Ground* will propose a "dark hope"—informed by the dark richness of soil science, the critical theorizations of Black feminist futurities, and the mysteries of apophatic *poiesis*—that is not so much emotive as a catalyst for work, for weaving.[10] This practice of hopeful world-mending, indeed an ember in the task of *tikkun olam*,[11] is not so much salvation-seeking as way-making,[12] granting attention to the contextuality of agency. This process is not fully nameable or sayable, but it continually folds back in hopes of multiplying present efforts seeking better worlds. The third chapter will weave Chapter Two's reflections on apophasis into this exposition on hope, linking the wisdom of apophatic thinking with the teachings of critical negativist theorists like Jack

Halberstam, Lauren Berlant, Stefano Harney, Fred Moten, Anna Lowenhaupt Tsing, Tina Campt, and the Invisible Committee. With their help, this dark hope may yet materialize in unexpected ways: not through pursuits of "progress" so much as precarious modes of habitation grounded in resistant rejection of unjust systems and structures. This is not to idolize or idealize the vulnerabilities that accompany the Anthropocene and have long accompanied the experiences of those forced to the margins. Rather, this is to highlight, to use Berlant's rhetoric, the cruelly optimistic forms of political engagement that reproduce the injustices of the present. This dark hope will serve as a spirited seed, with careful cultivation, to inspire the ethical practices proposed in the fourth chapter.[13]

The proposed planetary ground will take shape as nothing less than interconnected particularity, fragmented entanglement; in other words, ground connects but is contextual, links widely but is ever-local, ever-located. This project will maintain that ground can serve as an operative conceptual tool for activist movements and political coalitions that seek solidarity across diverse social locations without forgoing attention to specific needs and differently experienced circumstances. The intensities of the underway planetary disasters require critical responses: The planetary cannot be "saved" in any pure sense as if all of the toxic effects of human hubris (especially—though not exclusively— as a result of the industrialized West, in its whitest sectors[14]) could be remediated. But, further, the planetary cannot be "saved" wholly or universally, per se; what *may yet* be possible, however, is the renewal and processual repair of countless contexts, myriad milieus, limitless locales—each of which intersects, meets, overlaps, blends, blurs, and melds. These amorphous local zones—each with distinct characters, characteristics, ecosystems, and niches— are linked by the grounding principle of the earth-ground. Yet not a single one rises to serve as some sort of universal. Nor does there exist any sort of total panacea. Particular needs demand particular responses, but these needs and responses remain entangled in and by their eco-political connections. There's a certain porosity at play here: Each context is unique but not impermeably bounded; each community is discrete but not imperviously bordered.[15] Here Eva Haifa Giraud's "ethics of exclusion," in conversation with Bruno Latour's "Terrestrial," will help the particularities of eco-contexts remain distinct but not rigid, such that their nuances resist erasure by the overwhelming connective capacities of the earth-ground. Neither universals nor silos will suffice here; ground, as figured in and by the earth-ground, may yet be a mode of resolute resistance to both universals and silos for the sake of a pluralistic justice to come. *On the Ground* will make the case in Chapter Four for ground as prefiguring politics and as a useful symbol for engaged action.

Which Ground? Whose Ground?

The central goal of this project is the genesis of theoretical tools for the sake of environmental justice. I intentionally use the term "environmental justice" over against "environmentalism" to highlight the entanglement of social and ecological location. As has been argued in various ways, "environmentalisms" often elide or overlook matters of intersectional social justice; alternatively, "environmental justice" meaningfully develops concepts and measures that account for the differential and disproportionate effects of environmental degradation as a function of race, class, gender, ability, and so forth.

If this is the case, then the questions of "Which ground?" and "Whose ground?" must be addressed at the outset—which is to say, here-now. To offer "ground" as a conceptual metaphor and theoretical metonym does not (or at least should not) imply universality, either sociologically or ecologically—let alone theologically. Ground itself, as will be shown, is not *one* thing, and relating to it does not imply a prescriptive set of actions. What's more, human relations to soil cannot be referred to in the singular, as relations to ground are vastly affected *not just* by geography *but also* by histories of trauma, enslavement, displacement, exile, colonization, and so on. So, too, must the interconnections between environmental abuse and gender-based violence—rightly noted by ecofeminists, ecowomanists, and others—be acknowledged.[16]

As a white North American, it is vital for me to contend with narratives of those who have been dispossessed of land by those whose image I bear to some degree—and to offer a critical rebuke of those who have enforced this dispossession—to ensure that the theoretical tools I aim to offer here are not limited in scope or application exclusively to those of the positionality I inhabit. This project strives to learn from and be in deep solidarity with the work of anti-racist educators and practitioners to resist white supremacy and abolish its many manifestations. But neither is this an attempt to speak for communities of color or folks of other positionalities whose relationship to ground has been impacted by white supremacy, colonization, or enslavement; rather, I intend here, as faithfully as I can, to take seriously the challenges posed by these communities and to ensure that my arguments in this project remain accountable to them.[17] To do so, I turn now to U.S.-based Black scholars of religion and ecology to address the queries: Which ground? Whose ground?

To inherit or bear the familial narrative of having been unwillingly bound to land can deeply impact one's relation to ground. For some Black and Brown communities, ecological work, broadly, and agricultural work, specifically, carries not only the general stigmas associated with manual labor but, more pointedly, the cultural traumas of chattel slavery, the painful memories of sharecropping, and the narratives of communal displacement both to the U.S. and within the U.S. Religious environmental ethicist Christopher Carter's 2018 essay, "Blood in the Soil: The Racial, Racist, and Religious Dimensions of Environmentalism," addresses these concerns, arguing that "the ecological burden for black people emerges out of their racialization as a people particularly suited for agricultural work and the psychological trauma of chattel slavery."[18] Carter's work examines:

> ... the impact slavery and segregation has had on black people with respect to ecological care, the role whiteness has played in reinforcing problematic notions of humanness as it relates to black bodies, and how these beliefs have contributed to the overwhelming whiteness of the environmental movement.[19]

Recognizing the differential relations to ground on account of racism will remain a necessary component of the conceptual matrix offered in this project and will find further explication in the chapters to follow.

And yet, at the same time, it is unfair to essentialize or naturalize the reality of environmental degradation and environmental racism as the *sole* experience of Black communities' relation to the ecological. While a comprehensive literature review of this argument is not possible in this space, I offer two examples of this line of argumentation from scholars Elonda Clay and Monica M. White. They argue compellingly for the recovery of the ample narratives of Black ecological wisdom and relation—often erased or undermined.[20]

Elonda Clay's 2011 essay, "How Does It Feel to Be an Environmental Problem," insistently asks: "How did the phrase 'environmental racism' become a signifier *and substitute for* people of African descent as *religious and environmental agents* in much of Religion and Ecology literature?"[21] Clay, of course, does not deny the insidious violence of environmental racism. But she does present a crucial analysis of how this general assumption of the scholarly conversation limits, naturalizes, and essentializes Black environmental perspectives and narratives as solely ones of harm or devastation; in other words, scholarly discourse's treatment of environmental issues related to or affecting Black communities tends to "limit the discussion of religious and environmental themes among African Diaspora peoples to environmental racism and justice" and unintentionally "oversimplifies the complex cultural and communal contexts in which Blacks experience nature and live out their environmental ethos."[22] This limitation replaces the ways in which Black communities and religions are constructive, agential sites of contribution and not simply sites of degradation. Forcefully, Clay reminds, "Environmental racism remains a structural and existential component of black life. Racism is not, however, the totalizing defining cornerstone of African diasporic religious practices or cultural engagements with nature."[23]

Monica White's 2019 book, *Freedom Farmers: Agricultural Resistance and the Black Freedom Movement*, highlights the role of Black agricultural brilliance in the U.S. as a form of socio-economic resistance to the hegemonies of white supremacy and neoliberal capitalism.[24] White begins by surveying the agro-ecological contributions of Black intellectuals like Booker T. Washington, George Washington Carver, and W. E. B. Du Bois before analyzing the rich traditions of Black agricultural cooperatives in the U.S.—arguing that these cooperatives served not only as a form of resistance but, further, of Black flourishing. In line with Clay's assertions, White's excursus reframes Black agrarian relations as defined by solidarity and resistance, not degradation or unconcern. *On the Ground* hopes to hold these important and intense tensions: taking environmental racism seriously—in its multiplex manifestations across diverse communal lines—while not essentializing it. To downplay one or the other is to diminish varieties of terrestrial experience, to devalue legacies of legitimate harm *and* legitimate health.

Finally, Christian theology plays no small role in the nefarious intersections of white supremacy and anthropogenic climate change, impacting potential responses to the queries "Whose ground?" and "Which ground?" Offering a constructive account of ground and its philosophical, theological, and ecological consequences risks the replication of centuries-old dogmas that manifest at once in the purported universality of divine power—which, not accidentally, came to disproportionately benefit white folks—as well as the geographical particularities of xenophobic nationalism. Theologian Willie Jennings's seminal book, *The Christian Imagination: Theology and the Origins of Race* (2011), parses the functional interplay between Christian theologies of "creation" and colonial, white supremacist occupation of land. Referring to the work of sixteenth-century theologian and colonizer José de Acosta, Jennings traces the legacy of Christian theology's assertion of an ostensibly innocent "doctrinal logic"—"that God created the world"—as the theological "permission" sanctioning European colonizers' "classificatory subjugation of all nonwhite, non-Western peoples."[25] With the "discovery" of the so-called New World emerges the separation of "theology from the earth for the sake of theology's coherence," meaning that Christian theology's coherence required its detachment from land, from ecological wisdom, from grounded and native lifeways. (And none of this even begins to capture the vast histories of Christianity's classificatory exclusion, erasure, and eradication of non-Christian practices deemed pagan, heathen, savage, or similar.) Jennings explains that white Christian hegemony operates in and through the imagination and production of space—drawn and territorialized on actual land.²⁶ The purported universality, or *placelessness*, of the divine, in other words, grants legitimacy to white land grabs and other exploitative, extractive practices. This is duplicity par excellence. As Jennings notes, "That spatial dimension [of segregationalist mentalities] must be seen not as a product of behavior (that is, people that isolate themselves along cultural difference), but as the dual operation of the way the world is imagined and the way social worlds constitute the imagination."²⁷ There is, thus, a simultaneity at play here that remains impossible to disentangle: the imagination of worlds as effecting eco-social possibility and the effects of the world on eco-social imaginations.

Jennings's constructive turn near the end of the book opens a way to rethink "ground" in manners that maintain its paradoxical function as connective yet placed, as transversal yet contextual: "If Christianity is going to untangle itself from these mangled spaces, it must first see them for what they are: a revolt against creation. This recognition *turns toward a far more grounded vision of a doctrine of creation.*"²⁸ That is, "The moment the land is removed as a signifier of identity, it is also removed as a site of *transformation through relationship.*"²⁹ Christianity, Jennings argues, must reimagine its bonds with the terrestrial in ways that foster wholesome relations—both socially and ecologically. More broadly, he expresses, conceptual registers cannot function out of relation with the terrestrial—whether as a cause of (willful) ignorance or assumed transcendence—and must begin to recognize that which grounds material possibility. Of course, the potential danger lurking here is that renewing land as a crucial signifier of identity could re-calcify into new and newly violent iterations of "blood and soil." To return to ground could yet imply a (re)turn to territoriality, to jingoism, to colonization. This is far from Jennings' intention—or that of this project—but the risk remains and must be guarded against.

What does a return to the earth-ground look like if not xenophobic nationalisms and their effectual regimes? This project—through its reimagination of ground as process, as ungrounding, as (de)compositional³⁰—hopes to open new ways of theorizing terrestrial relation that do not lead to the evils of nationalism or fascism. Ground, understood in the ways articulated in this work, serves as the site of Jennings's hope for "transformation through relationship." Such a change of imagination, returning to the terrestrial as an integral factor in one's theologizing (and so much more), remains necessary despite its risks, Jennings reasons. He asserts that this change of imagination "is not only necessary but now stands before human communities *as the only real option for survival* in a world of dwindling natural resources and tightening global economic chains of commodification."³¹ *There is no hope outside of, away from, or out of touch with the terrestrial.* The gravity of the Anthropocene leaves no other option for making a way than by tending to the earth-ground. And toiling for environmental justice in this way constitutes an opportunity to embrace and repair the communion of the eco-socio-located differences of and by which we are constituted.

The conceptual metaphor of ground thus does not seek to erase the histories of land and its exploitation. In fact, ground as a storied milieu, as a narrativized matrix, can only reckon with these histories if it is to take on the processual, affective, and affecting capacities of and as earth-ground—distinct from the erasure of these placed accounts as realized under the auspices of "*foundation.*"

It is my hope that *On the Ground* will catalyze new possibilities for thought and action, theory and praxis, dedicated to environmental justice. This project represents but a minute kernel of the toil necessary in and against the Anthropocene. Echoing in deep humility the words of theorist and organizer adrienne maree brown, "If this is being read in a future in which this language has evolved, then please know I would be evolving right along with you."[32] Or such is my prayer. With that, I invite you into this work, exploring the possibilities sprouting forth from ground, hoping that it might inspire coalitions working faithfully toward more just futures.

Interlude
The Differences of Our Soils, the Soils of Our Differences

The rich auburn hue of that soil is nearly impossible to forget. Padding along the ridgeline—steep hillsides on either side dotted with *gana'o* (livestock) seeking shade under *guanacaste* trees—I followed the short but sturdy man I had been living with for a few weeks at that point. What he lacked in height, he made up for with an abundant, if somewhat abrasive, sense of humor, teaching me about the land, always punctuated with hearty laughs about whatever it was that we had encountered. Tracing the spine of the hilltops, we made our way to a rare bit of relatively flat land with the intention of sowing *chayote* seeds. Bare hands in the deep red clay-laden soil, we placed two or three seeds in each small hole we had dug, hoping that at least one would sprout in the coming weeks—*si Dios quiere*, God willing.

Nestled in the mountains outside of San José, about two hours—sometimes longer—by bus, Guaitil de Acosta, a town that hardly even appears on detailed maps of Costa Rica,[1] is similar to many other rural communities that tourists rarely visit: dirt roads, a small *soda* (a simple, traditional Costa Rican restaurant), a few *tienditas*, one church, and a quiet cemetery. I spent my time there living with a host family and joining them in whatever they got up to: attending mass, watching *telenovelas*, mending fences, milling wood, herding cattle on hillsides steeper than I once thought cattle could handle. I cherish the memories of this land and my "found family" there.

But I have noticed that one of the memories lingering on my mind most often is of the soil there. Initially, I think it was simply because of how vivid its colors were. Having been raised among the coastal scrub of Southern California—sagebrush and chaparral and buckwheat—I had grown accustomed to thinking of soil as sandy, silty, and perpetually dry. Prone to erosion and interspersed with sandstone formations, the soils of my home could hardly be more dissimilar to the burgundy clays of Guaitil. Surely these two substances could not be referred to by the same name—soil, ground. And yet.

As years have passed, I think my memory of Guaitil's soil has stayed with me for other, deeper reasons. The ravages of climate change portend cataclysms for places like Guaitil—unbearable heat, yearly record-breaking rainfall, and the potential for unthinkably massive landslides. So, too, does climate change promise even greater destruction to the Californian hills of coastal live oaks and black mustard that raised me—more than they have yet faced, as any time of the year now is apparently "fire season," as it's called.

How does one conceive of how radically shared yet vastly differential the effects of climate change are? We endure it planetarily, sharing a certain reality of violence, and yet it is radically particular, driven by particular regimes—corporate, gubernatorial, militaristic, and beyond—and impacting particular communities. It appears, then, at least to me, that the following claim is simultaneously both amply true and utterly false: "We share a planetary fate." Yes and no; no and yes. Those who endure the worst of climate change's effects seem to be (and, according to any reliable climate modeling, *will be*) those who have contributed least to its causes; those who have contributed most to its causes seem to be (and, if the structures of globalized finance capitalism persist, *will be*) those who are most capable of insulating themselves from its effects. And yet there is no transcendent escape, at least for the 99 percent. What, then, of the transcendental?

How might one adequately figure the impending and already-here burdens of the Anthropocene without flattening the crucial differences therein? Surely the United States and Costa Rica, broadly speaking, are substantially uneven in their culpability and thus responsibility for this climate crisis. And yet the two remain inescapably, planetarily entangled.

What precisely is it that grounds relations—whether human or climatic? What exactly was it that transversed my host family and me, a communal bond persisting in spite of—or is it because of?—the differences by which we're constituted? Surely it was something more than a shared language, native for them and laboriously learned for me.

To what extent can we relate across the differences by which we are constituted? How radically diverse can pluralistic coalitions become before those critical differences constitute impossible ruptures? Where are there edges of empathy, the limits that constrain how deeply one can feel or attune to the experiences of another? What are the bounds of a bioregion and thus the corresponding eco-ethic in relation thereto?

INTERLUDE: THE DIFFERENCES OF OUR SOILS, THE SOILS OF OUR DIFFERENCES

The red clay of Guaitil makes me wonder about that which undergirds our becomings, the ground itself surely eluding the trappings of a selfsame substance. The sandy soils of my fire-scorched home testify to the fallacies of that mindset. Neither solid rock nor sinking sand, this milieu of milieux transmutes differentially, yet sustains all the same (though it is never, in fact, "the same"). The disasters that were and are and are to come demand attention to the simultaneity of contextuality and mutuality: the entanglement of difference, the differences of entanglement. And I think that mystery is what I sensed in those surprisingly bright yet luminously dark clays of Guaitil: *Perhaps there's something in the soil worth listening to.*

1
Planting
Ground Is Not Foundation

> It turns out that groundedness requires *actual ground*.
> —JENNY O'DELL

Beginning—On the Ground

Anthropogenic climate change demands collective action on an unthinkable scale. To limit global temperature increase and thereby mitigate associated, consequential feedback loops, it is necessary to conceptualize a transversal terrain upon which to organize and resist both present and impending environmental injustices. There must be some sort of ground upon which to stake one's truth claims to make meaningful change for the sake of sustainability, wholesomeness, and even repair. But neither can this ground calcify into some unyieldingly violent foundationalism, upon which all truth claims appear as flags planted for the sake of domination. Still, what would it look like to theorize the co-constitutive nature of planetarity and particularity for the sake of environmental justice? What are the grounds for such a preposterous possibility?

In light of the potential prospect of misreading these claims, there is perhaps no single phrase more important to this project than the following: *Ground is not foundation*. This chapter intends to argue this very point, to experiment with this earthy hypothesis. That is, this chapter will contend for the earth-ground as the grounding principle—or, as Jenny O'Dell puts it, "an *actual ground*"—for any sort of philosophizing, theologizing, politicking, resisting, and so on. And yet that grounding principle must not be equated with foundation.

To fail to make this case adequately, if not compellingly, will mean the failure of the project as a whole. Behold, the cornerstone.

But, for what reasons is "ground" important conceptually, if not ethico-politically? Ground gives us something to stand on—something to take a stand on. In this moment of global climate crisis—coupled with the delegitimization of truth, the dismissal of science, and the amplifications of racial capitalism—it is most necessary to conceptualize and construct a plane upon which to make claims, to organize collectives, and to resist regimes. There is a need for ground in a material, eco-political, and perhaps even eco-spiritual sense. Ground, when figured as the earth-ground, allows for the genesis of concepts that are immanently earthen and that refuse to envisage the ecological as an accessory to one's theorizing.[1] The Anthropocene requires terrestrial concepts: ideas thoroughly suffused in and as the earthen—ideas that craft possibilities for sustaining, regenerating, and so on. It is for this reason—the political vitality of ground—that this project is not *solely* concerned with a politics of soil—that is, this work maintains that soil and ground must remain thoroughly entangled and, thus, seeks to contribute the notion of ground to extant soil-centric political theories.[2] Hence the term "earth-ground" when referencing this vibrantly muddled mesh of terms. While soil is, indeed, ground, it is crucial to maintain the relational capacities and political potencies of the term "ground" without diminishing the terrestriality of such a notion.

Such a declaration—ground is not foundation—represents a meaningful distinction with a meaningful difference, but it is one that I cannot claim to have invented. Constructive theologian Catherine Keller, in her 2007 *Ecospirit* chapter, "Talking Dirty: Ground Is Not Foundation," makes this very assertion.[3] She contends, "So what if we now declare: *let the earth itself be the ground*; let every grounding metaphor acknowledge its place, its earth, and its planetary context."[4] Such an assertion, we will find, shakes the foundations of crucial elements of human experience: that of epistemology, of economics, of religiosity, of ethics, of . . .

This chapter aims to explicate and extend Keller's argument distinguishing ground from foundation in primarily philosophical registers. Here I will parse the distinctions between these two concepts that have long been assumed to be synonymous and, therefore, often functioned as such; yet, these two terms operate with entirely different theoretical symbols and thus entail vastly differing ethical consequences.

This relational assemblage called "ground" will emerge throughout this chapter through engagement with continental philosophy, materialist theories, and, crucially, ecologically and agriculturally committed writings. To put it tersely, not only will I distinguish ground from foundation, but I will make a case for the *metonymic materialization* of ground as the earth-ground—or, soil. I intend to construct here the concept of "ground" by asking: What concepts can soil create? What can soil science teach philosophy?

If any meaningful nurture of the earth-ground is to be possible, it will come with, in David Macauley's terms, its "re-story-ation."[5] With the conceptual lenses constructed here, I hope to contribute to ground's restorative re-story-ation, re-narrativizing it as vibrant, vitally *prefiguring*, and *constituting* human experience and identity. Ground will be figured in this project as sensible and symbolic, material and metaphoric: a "matterphor."[6] Sought here is the entanglement of the material and the discursive, the weaving of *ecological location* and *social location*. Hence, the ground conceptualized here will sprout forth in the transdisciplinary nexus of critical theory, biological science, and eco-ethical praxis.

Eroding Ground as Foundation

Ground is not foundation. To introduce the difference, foundation concretizes, imposes, constrains. Foundations are situated thoroughly in the *anthro-*, often as attempts to control, mitigate, restrict, settle. Ground, nestled in the *geo-*, bears the promise of renewal, of ongoingness, of fecundity. Foundations homogenize and flatten difference, seeking sameness, immovability, and linearity. The earth-ground, the grounding principle of this project, is a cycling assemblage of relations, processes, affects, and animacies. Ground, unlike foundation, is irreducible—a confluence of principles, minerals, cycles, disturbances, and species.

With the advent of poststructuralism and its multiple offshoots thereafter comes a fierce critique of foundations and foundationalisms. Taking cues from Keller, I will argue two points in this section: (1) poststructuralist (et al.) philosophies, in their indispensable critique of foundations, improperly collapse the difference between ground and foundation, and (2) the foundation-breaking force of these philosophies actually, and perhaps somewhat surprisingly, informs the concept of ground constructed here. I must, therefore, work against these critical theories' tendency to throw the baby (ground) out with the bathwater (foundation), all the while making the case that this ground develops and even multiplies the vital deconstructive and deterritorializing capacities of these theoretical modes. To be terse about it, and perhaps surprisingly, I'll propose a Derridean notion of ground in this chapter.

On multiple occasions, Jacques Derrida decried the ontotheological essentialisms pervading the false assumption that there might be some sort of foundation purportedly buttressing the endless process of signification in language: "The genetic root-system refers from sign to sign. No ground of nonsignification—understood as insignificance or an intuition of a present truth—stretches out to give it foundation under the play and the coming into being of signs."[7] It is not the Signified that "grounds" the signifier; nor is the Signified that which founds the possibility of meaning for that signifier. Nothing stretches below; nothing superintends from above. There is neither Transcendental nor Transcendent.[8] According to Derrida, it is simply the horizontal processes of signification that generate meaning; anything more than this, and it inevitably calcifies into some ontotheological foundationalism. Even Derrida's "trace," the specter that persists in a sign but is not purely present, cannot be equated with even any residue of foundational origin:

> The trace is not only the disappearance of origin—within the discourse that we sustain and according to the path that we follow it means that the origin did not even disappear, that it was never constituted except reciprocally by a nonorigin, the trace, which thus becomes the origin of the origin. From then on, to wrench the concept of the trace from the classical scheme, which would derive it from a presence or from an originary nontrace and which would make of it an empirical mark, one must indeed speak of an originary trace or arche-trace. *Yet we know that that concept destroys its name and that, if all begins with the trace, there is above all no originary trace.*[9]

In *Positions*, Derrida decries, ". . . have I not indefatigably repeated—and I would dare say demonstrated—that the trace is neither a ground, nor a foundation, nor an origin, and that in no case can it provide for a manifest or disguised ontotheology?"[10] Until this point, Derrida and I are very much in agreement. My major qualm, though, is that Derrida unfortunately synonymizes ground and foundation here, and he does the same in his description of *différance*:

> The ontico-ontological difference and its ground [*Grund*] in the "transcendence of Dasein" [*Vom Wesen des Grundes*] are not absolutely originary. Différance by itself would be more "originary," but *one* would no longer be able to call it "origin" or "ground," those notions belonging essentially to the history of onto-theology, to the system functioning as the effacing of difference.[11]

Deconstructing Heidegger's foundational concern, the "ontico-ontological difference," through the fissuring-principle of différance, Derrida moves to shatter any possible underlying or overlording *fond* that would make meaning *final* and *present*.[12] This Derridean criticism makes all kinds of sense, as any sort of foundation or origin tends to concretize the free-play of signification into hierarchies ever-bound in static relation to some sort of absolute Logos: be it God or, God forbid, some other transcendental Signified. But, I maintain that *even a Derridean antifoundationalism need not dispose of ground*, for its eradication also removes the crucial eco-political plane upon which we must somehow persist. One can see the relations between the processes of undesired concretization, of substantive solidification, of the spatial (foundation) and the temporal (origin). It is this understanding of *foundation as origin* that begs deconstruction—but not at the expense of, not by *dispensing with*, ground. In a word, the ground argued for here shares Derrida's antifoundationalist concerns, all while maintaining the acute necessity of "ground" as a terrestrial plane for engagement across lines of critical difference. As will be conveyed below, ground, far from mere support for a foundation, *actually performs* a fissuring, deconstructive force while serving as a milieu of intra-active becoming; what will materialize, then, is the alluring alternative: *ground as beginning*.

Particularly pertinent to this project's concerns are the ways in which Derrida's argument, as has been amply shown, resonates with many postcolonial theorists' contention that the foundationalisms inherent in founding narratives and origin stories articulate trajectories of power and hierarchies of value for the present. Postcolonial theorist Edward W. Said memorably deconstructs the distinction between "origin" and "beginning" in his 1975 *Beginnings: Intention and Method*. Said is understandably wary of any iteration of "origin," illustrating how such normative universals serve as weapons against marginalized and colonized communities.[13] Origins connote linear projections, unbending principles. These origins congeal the value-systems of the powerful into unshakeable, often theological, dogmas. Put differently, these narratives say more about present organizations of power than they do about the past. More recently, geological theorist Kathryn Yusoff's indispensable book, *A Billion Black Anthropocenes or None* (2019), practices this critique of origins, questioning the reasoning behind variously selected "start dates" for the Anthropocene, each of which elides the experiences of those whose worlds have, for all intents and purposes, already ended:

> Origins draw borders that define inclusion and exclusion, and their focus is narrow, narrating a line of purpose (read: Progress) and purposefulness (read: Civilization), while overlooking accident, misdirection, or the shadow geology of dispensable lives, waste, toxicity, contamination, extinction, and exhaustion.[14]

Yusoff maintains, "Origins configure and prefigure the possibility of narratives of the present. . . . Origins, then, are another word for an account of agency or a trajectory of power."[15] Is there any way to separate ground from this colonial legacy of origins? Do these critiques not wholly undo any possible move to conceptualize and construct with this "ground"? Does it not hopelessly replicate these violent founding narratives with no promise of creativity, of fertility? To the contrary . . .

Said offers a crucial distinction between origin and beginning, which mirrors that of foundation and ground: "Whereas origin centrally dominates what derives from it, the beginning . . . encourages nonlinear development. . . ."[16] Beginning connotes ongoing creative processes—unfolding, spiraling, *activity*. As Said notes, "The beginning . . . is the first step in the production of meaning."[17] Beginnings grant agency; origins strip away capacity. "In short, beginning is *making* or *producing difference* . . . ," Said succinctly conveys.[18]

Beginnings are a fertile ground whereas origins are impervious foundations: One offers the potentiality for organic emergence, and the other forecloses any such possibility. Temporality breaks open in beginnings, granting possibility for growth—as opposed to the foreclosing thereof as performed by origins. A beginning is not from no-where (nor is it *ex nihilo*) but instead emerges from an extant milieu, from existing soils—however rich or contaminated. That is, because there is no adequate or possible definite article which will suffice, there is no longer "The Beginning" but only ever "when beginning. . . ."[19] To begin is only ever to begin again. A beginning is not a colonial universal but a shared transversal of connected difference—crafted, woven. As Keller argues, beginning "presupposes always a tangled complexity of relations" over against the undeviating singularity of origins.[20] Beginning is neither origin nor cemented certitude. Origins are passive—they pacify, signifying that "what is" is given, that "what is" is the rule. In Said's words, "I use *beginning* as having the more active meaning, and *origin* the more passive one: thus 'X *is the origin of* Y,' while 'The beginning A *leads to* B. . . . [O]rigins, because of their passivity, are put to uses that I believe ought to be avoided."[21] Rather than a singular source of creation, "beginning" is a space of starting together, of co-constitutive becoming, far from the calcified sterilities of ontotheologies, of colonial regimes, of oppressive norms. The cycling and recycling of beginnings prevent such calcification: ". . . beginning is basically an activity which ultimately implies return and repetition rather than simple linear accomplishment. . . ."[22] "Linear accomplishment" suggests the assumed, placating norms put in place by—but often pretended to be a priori, given, foreordained—extant Powers that Be. Beginnings readily multiply, whereas origins are in service of the One. As will become apparent in the materialization of ground as soil, ground is active *and activates*.

The violences of foundations and their respective "isms" clearly abound. They not only propose fixed origins inexorably joined to their transcendent form, but these conceptual registers materialize in political praxis in ways that systemically harm those who don't fall into or, perhaps better, those who have been *displaced from* and *pushed out of* the neat categories, straight borders, and tidy boxes of the powerful, the privileged. The ground posited here hopes to rupture these very matters, all the while advancing a concept that maintains a sense of both relational becoming and contextual particularity. But before this can be argued, we must turn once more to Derrida's critique of ground.

Derrida consistently tosses out any promise of ground—utterly too similar to the foundations he seeks to undermine. As he curtly reflects in *Rogues*,

> I don't need to remind you of the proximity between many of the figures of reason and those of the bottom or the ground, the foundation, the groundwork, the principle of sufficient reason, the *principium rationis*, the *nihil est sine ratione* as *Satz vom Grund*, the *Satz vom zureichenden Grunde* of the Leibnizian theodicy and its reinterpretative repetition by Heidegger.[23]

It may be worth cutting Derrida a bit of slack here—as Keller notes elsewhere, in French, "*fond* in *fondation*, translates as both 'bottom' and 'ground.'"[24] This might explain the dissolving of one into the other. But still, Keller rightly questions Derrida's argumentative overreach: "... is it *essential* thus to reduce ground to the notion of 'origin' as absolute foundation?"[25] No! Or such is my argument.

A transversal ground, attentive to the particularities of being located ("to be" is always "to be *located*," "to be *somewhere*"), might yet pose a creative conceptual aid to contemporary crises. In a postmodern age (if such a term still applies) rife with accusations of "fake news," with disbelief of scientific expertise, and so forth, there is some need to generate a plane of engagement across critical difference. It is with good reason to suspect that the cooptation of the "groundlessness" of postmodernism and all of its however-caricatured relativisms have contributed dramatically to a general inability to meaningfully react to the pending disasters of anthropogenic climate change.[26] *Might some sort of ground be necessary?* Unequivocally, yes! The planetary crises, both here and to come, necessitate a ground on which to stake truth claims—while also resisting territorial impositions of, say, blood and soil. Anthropogenic climate change warrants the theorization of ground as a planetary interconnectedness that remains irreducible in the multiplicitously contextual experiences therein. How might this be possible? This ground, in its deconstructing and decomposing capacities, resists recapitulating or reinforcing the damaging effects of foundationalisms, past and present.

So what, then, is ground if it is not synonymous with foundation? Let me define it provisionally: Ground is a processual, circulating milieu of forces, affects, animacies, matters—a beginning. Ground is thus liminal in that it is neither some Modern foundation nor some postmodern groundlessness; ground is thoroughly material but is not reducible to substance—physically or metaphysically. Paradoxically, then, ground may be read as always already a sort of "groundless ground."[27] There is a deeply mystical theological precedent for this sort of thing: *Ungrund*, a ground without a ground, a grounded groundlessness.[28] The groundlessness of this ground, in a way, performs the aporetic phenomenon of the Derridean *khora*, defying the "either/or" binaries of noncontradiction—making space, carving room, allowing roots to multiply in fractal fissures.[29] In a word, ground as always already groundless reflects its porosity even as it cradles, its hospitality even as it quakes.

Ground does not solidify into a stable, unchanging substance even while it continues to serve as a matrix for engagement and navigation. It offers footing, however tenuous; it is resolute but not Certain—*terra infirma*. In fact, *as a function of* its multiplicity of complex processes, ongoing activities, cycling relations, ground exhibits the very crucial characteristics of that Derridean *différance*. Keller curiously sketches this very point:

> Difference . . . opens an interval or space of irreducible alterity, freed from the naturalized foundation set in its empty "*Grund*." But deconstruction might force us to choose between a purified transcendent *Grund* and a purified transcendental *Différance*. However, doesn't the [Derridean] "originarity" of difference, as it fissures the foundations that had buried it, suggest a more elemental metonymy? Might it not expose to the air . . . a dirtier ground, in which the groundless is not nihilistically triumphant but mystically irreducible?[30]

Ground capaciously connects, simultaneously relating without erasing difference. This refusal, indeed inability, to erase difference (in Keller's terms, its mystical irreducibility) will emerge in the material illustration of ground as an assemblage of nonseparably different elements, matters, and creatures—which we refer to as soil. This will be demonstrated in due time.

What must be argued now, if ground is to be truly distinct from foundation, has already been hinted at: ground's depth—in contradistinction to foundation's one-dimensionality. The depth of ground is not merely for the sake of some sort of feigned profound wisdom so much as to point to how its heterogeneous porosity continually *ungrounds*, disrupts, unsettles. Ground's depth, its permeability, is precisely that which keeps it from stagnating into a bleak concrete slab. Indeed, depth explicates just what is so groundless about this groundless ground.

Depth has, or at least *can* have, an aversive ring to it: harkening the (re)constitution of hierarchical verticalities that homogenize those below into the normative standards of those above. This is the sort of arborescent structure of root, trunk, and branch of which Deleuze and Guattari sought to rid their conceptual world. Alternatively, they advance the fecund possibilities of the multiplicitous assemblage, forming heterogeneous and rhizomatic relations between and with other matters.[31] I won't rehearse their now-familiar argument. Nor do I wish to merely translate ground into Deleuzoguattarian parlance (X=Y, Z=α, ground=____, and so forth). Rather, I will use the conceptual tools they provided to summon a specter of ground that might incarnate here in our midst.

The first thing to note in their company is that if one thinks of ground in terms of substances or things, one is already amiss; even in the theoretical register, one must begin to think of ground in terms of interminglings, matrices, amalgamations, relations, fields, forces.[32] That is, of course, *not* to say that ground isn't amply material! But ground's materiality must be thought of as flux, as becoming. Becomings are not merely quantitative changes between fixed subjects. Deleuze and Guattari argue, "A becoming is not a correspondence between relations. . . . To become is not to progress or regress along a series. . . . What is real is the becoming itself, the block of becoming, not the supposedly fixed terms through which it passes."[33] If one thinks of becoming as change between two entities, two figures, two points, one simply predicates process on the foundation of, over, some sort of substance metaphysics.[34]

Experimenting now with these principles, I offer this hypothesis, this earthen intuition: *If foundation is substance, ground is process.* Even just this supposedly simple shift in focus yields a vastly different landscape with all sorts of depth: movements, flows, undulations, surges—none of which are possible with the fixed and shallow foundations of too many philosophical and theological systems. Any meaningful sort of flux implies added dimensionality—a depth—as is the case with this proposed ground. Ground is not selfsame substance; it is an assemblage, a multiplicity of nonseparably different matters, affects, relations. Foundation, having no significant depth to speak of, suggests transcendence, otherworldliness, supernaturalness, allowing one to abstract oneself from whatever one paved over to make that ostensible foundation by building upward—"away." That is, foundations could be metaphorically understood as but the stage upon which a play is performed, whereas ground could be understood as bound up in and as *integral to* the possibility of such a performance. Ground cannot be read as an additive or an accessory so much as that which actively enables elemental possibility. Distinguishing ground from foundation allows one, for example, to reject an understanding of "the environment" as some "wilderness" that is somewhere "out there" apart from webs of human influence, instead disclosing that "all that is" is terrestrial, is made possible with and by ground.

Ground indicates a tangible immanence that has depth, all the while resisting the hierarchical valuation of its entangled elements. As Deleuze and Guattari write, "An assemblage has neither base nor superstructure, neither deep structure nor superficial structure; it flattens all of its dimensions onto a single plane of consistency upon which the reciprocal presuppositions and mutual insertions [relations] play themselves out."[35] This flattening, paradoxically, is not an erasure of depth; Deleuze and Guattari's "plane of immanence" performs this aporetic function of grounding without erasing profound difference.

This plane is a horizon of events that holds together, that grounds; such a plane does not have borders but is continually woven as if on a gigantic, complex shuttle—ever open, ever unfolding.[36] And yet this plane folds and doubles back, a geology *both upon which and within which* concepts germinate. It is "the single wave that rolls [concepts] up and unrolls them."[37] It rolls; it roils. Indeed, counterintuitively, this plane, this ground, is deep not in the sense of above/below or surface/subterranean—both of which imply extension and substance; the differentiating capacities of depth—"difference itself," if you will—entail *intensive* differentiation. Deleuze limns, "Depth as the (ultimate and original) heterogeneous dimension is the matrix of all extensity."[38] What's more, "The ground [*fond*] as it appears in a homogenous extensity is notably a projection of something 'deeper' [*profond*]: only the latter may be called *Ungrund* or groundless."[39] There is a prior depth, a condition of possibility, a depth that implies not something "below" but rather a dimensionality that functions as a conceptually enabling matrix. This depth is nothing less than a prefigurative, constitutive condition of possibility. As Keller puts it, one might conceive of this depth *not* as a dimension *but rather* as "the dimensionality out of which the spatiotemporal dimensions unfold."[40] Or, in Deleuze and Guattari's own words, "The plane of immanence is like a section of chaos and acts like a sieve."[41] Thus their claim about flattening does not imply the erasure of difference so much as the deconstruction of the hierarchies associated with transcendence. The plane is a matrix for nonlinear connections, heterogeneous intersections of lines of flight, and knots of creative complexity.

Thus, the depth of the proposed ground is not a reinstitution of hierarchical heights versus unruly depths, overs versus unders, aboves versus belows.[42] The depth traced here invokes difference, rupture, ungrounding—all the while connecting.[43] It ultimately implies immanence. The immanence of ground, therefore, cannot be thought of as "immanent *to.*" Nor can it, itself, yield to internal gradations of value, at least in any linear sense, lest it wish to reiterate its relation to some sort of abstract Transcendent;[44] the incessant interminglings that contribute to the phenomenon of ground cut across it, deterritorializing, decoding, destratifying it—a fuzzy aggregate whose constituent elements, while remaining *located* and particular, are not points (read: stasis, substance) but lines (read: movement, processes).[45] Deleuze and Guattari helpfully frame this conceptual and methodological revolution, worth quoting in all their verbosity:

> One does not break with the arborescent schema, one does not reach becoming or the molecular, as long as a line is connected to two distant points, or is composed of two contiguous points. A line of becoming is not defined by points that it connects, or by points that compose it; on the contrary, *it passes between points, it comes up through the middle*, it runs perpendicular to the points first perceived, transversally to the localizable relation to distant or contiguous points. A point is always a point of origin. But a line of becoming has neither beginning nor end, departure nor arrival, origin nor destination; to speak of the absence of an origin, to make the absence of an origin the origin, is a bad play on words [*et parler d'absence d'origine, ériger l'absence d'origine en origine, est un mauvais jeu de mots*]. *A line of becoming has only a middle* [*un milieu*]. The middle is not an average; it is fast motion, it is the absolute speed of movement. *A becoming is always in the middle; one can only get it by the middle. A becoming is neither one nor two, nor the relation of the two; it is the in-between, the border or line of flight or descent running perpendicular to both.*[46]

Following Henri Bergson's lead here, this philosophical duo paints these in-motion lines—which tangle into this grounding network—*not* as a mere connection of points; they are pure speed, utter becoming.[47] Bergson, long before, invoked this very perspective: "There are changes, but there are underneath the change no things which change: *change has no need of a support.* There are movements, but there is no inert or invariable object which moves: *movement does not imply a mobile.*"[48] Bergson insists that there is *becoming*, solely, and *not* "things" or "substances" that become. Regathering some of the language used earlier in this chapter, to fixate on the point is to return to the Origin in search of paradigms of oppressive power to be recapitulated in the present; to think of change or radical flux, which possesses no substratum, is to think in terms of beginnings—always-already and only ever beginning from a context, a milieu, a middle, a location.

But we can still further emphasize the materiality of becoming, the becoming of materiality. Theoretical physicist and feminist philosopher Karen Barad, to this end, radically disrupts substance metaphysics in favor of an agential realism *not* of entities but of *phenomena*.[49] Barad's "intra-action"[50] undermines the very notion of separable parts, or mobiles, that change as if matter were utterly discrete and could inter-act: "Matter does not refer to a fixed substance; rather, matter is substance in its intra-active becoming—not a thing, but a doing, a congealing of agency. Matter is a stabilizing and destabilizing process of iterative intra-activity."[51] Even the essential unit of matter, the atom, is destabilized by Barad. Following the contours of experimental quantum theory, Barad exposes the epistemologically destabilizing intra-activity of material phenomena; matter is no longer fixed substance but rather is a process of relational becoming. In her words, matter refers *"not to an inherent fixed property of abstract independently existing objects of Newtonian physics. . . ."*[52] Shaking the very foundations of any object-oriented perspective, Barad contends, ". . . neither space nor time exist as determinate givens outside of phenomena. . . . Phenomena cannot be located in space and time; rather, phenomena are material entanglements that 'extend' across space and time."[53] Again, should it bear repeating, such a relational ontology of pure process, of groundlessly grounded phenomena (which shirk any notion of any sort of separable "entity"), *does not mean* that it is in any way non- or anti-material. Instead, it reveals another vital aspect of ground, distinguishing it further from foundation: It has the character of reciprocity and of simultaneity.

Foundation—objects, substances, even atoms—implies clear, determinate separability: *that* is foundation, *this* is edifice; *that* is below, *this* is above; *that* is *res extensae*, *this* is *res cogitans*; *that* is nature, *this* is culture; *that* is object, *this* is subject; *that* is passive background, *this* is active creation. . . . Ground dissolves these abstracted walls of separation, neither resolving into undifferentiated homogeneity nor allowing for the concretization of borders. As environmental philosopher Marjolein Oele puts it, soil "fosters a form of regenerative noncognitive, material affectivity that births and buries us all; it is one that in its direct touch still leaves open precious pores *to contest boundaries between what is and what is not.*"[54] In other words, porosity as simultaneously grounding and ungrounding. Just as "the environment" is not some "thing" that is somewhere "out there"[55]—for there cannot be any sort of "out there" other than that which *is made so* in the decision to *abstract* or *externalize* it—ground is that with which we're not just "surrounded" or "supported" but *suffused*. We're shot through with it, despite whatever sort of barrier one might wish to construct between nature and culture, materiality and discursivity, praxis and theory. As material feminist philosopher Stacy Alaimo relatedly conveys, "The walls of the domestic enclosure that would separate human from nature and define the human as such are nowhere to be found, as human corporeality and textuality effortlessly extend into the more-than-human world. *Word, flesh, and dirt are no longer discrete.*"[56] But this relation, even if it adequately considers the porosity of ground, *isn't* one-way. There's a simultaneous reciprocity at play here: We're permeated by ground, but the reverse is also the case. We're catalyzed by ground, enabled by its conditions of possibility; one can always trace one's aliveness back to the earth-ground. But ground is also affected by us, altered and influenced by our relations with and within it. This assertion is far from new; environmental historian Linda Nash limns this very phenomenon:

> When we focus on the human body . . . the boundary between the human and the nonhuman world, the actors and their objects, becomes much more fuzzy and the distinction much more tenuous. *Where does the body end and "nonhuman nature" begin? When we recognize that human bodies are directly affected by their environments, we are forced to acknowledge that humans are not simply agents of environmental change but also objects of that change. Conversely, the environment is more than an object upon which change is enacted; it is also an agent of sorts that acts upon the bodies inhabiting it.*[57]

There is only ever intra-action, only ever porous co-relations; ground is not simply *"background,"* but it sustains, prefigures, and *participates in* our becomings. This concomitant reciprocity is Alaimo's very point in her articulation of "trans-corporeality," ". . . in which the human is always enmeshed with the more-than-human world, [underlining] the extent to which the substance of the human is ultimately inseparable from 'the environment.'"[58] She maintains that we must recognize "that 'the environment' is not located somewhere out there, but is always the very substance of ourselves."[59] The border-walls of foundationalisms are rendered rubble in the recognition of trans-corporeal exchange, of simultaneous intra-action. To remind, these are not relations between discrete objects or between static points; rather, they are the intersections, the magnifications, the crisscrossings of movements, of becomings. That these relations exist *need not* mean that they're ones of sameness, of proportionality, of undifferentiated quality. Quite the opposite: These relations cut across and through, diving under and breaking over—waves that, at certain times, join and amplify and, at others, splash back and stifle.

Of course, environmental justice activists have been teaching about the differentially material consequences of contamination, pollution, and toxification all along—and Native Americans for far longer! The Warren County environmental justice protests of 1982 and the landmark "Toxic Wastes and Race" report by the United Church of Christ (UCC) in 1987 (which initiated the now-termed "environmental justice movement") exemplify the argument that there exists an undeniable trans-corporeality between and among humans and their grounded contexts; but, importantly, this relation is never selfsame or identical but flows according to the pipelines of power and privilege in operation—not for any "naturalized" or "essentialized" reason but because decisions were intentionally made.[60] These decisions were not made by, and generally *are not* made by, the directly impacted but by those who can externalize the damages and abstract the contamination as something somewhere "out there" affecting "others" who remain nameless, faceless. Thus, the point here is that ground draws our attention to, using feminist philosopher Nancy Tuana's language, the "viscous porosity" of the world[61]—a world that is not merely composed of interactions between detached objects but of intra-active becomings, a world whose becomings are neither singular nor homogeneous but shaped, affected, molded, redirected, and so forth—and not just by humans, either. These becomings are not neutral but are particular events, meaning that this ontological shift does not imply the erasure of certain becomings as violent or death-dealing.

If this argument isn't exactly new, its application to the conceptual matrix of the cultivated theo-philosophical ground *as earth-ground* presents both critical theory and critical activism with novel opportunities for a more robust engagement with the ecological. This grounded philosophy of becoming reconfigures the possibilities for conceiving of agency, animacy, capacity, and so forth; that is, to think in terms of flux as opposed to substance figures new modes for taking seriously, for example, the affects and effects of "inanimate" but nevertheless contaminating particulates, the toxicities of environmental racism, the animacies that move across but also emerge from the enabling-matrix of ground, the capacities that can be nurtured or exploited. This multiplies opportunities to consider the insidious potencies surfacing in the wake of forced dislocation and diaspora. These forces now read *as an effect of being coercively ungrounded* from familiar ecologies, alimentations, climates.

The present efforts to articulate ground as a fecund network that galvanizes, but is also *galvanized by*, the intra-active and simultaneous processes of theory and praxis, of word and flesh, would be inadequate, perhaps even hopeless, without allowing for this ground's rematerialization as the earth-ground. This grounded plane of becoming is no mere abstraction but materially incarnates in and as soil. To this, we now turn.

Materializing Ground as Earth-Ground

So far, I've dedicated this chapter to distinguishing ground from foundation—mostly philosophically. It bears repeating, perhaps now becoming a sort of liturgical refrain: *Ground is not foundation*. Another translation: Antifoundationalism need not imply utter groundlessness. It's primarily been a "This!" and "No, not that!" sort of argument, up till now. But what remains, in the space-time that remains, is an altogether constructive move: *the metonymic materialization of ground as earth-ground, as soil.* It is precisely here that I aim to craft with the concept ground—now offering an eco-political corrective of Derrida. This process will be reciprocal: the soiling of critical theory and the theorizing of soil, the muddying of concepts and the conceptualization of mud.

Here I turn to the wisdoms of agrarians, soil scientists, and ecologists to incarnate this ground as a properly material and evidently contextual web. Soil, we will see, disrupts any fixation on substance, instead redirecting one's gaze toward process, toward relation, toward networks. There is no "one thing" that is soil: there are sandy soils, loamy soils, clay soils, silty soils, peaty soils, chalky soils, rocky soils, acidic soils, alkali soils, saline soils, dark soils, light soils, platy soils, prismatic soils, granular soils[62]—and these are only the beginnings of how one might describe a soil.[63] Soil, veritably, is never any one thing.

Soil is process, assemblage, groundless ground, par excellence. *And yet*, at the same time, soil, as argued here, will disrupt any fixation on relation as the effacing of difference, as the whitewashing of particularity.

The earth-ground is not a thing but a process—meaning that it is not only open-ended in its unfoldings but also inherits and is affected by operative "pipelines of power." It is utterly material but irreducible: neither one thing nor many things. The mammoth fifteenth edition of *The Nature and Properties of Soil*, written by soil scientists Nyle C. Brady and Raymond R. Weil, defines soil in two ways; for the time being, I'll focus on the first: "(1) A dynamic natural body composed of mineral and organic solids, gases, liquids and living organisms which can serve as a medium for plant growth."[64] Soil is not simply "dirt"—not merely a discrete object or solely a singular substance—but a rhizomatic assemblage of matters, minerals, microbes, water, air, heat-energy, and so on. And soil is not universally enabling, either; the potentialities of fertility are contextually bound: fertile conditions for one species can easily be toxic for another. Soil illuminates the concern for a philosophical perspective of processual phenomena (over against ontologies of change that move through some sort of substratum or underlying substance) shared by Whitehead, Deleuze, Guattari, Barad, and beyond: This ground shifts, quakes, links, cycles, stirs, splits, relates. In this way, soil is a material multiplicity—a milieu of intersecting lines of flight, tangling transitions, and compositional processes of decomposition.[65] William Bryant Logan, a soil poet of sorts, reflects these paradoxical principles evident in humus,[66] stating:

Radical disorder is the key to the functions of the humus. At the molecular level, it may indeed be the most disordered material on Earth. No two molecules of humus may be alike. Though no one has difficulty recognizing a humus molecule, it is likely unique because it works upon fractal principles.[67]

Logan later claims, "Humus itself is a dynamic creature, comprising a fast-changing part that liberates nitrogen and micronutrients for direct absorption by plant roots, a slow-changing, stable part that holds water, and a porous material that is easy for roots to penetrate."[68] Interestingly, he (likely unintentionally) illustrates the earth-ground as a wave-like, Deleuzoguattarian plane: "It had never occurred to me that the surface of the earth was an assembly of holes. . . ."[69] This earthy matrix of relations blurs lines between organic and inorganic, animate and inanimate, active and passive, essential and superficial. Logan playfully quips, "Inert matter! As if there ever were such a thing."[70] Further providing support for the present process-oriented argument as he reflects on Hans Jenny, a soil scientist and former mentor, Logan writes: "A soil was not a thing to Jenny. It was a web of relationships that stood in a certain state at a certain time."[71] That is not to say that there are no gradations of vitality when it comes to minerals or elements or water content or drainage for the sake of particular vegetal life. Nor is it to expressly recapitulate any sort of flat animism of soil (though we can say that it is, at the very least, *ecstatic*). Rather, these matters only ever exist as relations, as cycles, as processes, as transitions—decaying, consuming, composing, decomposing, draining, absorbing, heating, cooling, and so on. And yet these transitions aren't between two points but are pure movement, sheer change.

Any static image of soil is just that: a snapshot of movement. It's pertinent to fold back for a moment here, turning to a bit of relevant early-twentieth-century continental philosophy on the question of movement and becoming. Henri Bergson contended that "we argue about movement as though it were made of immobilities."[72] That is, we tend to think of movement as a series of points traversed by a substance or subject. Bergson eventually refers to this incongruous procedure or way of thinking in *Creative Evolution* as "cinematographic," playing on how films are composed of fast-moving but demonstrably still, static frames.[73] Bergson quips that there are never "positions" but "suppositions."[74] He asserts, "Movement is reality itself, and what we call immobility is a certain state of things analogous to that produced when two trains move at the same speed, in the same direction, on parallel tracks: each of the two trains is then immovable to the travelers seated in the other."[75] He later states, "Thus, whether it is a question of the internal or the external, of ourselves or of things, *reality is mobility itself*."⁷⁶ This landmark perspective will later be echoed, and subject to some creative *midrash* in order to ensure the heterogeneity of movement and change, in Deleuze and Guattari's claim that "*flux* is reality itself."⁷⁷

It is this "snapshot" perspective of soil—the immobilization and compaction of the fluxes and flows of the world, broadly, and the earth-ground, specifically—that undergirds the hubris of exploitative agricultural practices and agribusiness models,⁷⁸ predicated on Enlightenment-style linearities and separabilities, which have led increasingly, almost exponentially, to the erosion of topsoil.⁷⁹ This is the primary logic undergirding practices of so-called conventional farming, with its countless "inputs" (fertilizers, pesticides, fungicides, etc.), which has, not surprisingly, led to all sorts of "unexpected" consequences such as oceanic dead zones caused by excess nitrogen and phosphorous levels due to agricultural fertilizer runoff. The assumption that one can hold a "snapshot perspective" of soil leads to the assumption that one can do the work of soil, fashion the conditions of soil, and adequately add X, Y, or Z input to one's field in order to "create" fertility. Indeed, any static "snapshot" of soil egregiously commits Whitehead's "fallacy of misplaced concreteness."⁸⁰

Soil, considered on its multiplicitous "own," is a tangled web of relations, a knot of indiscriminate matters, minerals, forces, energies, and so forth. But this assemblage, like any good assemblage, creates endless rhizomes. It would behoove us to turn to Brady and Weil's second definition of soil: "(2) The collection of natural bodies occupying parts of the Earth's surface that is capable of supporting plant growth and that has properties resulting from the integrated effects of climate and living organisms acting upon parent material, as conditioned by topography, over periods of time."⁸¹ What emerges here is an understanding of soil as a matrix, as a transversal milieu; it constitutes the immanental plane—or, perhaps better, plain—in and on which countless subjects live and move and have their . . . becoming. As Aldo Leopold, in his essay, "The Land Ethic," describes, "Land, then, is not merely soil; it is a fountain of energy flowing through a circuit of soils, plants, and animals. Food chains are the living channels which conduct energy upward; death and decay return it to the soil."⁸² The earth-ground is *not just* an assemblage of various matters cycling about but is always already constituted by *relations-between*—between what-we-think-of-as-soil ("dirt") and the ecosystem it hosts. Earthworms, root systems, nematodes, fungi, protozoa, springtails, mites, burrowing critters: each of these elements contributes to and, in some ways, *constitutes* the earth-ground. To put it another way, soil, as we know it, does not exist "in itself" but *only because of* its relations to vegetal, invertebrate, mycological life—relations often considered entirely "other than" soil.⁸³ To exemplify, I'll highlight three facets integral to soil but often considered "other than" soil: vegetal root systems, earthworms, and fungi.[84]

Roots, rhizomatic structures themselves, could not exist without soil—obviously; but roots function as a critical aspect of soil—crucial to preventing its erosion, vital for cycling nutrients.[85] Roots "typically occupy about 1% of the soil volume and may be responsible *for a quarter to a third of the respiration occurring in a soil.*"[86] Dramatically, in a way, soil would not be were it not for roots, and certainly *vice versa.* Roots hold soil in place, while simultaneously, perhaps paradoxically, creating rifts and pores that allow for the facilitation and communication of nutrients, matters, even creatures.[87] Not only do roots physically stabilize soil levels and prevent erosion, but they also chemically and biologically modify soil: "Roots chemically alter the soil around them by what they take out of it (depletion of nutrients and water) and what they put into it (root exudates and tissues). Root exudates better stabilize soil aggregates, both directly and indirectly by supporting a myriad of fungi and bacteria."[88] And while one may be wont to emphasize the importance of leaf litter and other matter involved in decomposition *on the surface* of our top-soils, *"root contributions are generally more important than the more visible (to humans) aboveground plant residues. In grasslands, about 50–60% of the net primary production (total plant biomass) is commonly in the roots."*[89] Without the presence of significant root systems—of the perennial but also even annual sort—soil could not exist, at least not in the generally-consistent and mostly-fertile states we've come to understand as "soil." Soil is not a thing; it is a rhizome, an intersection. The reciprocity here is undeniable and vibrant.

When it comes to invertebrates and the earth-ground, few are more important than earthworms, so I'll direct my attention there. Earthworms, of which there are thousands of varieties, often serve as a keystone species in soil, critically affecting soil functions. Although not exclusively or always a purely positive feature[90] (too much of a good thing isn't always so good, after all), earthworms' contributions to soil health are key: Burrows create channels for plant roots to extend as well as allow for better aeration and drainage, castings (or earthworm "waste") break down organic aggregates into smaller and more stable microaggregates, and earthworms generally hasten nutrient availability for plant life.[91] "Fertility" is unthinkable if not for these critical creatures. Soil as we understand it is predicated on the life and labor of earthworms; they are not "apart from" ground.

Although it may be a somewhat foolish, over-simplifying task to group fungi, of which tens of thousands of *known* species exist, into a single conglomerate, it'll be necessary for the sake of brevity.[92] Each of the three general "types" of fungi—yeasts, molds, and mushrooms—perform vital tasks for generating and maintaining soil health and consistency. Zooming in on the latter two, molds are critical to the decomposition of organic matter, and, surprisingly to some, much more so than mushroom fungi. Mushrooms, though, break down woody tissue and serve as a crucial symbiotic partner with plant roots, facilitating not only the "communication" of minerals but, as is becoming increasingly apparent, some *actual form of communication* between various plant organisms.[93] It can be argued that mycorrhizae, the symbiotic association that forms between a fungus and a plant, *enable* plant life to even exist.[94] As Weil and Brady note:

> Mycorrhizae *are the rule, not the exception*, for most plant species, including the majority of economically important plants. In natural ecosystems most plants are quite dependent on mycorrhizal relationships *and cannot survive without them*. Mycorrhizal structures have been found in fossils of plants that lived some 400 million years ago, indicating that mycorrhizal infection may have played a role in the evolutionary adaptation of plants to the land environment.[95]

There is clearly no soil "in itself," no single object that makes for soil; what's more, soil could not be but for its rhizomatic, interspecies intraconnections as a web of becoming. One cannot think of this ground as anything other than a heterogeneous matrix, thus preventing its calcification into a foundation if one takes the matterphor of soil seriously. In this precise way, this proposed terrestrial ground is utterly incompatible with and inimical to any sense of the concept "foundation." Not only are these relations amply different between contexts; they are always ever-changing even in "one" place. That is, not only is the earth-ground shifting differentially between contexts, but it is also cycling uniquely beneath our feet in any "one" place. The multiplicity of soil, it should now be somewhat clear, is the entangled minglings of various strata without parsable layers, definable borders, or isolatable elements, per se. Their characteristic relations differ, as do our relations to those relations.

Relations are not, and *cannot be*, universal; they are particular, placed, situated. Relations are only ever local, yet those locales are not bordered or delimited: They overlap, meld, blend, intersect, cut through, dissolve, commune. Human relations to the earth-ground correspondingly exhibit this paradoxical particularity *and* porosity, contextuality *and* transversality. What's more, there is a reciprocity, if only an asymmetrical one, performed here: One affects and is affected, shapes and is shaped—*intra-activity*, in a word. Cultures and agricultures are co-constitutive and co-creative—though not in any necessarily essentialized or totalized way.[96] The porosity of ground ungrounds these calcified categorizations, deconstructing that to which foundations give rise. Agrarian

Wendell Berry makes this claim and mobilizes it as a sharp critique against the homogenizing violence of agribusiness:

> The most necessary thing in agriculture, for instance, is not to invent new technologies or methods, not to achieve "breakthroughs," *but to determine what tools and methods are appropriate to specific people, places, and needs, and to apply them correctly. Application . . . is the crux, because no two farms or farmers are alike; no two fields are alike.* Just the changing shape or topography of the land makes for differences of the most formidable kind. *Abstractions never cross these boundaries without either ceasing to be abstractions or doing damage.* And prefabricated industrial methods and technologies are abstractions. The bigger and more expensive, the more heroic, they are, the harder they are to apply considerately and conservingly.[97]

The contextual nature of soil—never a "one thing" and ever differing across regions, even fluctuating in the space of a few feet—invokes the deeply eco-material phenomenon of difference-in-relation.

Aporia of, on, the Ground

Ground is not foundation. Ground is an earthy matrix of heterogeneous, symbiogenetic becomings. Ground is the condition of possibility—the possibility of possibilities, not in the sense of the superlative or the transcendent or the epistemological a priori, let alone any metaphysical foundation, so much as of the prefiguring, the undergirding, the empowering.

The Anthropocene demands philosophies and theologies that responsibly consider Earth not as an additive or addendum but as integral to *and grounding* their perspectives. Horizontality—which is the perspectival condition of returning one's concepts to the earth-ground—yields all sorts of consequences for theologizing, in particular, which will be the subject of Chapter Two. The ethico-political import of a grounded philosophy, entangling the social and the ecological, will manifest in Chapter Four of this project. What's crucial to consider now, at this moment, though, is how an agrarian fashioning of ground—as the earth-ground—markedly reorients the conceptual lenses of critical theory by exposing it to the inherent, multiplicitous paradoxes of soils.

Tending to soil involves entirely different ways of being—predicated on the becomings of relations, the cycles of nutrients, and the ecosystems of critters. One can only tend to soil *well* by developing a relationship with it, thereby uncovering modes of possible nurture.[98] But what's crucial to note here is how this paradigm shift exposes the fertile *paradoxes*, the fecund *aporias*, caught up in these concepts. Tending to paradoxes relies on the tension of mystery, not to be eradicated so much as held gently and faithfully. To "answer" these mysteries constitutes exploitative violence, as the "solving" of mystery only ever occurs by imposition, by brute force; to render the mysterious as anything less than mystery is to water it down, to erase its critical difference. Thus, to attempt to capture mystery, to force the paradoxical into some sort of box of comprehensibility, is to embody oppressive colonial logics. This reductionistic logic assumes a kind of "power over," a certainty that one "knows better." Agribusiness—much like any other exploitative, extractive, or colonizing industry—operates under these assumptions. Any such struggle to wrestle with mystery in an attempt to harness it, to "objectively understand" it (which is to say, to subject it to oppressive operative norms), soon bastardizes wisdoms into "orders of operation," degrades fecundity into desolation, and reduces nurture into exploitation. Attention to soil as an open system, as affected and affecting, as irreducible, as entirely *more* than the few parts that benefit human economic enterprise, is possible; but this possibility remains open only on the condition that it be treated as never fully knowable, as requiring the fluidity of humility toward *humus*.

The mysterious abounds: Ground connects but is contextual, links widely but is ever-local, ever-located. Ground has depth but is also surface. Ground animates but is not exactly "alive." Ground is porous but offers footing. As Logan discerns, "Hospitality is the fundamental virtue of soil. It makes room. It shares."[99] Such hospitality would not be possible, at least in the same way, without roots and worms and critters. And yet, a double-paradox folds therein: (a) these relations require soil as a necessary preexisting condition, even as soil needs these relations to respire, to cycle, to fertilize, and (b) this hospitality, this permeability, is precisely what enables ground's erosion, its loss—that is, when mistreated or exploited.

Berry draws our attention to the paradoxes of the earth-ground. As Berry ruminates,

> . . . we cannot speak of topsoil, indeed we cannot know what it is, without acknowledging at the outset that we cannot make it. We can care for it (or not), we can even, as we say, "build" it, but we can do so only by assenting to, preserving, and perhaps collaborating in its own processes. To those processes themselves we have nothing to contribute. We cannot make topsoil, and we cannot make any substitute for it; we cannot do what it does. It is apparently impossible to make an adequate description of topsoil in the sort of language that we have come to call "scientific." For, although any soil sample can be reduced

to its inert quantities, a handful of the real thing has life in it; it is full of living creatures."[100]

As Berry notes, soil is not something that we can "make." Nor is it something "out there"; the earth-ground is only ever a relation, a becoming within which we interact. It affects and is affected, but it cannot be made, only nurtured. He writes, "Even in its functions that may seem, to mechanists, to be mechanical, the *topsoil behaves complexly* and wonderfully. A healthy topsoil, for instance, has at once the ability to hold water and to drain well."[101] He continues a bit later, indicating the unnamable nature of ground,

> we must improve the soil, which is not a mechanical device but, among other things, a graveyard, a place of resurrection, and a community of living creatures. Devices may sometimes help, but only up to a point, for soil is improved by what humans do not do as well as by what they do.[102]

Soil is, hence, nothing less than aporia.[103] Soil confounds substance metaphysicians in the same way that it confounds neoliberal economists. It refigures attention to the interconnectedness of particularity, the relational fragmentation of transversality. Just as soil is not a "one thing" or a "universalizable" thing, *neither is a just relation to the earth-ground*: soil-care cannot concretize into norms, cannot universalize into categorical imperatives, at least if one wishes to be faithful to ground as flux and not as snapshot. As Berry states, "The land is too various in its kinds, climates, conditions, declivities, aspects, and histories *to conform to any generalized understanding or to prosper under generalized treatment*."[104] General use, much like most generalities, constitutes a form of violence, for the "general" can only come at the expense of nuance, of particularity, of contextuality.[105] Hence the resolutions aimed toward regenerative nurture may come in surprising and nigh-paradoxically small ways; they may come *not* from soil scientists (often, but not always, steeped in the traditions of mechanistic thinking, taxonomic categorization, and neoliberal concerns[106]) but instead from organic farmers,[107] permaculturists,[108] indigenous teachers,[109] plant medicine stewards,[110] and beyond.

The contextuality of relating to Earth also multiplies as one considers *who* is performing that work. That is, differences in experience, class, access, skills, race, shape, religiosity, health, gender, available tools, time, place of origin, disposable income, culture, intuitive capacities, traumatic histories, and beyond *all affect one's relations to Earth*. None of these do so in any sort of necessary or naturalized way, but they certainly do play into one's narrativized matrix of location, even if in an unconscious—or, perhaps better, *underground*—sort of way. One's social location influences one's relation to geographic location—braided together are the material questions of colonialism, enslavement, dislocation, diaspora, and trauma. For example, as Leah Penniman writes in her brilliant book *Farming While Black* (2018), "To farm while black is an act of defiance against white supremacy and a means to honor the agricultural ingenuity of our ancestors."[111] To "farm while black" in the contemporary U.S. context where now "less than 1 percent of farms are Black-owned"—not because of "happenstance" but because of the theft of land, the robbery that is sharecropping economics, the discriminatory lending practices at the heart of U.S. banking, and the general persistence and elasticity of white supremacy—generates an entirely different relation to the earth-ground.[112] O'Dell's call for groundedness as requiring "actual ground" thus complicates in the wake of the colonial legacies shaping land use, ownership, and the like.[113] Relations to ground emerge from the locations of the social and ecological—intertwined. Tapping into the agricultural side of this point, Berry notes,

> One thing we do know, that we dare not forget, is that better solutions than ours have at times been made by people with much less information than we have. *We know too, from the study of agriculture, that the same information, tools, and techniques that in one farmer's hands will ruin land, in another's will save and improve it.* This is not a recommendation of ignorance. To know nothing, after all, is no more possible than to know enough. *I am only proposing that knowledge, like everything else, has its place, and that we need urgently now to put it in its place.*[114]

It is not only the earth-ground that refuses any sort of static depiction and eschews any "generalities" or "universals" but also the human subjects—ever different across the tangled, intersecting lines of social location—who relate differently with the earth-ground in response to and as an effect of contextually available resources, agency, and power.

The aporias of the ground do not mean that one cannot "do" anything when it comes to relating to soil, but that one must be wary of the solutions thrown at this great problem—solutions that emerge from the very logics and systems that caused it.[115] That is to say, there is something to learn, something to do, but this "something" (which is always multiple, ever-plural) may come in surprising ways, in unexpected fashions, in unthinkable, even paradoxical manners. These are the only comprehensible consequences when one reassumes the horizontal and eschews the fallacy of any sort of removed, bird's-eye, overlooking perspective. Horizontality, or being grounded, reintroduces and indeed requires horizons. As will emerge in Chapter Two, in the horizontal, an encounter with the shock of aporia elicits apophasis. What should be beginning to emerge here-now, though, is how a reconceptualization of ground entails, simultaneously, revolutions of metaphysics, reimaginations of agency, and transformations of ethics.

One only ever materializes from the ground—even as one reciprocally affects it. One is never anything "other than" or "more than" that which the earth-ground has enabled—the upshot of web-like ecologies. It is only *because of* this matrix whence life emerges, this net upon and within which life has its becomings, that one can read this sentence. And yet, our relations to the earth-ground—for reasons both chosen and forced, willed and colonized—are endlessly different. The ground is not impervious to our relations, affected as we intra-act with and within it. Still, the paradox *continues to unfold*: Even as one is given rise to *by the ground* via one's intra-activities with it, who among us comes from a context of identical soils? Of fully relatable similarities? Of utter same-nesses? Of indistinguishable social locations? No single being, no single becoming. The transversal connections between and among do not negate the particularities of location—social and ecological. Rather, they're grounded in and by them.

The following chapter will trace the theological consequences emerging from this reconceptualized and rematerialized ground—inviting the way-making process of *theopoiesis* on this soiled plane of elements, of immanence. It is at the edges of articulation where we will find the way-making fold of a grounding apophasis, offering glimpses of a dark light not fully nameable.

Interlude

Poetics at the Edge

What happens when you reach a precipice? When you arrive at some unforeseen edge? Staring down, looking out, sitting in surprise, tracing along, navigating, seeking out some sort of way . . . Gazing into whatever sort of abyss one has approached, a paradox emerges: It is an obstacle-less obstacle. It is a nothingness that is also something—a nothing-incarnate.

But rare are these *extraordinary* moments—or so they are for me. They are striking, momentous. At a precipice, one reaches a sort of limit, a threshold. These edges are hard, prominent, final; these experiences tend to characterize most articulations of the inarticulable—the grandiose, the awesome, the magnificent. But one *need not* invoke the sublime to sketch the threads of some sacred ineffability. Indeed, these threads weave through all sorts of matters in *far less* spectacular ways. They manifest in the ordinary.

The edges of articulation, the borderlands[1] of communication, the porous liminality of interconnection—these zones of ambiguity exist in all sorts of ways in the mundane, the commonplace, the familiar—at least if one is on the ground, is an earthling. Treading on the earth-ground—the condition of one's perspective, the milieu of one's renewed becomings—the unknown and the mysterious become *all the more so*. There is a certain fuzziness,[2] an inbetweenness that pervades and transfuses dusty standpoints, soiled perspectives. On the ground, one cannot escape the phenomena of horizons.

At the edge of the unknown, what might it mean to approach that abyss interrogatively as opposed to declaratively?[3] In other words, as Catherine Keller inquires, "... what is the actual work of theology—but an incantation at the edge of uncertainty?"[4] From the fallacious "Above," one "Knows," one masters. But from the earth-ground, one senses, one seeks. *This is the only way it's ever been*—here on the earth-ground—but this is the dust that many since, at least, the Enlightenment have sought to sweep under the rug. Religious institutions have hardened these intuitions of irrepressible mystery into cold dogmas; sciences have overlooked and under-acknowledged the necessarily perspectival human subjectivity functioning as an integral part of the apparatus or mechanism of science;[5] economists have calcified Earth into separable "resources" to be taken at will—the only obstacle being whether one has sufficient capital to do so.

In a letter of advice to an aspiring young poet, the twentieth-century German poet Rainer Maria Rilke writes the following:

> You are so young, so much before all beginning, and I would like to beg you, dear Sir, as well as I can, to have patience with everything unresolved in your heart and to try to love *the questions themselves* as if they were locked rooms or books written in a very foreign language. Don't search for the answers, which could not be given to you now, because you would not be able to live them. And the point is, to live everything. *Live* the questions now. Perhaps then, someday far in the future, you will gradually, without even noticing it, live your way into the answer.[6]

This faithful task of living questions opens new affections and greater depth of feeling. And yet, "living the questions" does not suppose the impossibility of response so much as the paradoxical mode of responsive way-making.

Is it yet possible to instill this sense of paradoxical mystery, of divine ineffability, in the toil of environmental justice? How might this inexplicable process of edgy incantation infuse the efforts of environmental justice with new spiritual resonances that do not take this work "up and away" but generate, instead, more acutely intimate interconnections with the terrestrial? Resolution remains a fecund potentiality, even in this unexpected framing; put differently, living the questions may not undo the necessary and necessarily resolute claims for justice made by environmental justice advocates but rather may actually catalyze possibilities yet unforeseen. That is to say, sensing novelty is paradoxically predicated on uncertainty.

The following chapter explores these themes in greater detail.

2
Rooting
Terrestrial Theopoetics of and for the Planetary

> Culture is the precaution of those who claim to think thought but who steer clear of its chaotic journey. Evolving cultures infer Relation, the overstepping that grounds their unity-diversity. Thought draws the imaginary of the past: a knowledge becoming. One cannot stop it to assess it nor isolate it to transmit it. It is sharing one can never not retain, nor ever, in standing still, boast about.
>
> —ÉDOUARD GLISSANT

Opening—Trajectories for this Present Poetic

The perspectival reorientation posed by ground as earth-ground—and by ensuring that one's feet are gingerly placed on it—requires attention to immanent materiality, all the while carving space for the ineffable unknown, the alluring mist. Re-grounding constructive theology in and on the earth-ground breaks open the transcendent, scattering its shards across the horizons of possibility.[1] That is, the transcendent is not erased so much as rematerialized, dispersed, across this loamy plain of immanence. The task of discernment associated with traversing this ground and relating to it *wholesomely* is one of *poetics*, of *poiesis*.[2] Following the footsteps of Caribbean poet and theorist Édouard Glissant, a central figure in this chapter, poetics signifies this very process of rupturing and gathering, of breaking and collecting, of disturbing and assembling: in short, sense-making without ever entirely, completely, "making sense."

A few preliminary disclaimers are in order. The first contribution I hope to make here is this: The exploration of that which grounds thinking and, hence, creativity, the investigation of that which grounds sensing and, therefore, revelation. To study the grounds of epistemological experience, thusly reoriented when one integrates the realities of ecological and social location, ever poses serious consequences for the work of theologizing. If the divine is *not* that which lords over—pulling puppet strings or conducting some orchestra of events, cosmic and terrestrial alike—but that which grounds, that which catalyzes and receives,[3] that in which one grows and is rooted, then that divinity must materialize in wholly different manners of holiness. In other words, that which sets the divine apart[4] then *would not be* the distance between the immanent—or "here"—and the transcendent—or "out-there"—so much as the aporetic mystery that muddles, that muddies. This mystery, perhaps counterintuitively, can only amplify when one's feet are on the ground, when one's concepts mind the ground, when one's theology considers the ground— materially divine, divinely material. What one can sense on the ground is limited to one's immediate ecology, that micro-*oikos* where one is—and, to a certain degree, whence one emerges. To be grounded is to attune to the horizontal and to the phenomena of horizons. A terrestrial perspective necessitates a horizon, some sort of mystery at the threshold. *To be on the ground is to reintroduce the phenomenon of the horizon, to refigure the unknown as intimately a part of the very experience of having a perspective.* And yet this out-of-reach horizon, when treated as that which cannot be "grasped" even as it remains constitutive of one's milieu, does not make it an object of conquest so much as a provocation toward apophasis.

To get a bit more material, though not to say "concrete," then, and offer the reader a sense of direction in the luminous dark of this chapter, here's the plan: Before fleshing out these theological musings, we'll need to wander through questions of poetics, of wonder, of apophasis. This chapter explores the theopoetic capacities emerging from a philosophical theology rooted in the earth-ground. I will begin by outlining my use of the term "poetics" as something more than a style or method of writing—tracing Glissant's understanding of "poetics of relation" and how this poetics concerns epistemology and ethics. That is, Glissant will help direct our attention to how "poetics" is not merely an artistic adventure or theoretical tool but opens newly possible manners of confronting systems of violence, rebelling against neocolonial forces, and creating new lifeways amid and with rubble. As Glissant reminds, "Let us not stop with this commonplace: that a poetics cannot guarantee us a concrete means of action. But a poetics, perhaps, *does allow us to understand better our action in the world.*"[5] While Glissant's work is motivated by the particularities of Caribbean contextuality, I believe that his articulation of poetics' relation still deeply informs my present arguments concerning the fecundity of aporetic mystery for the work of environmental justice. Following this theoretical foregrounding, I'll use these poetic concepts to explore one of the facets studied in the previous chapter: the paradoxes of ground, linking them to the organic processes of apophasis through philosopher of religion Mary-Jane Rubenstein's reflections on "wonder." Aporias imply—indeed, *insist on*—apophasis. And yet, apophasis, even in its unmaking, constitutes a making: for in disruption emerges the possibility for creativity—folding and unfolding. This insight will materialize as poetics and soil muddy one another: a terrestrial poetics.

Such meditations on the aporetic will lead into a discussion concerning the ways in which a terrestrial perspectivalism—horizontality, in a word—entails theological *activity*, sacred-seeking *crafting*. Poiesis, if nothing else, is a creative way-making, a carving of space, "an incantation at the edge of uncertainty. . . ."[6] The cycles of the earth-ground's fissuring and assembling and of apophatic theology's unsaying and creating present mirrored processes that will be braided together here.

Woven throughout will be a critique of the entangled relationship between transcendence and abstraction, each of which allows for the extraction, externalization, or extinction of matters deemed extraneous, unnecessary, expendable, disposable.[7] The transcendent as above, "away," "out-there," enables a necropolitical calculus aimed at maintaining the status quo of anthropocentrism, generally, and of elite, white heteropatriarchy, particularly. Integral to this argument concerns the remembrance and reclamation of *that which* and *those whom* have been forsaken by these systematic doctrines; this terrestrial theopoetics is aimed at offering a remediation of these systemically carcinogenic particulates to recondition the material as both vital and *vital to* the creative processes necessary to fecundity, to survival. This act of remembrance and reclamation aims to address and ultimately disrupt the practices of the privileged elite who have profited from the dispossession and desecration of the earth-ground. This terrestrial theopoetics thus strives to dismantle these structures—theoretical and material—by which many, undoubtedly including some of my own ancestors, have benefited and continue to benefit.

Muddying—Poetics on the Ground

Poetics isn't merely some fanciful writing or frilled-out discourse; poetics—particularly in the work of Caribbean authors like Glissant, Derek Walcott, Aimé Césaire, and Sylvia Wynter[8]—carves space for the making of new meanings, novel modes of living, inventive practices for collecting, for resisting.

Here, I'll dive into Glissant's reflections on his "poetics of Relation," which will help not only stage what is meant by poetics (and, eventually, *theopoetics*) but, further, will refigure poetics as the process of sensual reorientation posed by replanting oneself in the earth-ground. In constructive theologian Mayra Rivera's assessment of Glissant's poetics, "... poetics refers not only to styles of writing, but also to modes of knowing, being, and acting in the world. The poetic approach is indispensable for addressing histories marked by disruption, displacement, and irrecoverable loss...."[9] Glissant's writings centrally concerned Caribbean peoples and those forcibly displaced through the transatlantic slave trade. But his reflections can now readily be extended to those facing disruptions caused by anthropogenic climate injustice. Not only are peoples already being forced into exile through deforestation, desertification, rising tides, and so forth,[10] but Earth itself is going into a sort of exile: The topsoil beneath our feet is eroding at rates that may well make agriculture impossible in just decades.[11] Humans and other creatures are forced into diaspora by the disproportionate emissions, habitat destruction, and greed from the wealthy elite, but so, too, is the earth-ground *itself* becoming undone and displaced.

Such impossible matters demand elasticity in the face of the unknown, resilience in the fog of ambiguity. To this end, as Rivera writes of Glissant, poetics aims to construct a way of knowing that is "attentive to loss and opacity, interruption and silence."[12] In this way, "instead of privileging the genres of stable, ordered unity," poetics "questions the search for legitimacy in genealogies and the drive to produce ontological systems, theories of the nature of being itself."[13] Thus the terrestrial ground and the soily theopoetics it inspires ruptures ontological systems, doing away with "things" (especially "things in themselves") and instead cultivating concerns for relations, becomings, movements, cycles—never stable, ever at the edge of chaos. The dark light, the luminous dark, exposed by tending to histories of colonialism, oppression, domination—over humans and Earth—does not reveal any sort of holism or salvific redemption of the "pure" or "total" sort.[14] Trauma isn't "healed," per se. Instead, what's revealed in this ambiguous in-between are the shards of narrative, the fragments of meaning. Sensing and processing—both of which are integral to the process of poetic way-making—resist the dualisms of knowing/feeling, broken/fixed, useful/useless, saved/damned.[15] As Caribbean poet and Nobel laureate Derek Walcott writes, poetics is a sort of "gathering of broken pieces." He expresses, "Antillean art is this restoration of our shattered histories, our shards of vocabulary, our archipelago becoming a synonym for pieces broken off from the original continent."[16] Poetics are constituted by the activity of gathering, of cobbling together, of mending; Antillean poetics, in Walcott's words, are "this shipwreck of fragments, these echoes, these shards of huge tribal vocabulary, these partially remembered customs, and they are not decayed but strong."[17] Walcott's inheritance of Caribbean history prevents turning to any possible notion of completion, wholeness, or universality. As Rivera recapitulates, "Poetics is an approach to knowledge that values processes of creation from 'shattered histories' and 'shards of vocabularies' and acknowledges their discontinuities."[18] These memories are not about returning to some romanticized past but are instead concerned with the remaking of, the patching of, the present, not *ex nihilo* but from the ground whence one emerges—social, political, ecological, racial, gendered, and beyond. This is why Walcott describes the "process of the making of poetry" as "not its 'making' but its *remaking*."[19] It is the past flowing into the present, remaking itself. This process only works if one locates oneself on the ground, acknowledging the inheritance of the past, of a narrative, of a location.

Poiesis is thus a process of open-ended interactivity in the present from the grounds, the resources, and the landscape of the past—flowing into the present. The function of poetics is not an abstraction but an incarnation: *making present, embodying, emboldening*. Glissant contends, "Just as Relation is not a pure abstraction to replace the old concept of the universal, it also neither implies nor authorizes any ecumenical *detachment*. The landscape of your word is the world's landscape. But its frontier *is open*."[20] In other words, "the poetics of Relation remains forever conjectural and presupposes *no ideological stability*. . . . A poetics that is latent, open, multilingual in intention, *directly in contact* with everything possible."[21] For this reason Glissant relies on the paradoxical framing of "unity-diversity" in his articulation of that which grounds relation. Tuning into relation in this way precludes the possibility for the delineation of externalities—of "collateral damage."[22] Poetics does not sweep us away but roots us, puts us "directly in contact" with Earth. Yet—and this is crucial!—this rooting does not presuppose the ideological stabilities professed by foundations and their respective isms but instead "rests" in the groundlessness of a cycling soil—making, unmaking, (un)making. As Rivera aptly describes this process, poetics "can give voice to injuries suffered, challenge received certainties, and conjure new possibilities."[23] Extending this argument to the work of environmental justice, for example, these "new possibilities" make room to refuse static and domineering environmentalisms—particularly those of liberal white folks from the Global North, generally—given their oversight and, worse, malicious subjugation of the complexities of social location when it comes to ecological concerns.

Glissant's "poetics of Relation" sketches an organic ground, but it rightly resists the tendency to idealize these lessons as universal, as anything other than contextually located. Glissant seeks "an aesthetics of earth" that remains fecund even in "landscapes of desolation," in settings of undeniable violence and oppression.²⁴ This would have to be, Glissant contends, an aesthetics "of rupture and connection," an aesthetics "of a variable continuum, of an invariant discontinuum."²⁵ This transversal disturbance, this fragmented interconnection, extends the possibility of Relation without colonization: an interactivity in which one "does not think of a land as a territory from which to project toward other territories *but as a place where one gives-on-and-with rather than grasps.*"²⁶ The chaotic milieu of these shards of the present ensure land is not transformed "into territory again." For, "Territory is the basis for conquest. Territory requires that filiation be planted and legitimated. Territory is defined by its limits, and they must be expanded. A land henceforth has no limits. That is the reason it is worth defending against every form of alienation."²⁷ To embody this poetics of Relation is thus to acknowledge one's relation to the earth-ground without rendering that ground into a foundation—a background or Territory—upon which one acts, coerces, colonizes. And yet, such a ground does not remain "other," as if there were a discrete "I" imaginable as distinct from a separable context: Relation remains intransitive, intra-active.²⁸

It almost goes without saying that anthropogenic climate change—now already upon us, ever-differentially—necessitates all of these things: new meanings, new lifeways, new models of organizing, and so forth.²⁹ Everything is changing: It's not that it hasn't always been changing, but it's that the *very rate of change is changing impossibly quickly*. In light of this, any presupposed static model concerning knowledge production, ethical conduct, political engagement, or so forth will become undermined by these rapidly changing rates of change. The false lure toward the linear and static "works" only to the extent that it can dominate and maintain control: hence the real and pressing danger of fascist resurgence with the coming calamities of climate catastrophe.³⁰

Poetics constitutes the rupturing of the fixed, the objectified, the simplified, the abstracted. The imaginative capacities of poetics do not make it in any way a- or anti-material; these dimensions do not point toward some transcendent "away" or "beyond" but rather uncover alternatives, opportunities, and change—here-now. Poetics configures new visions; the poetic is visionary not because it leads us away from the earthen, but because it offers new angles, unique lenses, and reimagined perspectives. These novel optics trace the interconnections between phenomena thought to be "disparate" or "not correlated": coal-fired power plants and respiratory illness, landfills and cancer rates, wolves and riparian health.³¹ The grounded poetics here at stake minds these relations even as it concedes that mysteries remain and that there will ever yet be mysteries that remain; this is not for the sake of mystification itself but because it admits to having a perspective, *which means* that it is *the effect of* material histories, of enfleshed stories, of earthy geographies—making them particular, contextual, located. To be grounded and to ground one's philosophical theology in the earth-ground thus marks the need for poetics as a mode for navigating landscapes, for negotiating terrains. The definitiveness, the finality, of Logos decomposes on the porous ground among vital matters, decaying into organic, expressive elements for way-making.

Cultivating—Aporetic Ground, Apophatic Soil

The poetic pushes us to the edges of language, carving room for sensing differently, newly. Sensing includes but also extends beyond "knowledge" into experiences of corporeal feeling, embodied affect, and intuited concern. Yet, horizons remain—deferred limits that are the very result of having a perspective. What's more, the earth-ground on which we tread presents itself as nothing less than an aporia: to recall language from the previous chapter, a groundless ground that is sturdy and fragile, material and relational, particular and connecting, contextual and transversal, organic and inorganic, life-giving and life-receiving, decomposing and animating. One can *wonder* at these poietic matters, or one can foreclose them into taxonomic boxes or reduce them to static "natural resources." This section is dedicated to arguing for the fecund promise of "wonder."

The series of paradoxes just referenced aren't new by any stretch of the poetic imagination; they've held a critical place in the history of Western philosophy since at least Heraclitus. And it was Socrates, or at least his Platonic literary incarnation, who so poignantly reflected on the ways in which philosophy rests on these impossible grounds: "For this is an experience which is characteristic of a philosopher, this wondering [*thaumazein*]: this is where philosophy begins and nowhere else."[32] Mary-Jane Rubenstein's 2008 *Strange Wonder: The Closure of Metaphysics and the Opening of Awe* dwells on this Socratic wonder as the very opening of philosophy. Wonder "comes on the scene neither as a tranquilizing force nor as a kind of will-toward-epistemological domination, but rather as a profoundly unsettling pathos."[33] Rubenstein even describes wonder as a "groundless ground" that constitutes the *beginning* of philosophy.[34] But wonder can remain open, or it can close itself off; according to Rubenstein: "Wonder either keeps itself open, exposing itself to all the raging elements, or it shuts itself down, shielding itself against all uncertainty within the comfortable confines of the certain, the familiar, and the possible."[35] As she argues,

> There is an irreducible difference between a rigorous, investigative thinking that sustains wonder's strangeness and a rigorous, investigative thinking that endeavors to assimilate that strangeness. To the

extent that thinking remains with wonder, it is not inimical to all propositions, but rather keeps propositions provisional, open-ended, and incomplete. This is because wonder wonders at the strangeness of the most familiar: at that which, *within the possibilities of determinate thinking*, still remains indeterminate, unthinkable, and impossible.[36]

Wonder is that which opens thinking itself, that which conditions possibility, that which grounds thinking precisely by *ungrounding*, by *opening*. Wonder *is* perpetual openness, the very condition of change, of relation. Openness, or groundlessness, serves as the catalytic function propelling philosophy, animating organic life. To this end, Rubenstein writes,

> . . . wonder is only wonder when it remains open. Wonder opens an originary rift in thought, an unsuturable gash that both constitutes and deconstitutes thinking as such. To open the question of wonder, then, is to open thought not only to the fantastic and amazing but also to the dreadful and the threatening.[37]

To stay with wonder, in other words, does not transport one away from the shards of history or the way-making necessitated in the ruptures of life. The resonances between Rubenstein's wonder and Glissant's poetics abound. To create with and among the rubble, the wreckage, demands a certain double attention to impossibility—both in the sense that any sort of wholeness is impossible when one is dealing with debris and in the sense that that which grounds also *ungrounds*. That is, one cannot "think" wonder, despite the reality that wonder constitutes the very possibility of philosophizing—in the same way that one cannot "think" ground as extricable from its implicit groundlessness. On this point, Rubenstein contends,

> Any thinking of wonder is destined to miss its mark, and yet thinking cannot *not* think with wonder. One hopes, therefore, that even if the difference between the thinkable and the unthinkable will never be closed, attempting to think the unthinkable *as such* will at the very least expand the limits of thought before collapsing back into them.[38]

Wonder extends its tendrils just past the edge, searching and curling back. The process of poetics, then, isn't ever linear; the process of poetics is spiraling, weaving.[39] To explore at the edge entails a simultaneous and reciprocal folding-back, necessary in order to remain open, conjectural, in-process, on-the-way. Rubenstein's "wonder" constitutes the grounds of epistemology and its thresholds: That which opens thought itself also limits it. In the vernacular of this project, one could then say that wonder opens transversal possibilities even as it contextualizes them; wonder opens potentiality even as it perspectivally particularizes that potentiality.

Here, at last, bumping into one another in the luminous dark of the aporetic edge, the poetic meets the apophatic. The two intermingle and intertwine, ever gesturing toward the unnamable while at the same time folding back on itself in the face of this impossible task. The poetic points toward that which lies beyond the sayable, simultaneously *making* as it itself becomes *unmade*. In its way-making gesture, poetics comes undone in its aim to express what it cannot possibly articulate; this poetics produces a way that cannot be confined to its articulations or organization, creating something that transgresses the limits of communication. It frays—indeed, remains open—at the edge. The poetic makes insofar as it is unmade and broken in its collision with a horizon. *Poiesis* composes a way—creatively—not straightforwardly or straightly but by queerly pointing toward that which remains unnamable. This process of unsaying is integral to a wonder-full *poiesis*; Rubenstein muses, "Wonder wonders at that which conditions—and for that reason ultimately eludes—the mechanisms of calculation, comprehension, and possession themselves."[40] Put differently, *poiesis* necessitates apophatic folding lest it become some mechanistic program or linear course of action. The fold here, making and unmaking at once, constitutes creativity—without it there would be no difference, only selfsame repetition.[41] But unsaying should not be equated with a rejection of resoluteness, of a commitment to liberation.

Closing down wonder, even as it exposes the terror-inducing and awe-striking, only exacerbates the linear progress narratives so often accompanying the hegemonic. Glissant leans into the promise of poetics in the face of injustice:

> ... we are just barely beginning to conceive of this immense friction. The more [this turbulence] works in favor of an oppressive order, the more it calls forth disorder as well. The more it produces exclusion, the more it generates attraction. It standardizes—*but at every node of Relation we will find callouses of resistance. Relation is learning more and more to go beyond judgments into the unexpected dark of art's upsurgings. Its beauty springs from the stable and the unstable. . . . The more things it standardizes into a state of lethargy, the more rebellious consciousness it arouses.*[42]

Foreclosing the abysses that poetics opens *shuts out* creative modes that resist the generalized, the standardized, and the universalized—all of which are inimical to sensing the particularities of being on the earth-ground. Rubenstein suggests, "The progressive eclipse of wonder is therefore related to a certain will toward mastery, even toward divinity: by *comprehending* the source of the wondrous, the thinking self in effect *becomes* the source of the wondrous...."[43] One can, in other words, criticize the "self-mastery (and, by extension, the mastery of others) that characterizes the thinker of clear and distinct ideas" in favor of a poetic way-making that concomitantly admits to the fuzziness of the world, to its rhizomatic relationality, without forsaking poetics as inherently *entangled in* and *prefiguring* efforts to upend oppressive hegemonies.[44] To concede that the ordinary is wondrous, is strange—and not in some romanticized sense, either—is to concede that one does not have mastery over it. And yet, this does not mean that efforts aimed at radical justice need be any less resolute or steadfast in their demands. If the goal here is, as Rubenstein puts it, to "stay with the perilous wonder that resists final resolution, simple identity, and sure teleology," then this process of apophatic folding as one navigates the edges of possibility may bear the promise for greater creativity.[45] Apophasis grants opportunities to regroup for the sake of reimagining and amplifying one's cause, to remain open through sensing, through listening. Taking on the lessons offered by activist and queer theorist adrienne maree brown's "emergent strategy," apophasis extends moments for communities to practice intentional adaptation and nonlinear, iterative growth for the sake of a resilient resistance.[46] That is to say, apophasis allows ongoing justice-seeking efforts to remain dynamic, responsive, elastic.

Rubenstein, in proper Kierkegaardian fashion, describes wonder as a "double movement" that "takes us out of the world *only to put us back into the world*, dismantling old possibilities to uncover new ones...."[47] Here a familiar echo returns: *poiesis*, even as it pushes one to the edge while ever carving space thereat, does not take one into some transcendent "elsewhere" but steers one closer to matters at hand, entering into deeper and more intimate—indeed immanent—relations on and with the ground.[48] But this is only possible by remaining open, by predicating one's way-making on, by planting it in, these aporetic grounds that oscillate and flow in ways that inspire, if not provoke, apophatic folding.

The edge of the sayable prompts a *gesturing* for which words are inadequate; poetics must then *materialize* in the rift of that which remains unutterable. The incarnational implications of these matters yield all sorts of complications for any who wish to hold to that which prefigures the prefix *theo-*. The mist of the divine descends altogether differently if one adopts a terrestrial perspective.

Navigating—Horizontality and Divinity

The practice of theology on the ground, in the disorienting reorientation of a terrestrial horizontality, may yet find itself fracturing in an encounter with aporia. The "systematic"—or, otherwise, the adjectival counterpart oft-accompanying theological work—cannot contain the paradoxical mysteries that persist; at this mystical edge, one has few options: box in, wall out, or *stay with*.[49] Obviously the last of these is the most desirable, at least if one doesn't wish to reduce the sacred, diminish the aporetic, or shut in the enlivening.[50] The work of theopoetics is to *stay with, to abide*, which promises the capacity to remain open to divine lures.[51] Systematization constitutes compartmentalization, fixing rigid margins and relegating accordingly; poetics composes precisely through decomposition, opening at the edges to ruin any notion of the "Center."[52] Recalling Glissant's efforts to disrupt ideological stabilities—undoing foundational centralisms in favor of errant rhizomatic connections—an earthy poetics attempts a filiation with and in networks of relation in an effort to "give-on-and-with" as opposed to "grasping."[53] Systematicity is this very attempt to "grasp," to comprehend. Poetics instead traces the web-like tangles of sensed lures; it envisions "knowledge" as far closer to *imagination* than "intellect."

The question at hand here—if not to be answered, at least *addressed*—is this: What are the implications for the *theos* of theopoetics if one treads on, is rooted in, the ground? I hope to explore this query in search of a *terrestrial theopoetics* that neither elides the immanently material nor renounces the lures of a divine creativity.

Navigating these tenuous grounds warrants both precision and ambiguity. One must precisely illustrate the vital elements of these musings while preserving a bit of the ambiguity that shrouds the sacred. To do so is not to refrain from plumbing the depths of what can yet be known for the sake of reifying some status-quo-preserving mysticism but rather to fold apophasis back into the mix, aiming to avoid perpetuating some mechanistic logic or anthropomorphic projection or unfeeling rationalism or . . . Such navigation, even as it remains ever on-the-way, does not "succeed," per se; one does not "arrive at" Justice or Truth or Beauty, for these remain, in part, concealed, deferred, and open-ended. There is no Final Truth, just as the divine is not Final in its eternality. Isn't this what it means to have a perspective: the acknowledgment that one's vision is incomplete, is at an angle, is located? Contextuality merits horizons, not walls or borders.

If one is to take context seriously, then, it must be said that there is a preexisting porosity implied: One is composed of, constituted by, and grounded in context. This is not some mere external influence seeping in but is a constant intra-activity in which a subject always includes not only other subjects (historical, social, political, and beyond) but also its ecologies (geologies, minerals, contaminants, and beyond). What I mean is that a subject is not only ever intersubjective (or, more accurately, intra-subjective) but is also always unspeakably ecological. Any "bounded" subject is *undone* by the ecological. As material feminist Stacy Alaimo theorizes in her book *Bodily Natures*, "Imagining human corporeality as trans-corporeality, in which the human is always intermeshed with the more-than-human world, underlines the extent to which the substance of the human is ultimately inseparable from 'the environment.'"[54] Trans-corporeality implies "a recognition *not just* that everything is interconnected but that humans are the very stuff of the material, emergent world."[55] That the human is porous in a trans-corporeal sense does not mean that the effects incurred are universal; to the contrary, trans-corporeality doubles-down on the physicality of context, acknowledging the materiality of location generated differentially by political systems, toxic substances, access to alimentation, and so forth. As Alaimo writes, "Environmental justice movements epitomize a trans-corporeal materiality, a conception of the body that is neither essentialist, nor genetically determined, nor firmly bounded, but rather a body in which social power and material/geographic agencies intra-act."[56] In this way, one might begin to observe the deconstruction of the exceptionalisms inherent in anthropocentrism, all the while emphasizing the persistent need for remediating the damages of environmental racism. In light of this reality, what might it mean to *stay with* the aporias of ground—and to do so in a way that does not erase but actually bolsters environmental justice activists' legitimate desire for greater capacities in the face of vast inequity and harm? Does an appeal to any sort of *theos* imply an escapism, simply "passing the buck" to that immaterially material Character who will surely fix things in spite of, and maybe even through, my own inactivity? Sarcasm aside, how might one apophatically imagine the divine without pulling the rug out from under those theologically inclined folks who seek justice for "the least of these?"

The central premise in this section, in hopes of responding to the above queries, is this: There may yet be a fertile relation between the apophatic construction of the divine and the aporetic processes of the earth-ground. Each offers lessons for the other. The earth-ground is stable yet moves, is firm yet full of holes, is organic yet inorganic, is animate yet not "alive," is active yet passive, is resilient but fragile; the divine is active yet does not orchestrate, is transcendent yet immanent, is here yet elsewhere, is particular yet eternal. Both offer modes of constructive, contextual way-making *by means of the paradoxical process of decomposition*: transfiguring composted matters, transmuting the immanent as mystically irreducible, incarnating the numinous.

Apophasis implies unsaying; but, if one has any enfleshed connection to one's speech-acts, this amounts to a *sensual undoing*. One is undone at the edge of the sayable; for this reason a poetics *does something* to us, precisely by *undoing* us. One is ungrounded by the abyss toward which the poetic points but does not—indeed, cannot—directly name. One cannot articulate the depth of feeling, of embodied ache, crafted in the work of, say, Claudia Rankine or Pablo Neruda or Ernesto Cardenal or Mark Strand or bell hooks.[57] To unsay is to resist the temptation toward Finality; to be undone is to *open* oneself to the relations that constitute all that becomes in this world. Being undone is the very condition of a precarious openness that allows for even the possibility of relationality; without openness—without, daresay, vulnerability—any sort of becoming would not be possible.[58] While the ethics of this precarity will be explored in detail in the two chapters to follow, the ontological queries grounding them rumble here-now, begging poetic explication. For this, we turn to Judith Butler's relational ontology, seeking a geo-muddying thereof.

Judith Butler and their proposed relational ontology, which centers a certain openness—indeed, vulnerability—in its gaze, is of paramount importance here. Writing in the wake of loss, a moment of grief, Butler claims, ". . . we cannot represent ourselves as merely bounded beings. . . ."[59] They contemplate what it means to think of oneself not as bounded but as utterly relational:

> It is not as if an "I" exists independently over here and then simply loses a "you" over there, especially if the attachment to "you" is part of what *composes* who "I" am. . . . Who "am" I, without you? When we lose some of these ties by which we are constituted, we do not know who we are or what to do.[60]

Could loss perhaps attune us to the relational web that composes us: Who am I without the relations from which I continue to emerge?[61] One is undone by the unspeakable weight of loss—the threads that weave through one's narrative fraying, slipping, unraveling. These revelations only multiply when one considers the ecological: Who am I, earthling, without Earth? Truly what am I without the earth-ground on which I tread, much less the life that emerges from it, thereby enabling my own?

Caribbean theorist Aimé Césaire merges these earthy stirrings with a cosmo-poetic vision:

> This is the right occasion to recall that the unconscious that all true poetry calls upon is the receptacle of original relationships that bind us to nature. Within us, all the ages of mankind [sic]. Within us, all humankind. Within us, animal, vegetable, mineral. Mankind is not only mankind. It is *universe*.[62]

Césaire isn't just waxing poetic: Earth, and "humankind" by extension, is composed of elements that are necessarily cosmic, for our sun cannot produce any elements heavier than helium.[63] Césaire is tapping into a cosmic wisdom here, offering a novel optic that seeks beauty and richness prior to "scientific knowledge," which "enumerates, measures, classifies, and kills."[64] Instead, if, as he writes, "poetic knowledge is born in the great silence of scientific knowledge," then it signifies an openness to that which cannot be *grasped* in word but must be *sensed* in flesh.[65] This same ethical import—or at least one very akin to Césaire's—mobilizes Butler's relational ontology, striving for "a relationality that is composed neither exclusively of myself nor you, but is to be conceived as *the tie* by which those terms are differentiated and related."[66] We are not—save for our relations. In Butler's potent words,

> . . . each of us is constituted politically in part by virtue of the social vulnerability of our bodies—as a site of desire and physical vulnerability, as a site of a publicity at once assertive and exposed. Loss and vulnerability seem to follow from our being socially constituted bodies, attached to others, at risk of losing those attachments, exposed to others, at risk of violence by virtue of exposure.[67]

Again, the magnitude of these arguments inches us ever closer to the edge of an inarticulable mystery, both ontologically and ecologically: *The vulnerabilities that threaten our undoing are the very phenomena that constitute possibility itself.*

The threat of being undone can lead easily down a wide path of seeking control, seeking to dominate. In fear, one might wish for a final Word, a Logos once-and-for-all, that might *explain* or *justify*. Wendell Berry links the ecological and theological along these very lines:

> . . . the most dangerous tendency in modern society, now rapidly emerging as a scientific-industrial ambition, is the tendency toward encapsulation of human order—the severance, once and for all, of the umbilical cord fastening us to the wilderness or the Creation. The threat is not only in the totalitarian desire for absolute control. It lies in the willingness to ignore *an essential paradox: the natural forces that so threaten us are the same forces that preserve and renew us.*[68]

This aporia compels a certain fear and trembling in this here author, for even as I am convinced by these ontological and ecological revelations, I am wary that they may be read as reifying the violences incurred disproportionately by those on the margins at social, ecological, and even, arguably, ontological levels.[69] But recognizing these vulnerabilities that open us to relation with- seems too crucial and too true to avoid, much less reject. To state clearly my presuppositions, this does not imply that this openness is non-differential or evenly distributed; such a claim would undo the very lessons made by intersectional feminism and environmental justice advocates, among others. Rather, by highlighting this openness, by bringing it to the fore, I hope to uncover how a materially attuned poetics might lead to more radically just ways of tending to the vulnerabilities that constitute us *without denying them*.[70] Bringing these matters to light allows for better ways to mend them. As Butler states,

> If my fate is not originally or finally separable from yours, then the "we" is traversed by a relationality that we cannot easily argue against; or, rather, we can argue against it, *but we would be denying something fundamental* about the social conditions of our very formation.[71]

And these conditions are not just social but are also ecological. In response to this paradox of an openness, a vulnerability that at once grounds and ungrounds, how might one respond in a way that aims toward nurture, toward justice? Butler offers one such poetic mode: "We cannot . . . *will away* this vulnerability. We must *attend to it, even abide by it*, as we begin to think about what politics might be implied by *staying with* the thought of corporeal vulnerability itself. . . ."[72] A relational responsibility of ongoing openness is the paradoxical mode Butler offers for tending to vulnerability: "I cannot think the question of responsibility alone, in isolation from the Other; if I do, I have taken myself out of the relational bind that frames the problem of responsibility from the start."[73] Responsibility tangles in the web of relations that ground the possibilities of our becomings. It is through the recognition of vulnerability—and, hence, contextual agency—that one recognizes that which precedes the autonomous "I," the detached *cogito*, the superior human. It is vulnerability as a body to the material conditions of the world, broadly, and of our immediate geography, specifically, that precedes any understanding of who "I" even am.[74] To be undone by the aporias of the theological and terrestrial alike can only find elucidation in an apophatic poetics: making by being unmade, constructing via deconstruction, composing by means of decomposition. Yet this claim is not a condemnation of relationality but is the revelation that relations are contextual, particular, and located: processes of making and unmaking, linking and disjoining, grounding and ungrounding.[75] These earthy lessons affect what it means to practice theopoetics on the ground.

So what, then, does a terrestrial theopoetics promise, or at least point toward? It offers a *way*, a *process*—not a "thing" or "goal" so much as *movement*. Yet this movement is neither free-floating nor abstract: It is embodied, incarnate, and ecological. It concerns itself with the material, meaning that it refuses the extraction of the immanent as a-relational, as expendable; it treads—lightly. Terrestrial theopoiesis offers not "Solutions" but fluid resolutions, not Final Answers but tentative, adapting activities. It recognizes that pursuing the lure of the divine is not only predicated on social contexts but also geological ones; there is, hence, no uniformity or universality to justice—though, *crucially*, even in its located-ness *it shares a transversal ground*. A terrestrial theopoetic justice concerns not just the particularities of socio-cultural matters but also of ecological place, and these "two" are neither two nor one but an entangled multiplicity! As Catherine Keller writes, "We—we humans at least—emerge complicated by a past that we cannot fully know, implicated in its distortions, its pathologies intimate and collective."[76] How vast this cloud of unknowing becomes as one attempts to trace the threads of ecological particularity, unnoticed affects, and unacknowledged animacies.[77] One is not only a complication of the milieux of race and gender and sexual orientation and class and ability and beyond, but, further, one sprouts from the folds of alimentation, watershed quality, synthetic particulate presence, and so on. There may be no universals even as there are linking particularities—placed but not fully known, immanent but mystically irreducible.

To practice a terrestrial theopoetics, to embody resolute activity, thus amounts to far more than words and extends far beyond, remembering Butler here, the myth of the autonomous "individual," without forgoing the need to infuse this practice with the vital integrities of liberative justice for those long denied the liberties of self-determination. Put simply, the practice of a terrestrial theopoetics unfolds communally, contextually, if it is to be done well. It is the communal that offers accountability, if one is *open* to being held accountable, if one is *moved by and with* one's community—human and otherwise. Recalling Glissant and Rubenstein, this is not a one-time openness but a continual carving of space, a constant praxis of sensing, a persistent openness to transformation.[78] The relational nature of *com/passion*—"to be moved" "with"—comes to the fore here. Hence the toil of theopoetics engages a collective—the intertwining of histories, the cross-pollination of contexts, the entangling of differences—without reducing that collective into an amorphous, undifferentiated, or homogeneous mass. This becomes all the more interesting when the divine gets folded in, not as some additive but as the ground that links, that intersects.

Theopoetics, as a task of communal discernment, minds relations not as that which is "between" otherwise separate entities but as that which *is*, that which *becomes*. Theopoetics defers the finality of Logos in favor of the decisiveness of faithful decision-making in the dark. And this extends far beyond the *anthro-* into the *eco-*, tending to the precarity of the planetary.[79] This deferral could be read as endlessly tempting by means of a carrot on a stick, so to speak; that is, the open-ended nature of *poiesis* may yet be accused of a certain incapacitation of meaning-making for those occupying most uncertain circumstances. In other words, such a delay, if not deconstruction, of Certainty could be considered a ceaselessly cruel decoy that never materializes as real—as a *really real* experience of equitable justice. But it is precisely the opposite that I take to be the case here.

If theopoetics does not dangle some tempting lure just ever out of reach, what does it purport to do? We might say that it offers opportunities for embodied action in ways that the abstract Logos of theology, at times, leaves free-floating, out-there, beyond, apart, not among—anywhere other than here-now. Being *apart*—in the sense of the *distance* between transcendent and immanent, between heaven and earth—characterizes many classical conceptions of holiness, thereby jeopardizing the material magnitude of divinity. Terrestrial theopoetics entangles the two—immanence and transcendence, earthly and heavenly—as nonseparably woven; put differently, this theopoetics imagines the transcendent "otherness" of divinity as that which remains aporetically irreducible, as that which refuses the inclination to coerce or to dominate or to possess or to "understand," as that which resists the disconnection of the world into clear-cut, externalizable, or separable parts.

Transcendence is not far off, is not outside, but becomes mystically incarnate in word and deed. This is Mayra Rivera's point when, in her earlier book, *The Touch of Transcendence* (2007), she argues that the divine is transcendent in that it is unable to be *grasped*—though it can be *touched*.[80] To *sense* holiness is far different than to "grasp" it. Rivera's "relational transcendence" creates *space* for the holiness—the otherness—of God as the coming of the new, as the advent of possibility, without doing so as the mere taunting of a groundless hope;[81] to translate her contentions into the vernacular of this present project, a theopoetics that attempts to take seriously the entanglement of the terrestrial and the theological can find both in the intra-relational web of a groundless ground that disturbs and embraces, that ungrounds and welcomes. If *theos* is to have any meaningful place in the *geo-*, or even the *anthro-* for that matter, the boundaries between the heavenly and earthly, the spirit and flesh, must pleat into a *complicatio*, a fold. In tune with Glissant's poignant contention that "Relation is the moment when we realize that there is a definite quality of all the differences in the world,"[82] the earthiness of ground as contextually, materially entangled difference discloses itself as the location whence one practices theopoetics. To practice a soiled theopoetics—in other words, an immanent perspectivalism that retains the need for incarnation and feeling as well as mystery and humility—ruptures any of the "all is well" affects accompanying any sort of top-down topography; terrestrial theopoetics is a first-person map (which is indeed something of a paradox in itself), not from-above but at-hand.

Hence theopoetic praxis carves room for one to entangle oneself with, to nurture the intra-active relations between, the divine manifested—*in the terrestrial*.[83]

Theopoetics does not constitute the end of work, the end of unveiling toil, but their *beginning*—a task that lasts lifetimes. For this reason, it remains perpetually open: not a conclusory Omega so much as a ceaselessly cantillated *b'reshit*. But a grounded theopoetics demands not only a certain toil—that one cannot superintend but must remain open to traversing, to navigating—but, what's more, it fosters a commitment to undoing, to becoming undone.

The work signified by a terrestrial theopoetics thus entails a faithfulness to the ambiguity of the aporetic, a recognition of the limits of horizontality and its respective horizons—indeed, a commitment to open-endedness. Ambiguity is not relativism. Nor does it mean to suggest a certain inescapability from violence or an incapacitation of agency. Ambiguity implies that *decisions* must be made and ought to be *rendered visible*. This ambiguity and its attendant "dark hope," amplified by the undecidable conditions presented by the Anthropocene, will be the subject of Chapter Three.

Interlude
Mountaintop Removal and the Impossibility of Hope

I *knew* what to expect. As we rounded that corner, the van rattling slightly on the rock-strewn dirt road, well-compacted by heavy machinery, I fully knew what we'd encounter. None of this was new to me; it should not have felt new to me. Even still, I could not have been more shocked. We came around the bend, and, just barely audibly, I heard myself whisper in surprise, "Oh my God."

I've never felt so out of place, as if instantly transported to another planet. The ground seemed to almost literally drop out from under my feet, transmuting suddenly into some alien terrain. Surely this could not be Earth; I recognized . . . nothing. Was this even still—clay? Stone? Next to the cold metal "Danger: Blasting Area" signs, I fully expected others to read, "If you've come looking for life, turn around now. You're in the wrong place for that." And yet, I was unmistakably—*here*.

By then, before that moment, I'd been taking college students to Appalachia for several years. Each spring break, a dozen or so students from the small liberal arts university in New Jersey where I was working on my PhD would pile into vans—overstuffed with sleeping bags, mucky boots, and, like any proper road trip, ample snacks—and together we would journey southward.

It was one of those "alternative spring break" trips that were a mix of environmental education and community service—an exciting opportunity to get outside of the liberal bubble so often surrounding college campuses to learn about the world by getting one's hands dirty. In any case, the students were inevitably a mix of those genuinely interested in environmental justice, genuinely curious about life outside of the Northeast, and genuinely concerned that they may not graduate without fulfilling their mandated "off-campus experience." There were freshmen and seniors, art students and biochemistry majors.

INTERLUDE: MOUNTAINTOP REMOVAL AND THE IMPOSSIBILITY OF HOPE   63

But, against all odds and in the face of every collegiate stereotype, the students would form a bond that few other school-initiated collectives could have rivaled. So, together, somehow, we'd spend a week in Appalachia, partnering with a local organization to learn about mountaintop removal coal mining and its associated injustices—human, ecological, and beyond.

The students would spend their days bouncing between lectures on everything from coal extraction processes to power plant health hazards, seminars with on-the-ground activists, various site visits, and some hands-on service work. One day they might be participating in a roadside trash pickup before a quick hike to learn about local flora and fauna, all before dashing off to an afternoon Q&A with community organizers, former miners, and local leaders.

Each year, without fail, the most striking moment of the week is a visit to a mountaintop removal site. To stand before the sheer violence of a destroyed mountain is surreal. It's an unimaginable sight: Where a mountain should have been—*nothing*. It's hard to feel that one's eyes haven't betrayed them: Surely there should be *something* here—a tree, even a shrub, literally anything at all. Even calling what remains "rubble" is an overstatement. It is barren, destitute, unnaturally flat land without a hint of life, of possibility. That destruction of this magnitude is possible, let alone legal, confounds: How did this ever become allowable? And by whom?

And so it would go each year; I'd invite students to spend time looking on this devastation in silence, in contemplation. They would scatter across whatever overlook we'd happened to be on and dwell on what was once a flourishing mountain—now ruins. We would circle up afterward, and I'd muster up some misty-eyed speech about the injustice we had encountered and the responsibility that comes with being a witness to that injustice. I'd encourage them to think about the systems and structures that have allowed this violence to not only "occur" but *persist knowingly* despite the grave consequences for humans, critters, watersheds, habitats. I would ask them to consider their place in those systems and structures—none of which they had consented to, much less constructed, as just barely young adults, but to which they were now bound in responsibility as *witnesses*. I'd urge them to remember this very moment, standing before that seemingly impossible but undeniably real terrain: once vibrant, now devastated.

To some degree, the trip worked. It did something. No student went on to single-handedly take down a coal company or pass legislation against mountaintop removal—at least, not yet. No, such violence continues—amply. But, for whatever reason, some students pursued careers as earth scientists; some went on to make environmental justice central to their studies; others wrote ecopoetry; still others made lifestyle changes for the sake of sustainability. At any rate, something changed in these students' lives. And so they told their friends about the trip. Some even got tattoos to remember it. And, year after year, in the face of financial crises, budget cuts, and far-reaching layoffs, this little university would continue to send its students to Appalachia under my care.

But, just before the beginning of the COVID-19 pandemic, our trip in the early Spring of 2020 was a bit different. A new legal team at that university—by requesting new insurance procedures, imposing finance capitalist-inspired contracts onto our partners and hosts in Appalachia, and requiring new restrictions on what activities could take place once there—caused enough commotion to ensure that the organization with which we'd been partnering for years would not be able to work with us. This perfect storm, all coming to a head only weeks before our scheduled departure, nearly canceled the trip; a somber email to the students notifying them of the trip's cancellation had been drafted, though not sent.

By some stroke of luck, it was then that we happened to get in touch with Coal River Mountain Watch (CRMW) in Naoma, West Virginia. With a sort of shocking gladness, they agreed to host our trip at a moment's notice. Not knowing much about their work or history, save for what was shared on their website, we decided to go all-in. Hardly a better decision's been made.

Once in Naoma, West Virginia, my co-leader and I quickly realized that things would be quite different that week. Situated in the heart of one of the most active regions for mountaintop removal, Coal River Mountain Watch constitutes something of a basecamp, actively organizing what feels like a last stand. This may seem hyperbolic, but it's difficult to exaggerate the gravity of the destruction already completed in the Coal River Valley. This valley is ground zero of environmental violence—and resistance.

There is but one mountain left in the entire Coal River watershed that's not been destroyed by surface mining: Coal River Mountain. Every other mountain has been exterminated: leveled, stripped, ravaged. Above the Coal River valley sits the Brushy Fork Coal Slurry Impoundment, over 900 feet tall (unofficially making it far larger than any other dam in the States) and holding back over 8 *billion* gallons of toxic coal slurry.[1] The devastation that this impoundment portends should it rupture for whatever reason, on top of the devastation it already represents, is almost unthinkable—flooding the valley with billions of gallons of coal sludge mixed with the carcinogenic chemicals used to "clean" coal during the preparation process, not to mention the toxic heavy metals that are present in coal. This sort of disaster is not unprecedented.[2]

Just down the road from the CRMW headquarters sits the old Marsh Fork Elementary School. The school lies in the actual shadows of a coal preparation plant's silos and sits at the very foot of the Shumate Coal Impoundment, nearly 400 feet tall and holding back 2.8 *billion* gallons of coal slurry.³ For decades, children learned amid noxious coal dust, noisy coal trucks, and the ever-looming threat of the dam's rupture. Activists—including Judy Bonds and others from CRMW—organized, protested, and lobbied for more than six years before finally succeeding in acquiring the land and funds for a new Marsh Fork Elementary School to be built in 2012. Of course, this victory does not undo or resolve the damaging health effects alumni continue to experience; nor does it offer a solution to the Shumate impoundment, much less Brushy Fork.

In the Coal River Valley, one could not avoid noticing the precarity of it all: earthen dams that cannot be meaningfully considered "permanent," children placed in the line of fire of toxic sludge, a local economy predicated on a deadly industry long automated and mechanized. "Precarity" is an understatement when one is dealing with billions of gallons of contaminants—in just a few square miles.

And so, for a week, we worked alongside the folks of CRMW, and it was partly my task to help students "understand" (as if such violence were "understandable") not only that all of this was *possible* but that it was the daily reality for so many. But this would prove all the more impossible once we drove through an active mountaintop removal site: Blackhawk Mining company's Panther Creek mine.⁴

And so, to resume the vignette with which I began this interlude, as we drove our vans up the washboard-rutted road, I anticipated simply another view of surface mining—only, this time, "up close"—as we'd already seen several other operations, active and "reclaimed," just from afar. I couldn't have been more wrong.

We rounded a nondescript left-hand turn—and the world fell apart. There is no "comprehending" this kind of wreckage: It's nothing short of terrestrial genocide. Surface mining obliterates—a hellscape incarnate. It shatters any semblance of familiarity, rending the fabric of Earthly possibility for the sake of—*what exactly?* Profit? Greed?

To describe an active surface mine approaches the inarticulable. To be there—not at-a-distance but at-hand, on-the-ground—splits words just as it splits worlds. These earthen shards, when one is *with* and *among* them, are not "seen," per se, in the same way as they might be from afar or in a photo. In a way, to view, to "look upon," implies a passivity of the terrestrial that's inaccurate—or at least unfitting. Rather, on the ground, the terrestrial, active and vibrant, *confronts*—*colliding* materially, corporeally, with one's senses.

This anthropogenic ravaging is otherworldly—not in any cosmically divine or ideal sense; it's the *unconditional* rupture of the entangled ecologies composing the very *conditions* of life, of *possibility itself*. That's the thing with strip mining: It's not just the eradication of life but the annihilation of the *continued possibility thereof*. This sort of violence unravels ancient threads, exposing truly primordial matter and wrecking relations that sustain and support—*it unearths Earth itself*. To describe the severity of mountaintop removal, as it explodes entire landscapes, as *irreparable and irreversible doesn't even begin to capture the magnitude of undoing, of uncreating*. It challenges any assumption of reclamation, much less restoration: "Reclaimed" strip mines are but gravelly lots sprayed with GMO grass seed, far from the complex biodiversity found in healthy Appalachian mountains—supposedly "reclaimed" by turning them into airports, strip-mall shopping centers, "desirable" flat land.[5] Even the incomparable resilience of Earth tarries in the wake of these blasts, disrupting untold eons of relational interchange.

What does it mean to have hope in blasted landscapes?[6] Is there any such inflection of hope that remains viable in any meaningful sort of way among these irremediable terrestrial scars? Or does any iteration thereof helplessly crumble as mountains slide away? What sort of way can be made where there is no other, where the networks of possibility themselves are blown apart?

The magnitude of environmental injustice, broadly, and mountaintop removal, specifically, demands a vastly reimagined notion of hope. Any concept sufficiently robust to remain practicable in this most unjust present cannot slip feebly into some naïve optimism nor fatalistic pessimism; what's more, if such a thing can exist, this precarious, catalytic hope must not reproduce futurities predicated on linear progress—for it was "Progress" and all of its attendant "efficiencies" that deforested and strip-mined and desertified and plundered in the first place. The following chapter explores these questions in-depth, proposing the concept of "dark hope" as the grounds for ethical decision-making in these undecidable times.

3
Sprouting
Dark Hope in Undecidable Times

> ... if time is not empty, continuous chronos, each present contracts at once its past with its potentiality. So if we then disallow hope, we may miss and so fail to embrace the possibility tucked in this very present.
> —CATHERINE KELLER

The Impossibility of Hope

The Anthropocene's trials, overwhelming and unthinkable in scale, demand entirely different, though not necessarily "new," lifeways. Microplastics are everywhere, even in remote areas;[1] ocean acidification threatens to decimate not only fisheries but phytoplankton, the source of a significant portion of Earth's oxygen;[2] keystone species' "disappearance" portend the undoing of ancient ecological webs.[3] The vastness of these problems, somehow only the surface of the threats posed by anthropogenic climate change, immediately reduces any naïve hope to rubble. And, sometimes, naïve hope prevents one from even seeing the calamity—past, present, future—in the first place.

The enormity of scope and the degree of severity that the Anthropocene poses demands radical theoretical and ethical overhauls: One must speak *not* in terms of saving so much as salvaging, *not* in terms of fixing so much as mending, *not* in terms of solving so much as resolving. At this juncture, the immense disasters—underway and impending, actual and potential—of ecological collapse, irreparable contamination, and civilizational breakdown require the examination and reimagination of the conceptual grounds upon which our ideas are built—concepts that have led to the disrepair of our very earth-ground. This insurrection across registers of the speculative and embodied, of the notional and corporeal, does not forfeit the future in some fatalistic nihilism or indifferent apathy; nor does such an ideational rupture extend opportunities for blissful optimisms. Neither satisfied with pessimism and its abject unconcern nor optimism and its unfounded certainty, one must make another way. This chapter aims to offer one such way.

Drawing on an interdisciplinary web of literature, the conceptual matrix of "dark hope" will emerge here through an engagement primarily with questions of critical negativism and pessimism raised by theorists like Kathryn Yusoff, Fred Moten and Stefano Harney, Joseph Winters, Jack Halberstam, Anna Lowenhaupt Tsing, Alexis Shotwell, The Invisible Committee, and Tina M. Campt. While these theorists do not necessarily self-identify as "negativist" or "pessimist," per se, they raise potent critiques of "progress" in their attention to the contextual nature of agency and possibility in uncertain presents. The deconstructive force of their work destabilizes white supremacist, capitalist logics of "progress" without forsaking the real need for a radical material justice—particularly for those who have suffered most gravely under those logics. And yet, can one give up on the idea of a "progressive" justice that aims for radical systemic overhauls for the sake of wholesomeness and equity?

I seek to learn from and think with these particular sources in this particular moment, given the twofold challenge they present to any notion of hope: (a) they upend any possibility of hope as easily achieved or simply realized, and (b) they disrupt the notion that hope might find materialization within the bounds of or as defined by the structures of the present. If an anti-racist, anti-capitalist, intersectional hope in the Anthropocene is possible, it must be shaped by the voices and concerns of the directly impacted; for this reason, I intend for those like Yusoff, Moten, Harney, Winters, and Campt to unsettle my learned tendencies toward hopefulness as a white man, instead opting to think with the challenge they present to those whose privilege may have shielded them from having to toil for any promise of hope. I speak only of my understanding of hope, which has been influenced by these thinkers, and thus aim to bear witness to their work; I offer here an articulation of hope in and for the Anthropocene that intends to remain faithful to the negativist critiques of these theorists.

This chapter will trace the contours of what I'll refer to as "dark hope," with the goal that it might serve as a seed that will germinate into a more robust grounds for ethico-political engagement in the following chapter. This iteration of hopeful world-mending (indeed an extension of *tikkun olam*), by granting attention to the contextuality of agency, seeks not pure salvation but a radically just way-making.

Dark hope seeks to take seriously the woes of the Anthropocene—and all of its differential effects—without conceding the future because either "it'll all work out" or "everything's fucked." Neither will do. Instead, dark hope, predicated on the concept of ground materialized in Chapter One and the earthy theopoetics limned in Chapter Two, strives to make a way amid and with—*not* "in spite of"—the uncertainties of the present and the aporias of the terrestrial. This hope refuses to give up on the future, even as it remains tenderly planted in the present; yet, at the same time, it rejects any sort of linear projection onto the future—be it of "Progress," "Growth," "Development," or the like. These precarious times make such projections unwise, if not downright foolish, as they replicate and reify those drivers that created not only the Anthropocene but its attendant violences of the white supremacist, neoliberal capitalist, heteropatriarchal, xenophobic sort. What's necessary, then, is a notion of hope that tends to and dwells with precarity, that catalyzes decisions precisely *because* they remain undecidable. This darkly hopeful activity is not fully nameable or sayable but continually folds back in hopes of multiplying present efforts seeking better worlds—amid and even because of their undecidability.

The question of hope braids matters of agency and temporality: What is dark hope's relation to agency or capacity? What is dark hope's relation to temporal structures and imagined futurities? What is dark hope's relation to ethical incertitude of the most critical sort—that is, undecidability itself? I aim to respond to these three queries in this chapter, and, while they are not in any way discrete from one another, it will be crucial to remember that these strands are but pleats in the intertwined threads constituting dark hope.[4] Grafting together these matters, I will make a case for dark hope, conveying its relation to the metonymic materialization of ground as earth-ground. This dark hope will serve as the grounds for the emergence of political engagement as offered in the following chapter; dark hope is that which grounds political resistance to the disasters of climate catastrophe.

Hope, Optimism, Pessimism?

Though I endeavor to clarify the nuances of dark hope in more robust ways at the close of this chapter, a few clarifying remarks about hope at the outset are necessary. These claims will receive far more substantial treatment as the chapter unfolds. But it is crucial to lay a bit of groundwork here to ensure that I have preliminarily clarified my use of "hope."

I situate hope as distinct from, as wholly other than, optimism and pessimism. Hope is a radical rift in the spectrum of optimism-pessimism, both of which promise everything and require nothing; because optimism and pessimism are predicated on certainty, they pacify, incapacitate, even debilitate: Either it's going to work out or it's not, but either way "*I am certainly not responsible*" to do much of anything. Hope, as the fecund alternative to this binary, emerges in the face of—indeed *because of*—uncertainty.

The instability of uncertainty provokes modes for one to embody and *participate in* hope. That is not to say that hope exists in a free-floating, abstract sort of way, but rather, it is meant to suggest how hope operates as a lure to becoming—a communion simultaneously *with* and *as* creativity. That is, hope does not exist independently "out there" but rather incarnates relationally in material manners. One cannot force hope—as if it could be grasped or arrested—but neither does hope "occur" spontaneously or on its own. A way must be made—though not necessarily a way "forward," as forward so often continues in the direction intended by extant structures of oppression. Hope, thus, is *adamantly not* reformist. What's more, hope as a way-making catalyst necessarily implies its emergence differentially from the grounds of context, which would mean that it sprouts forth from the webs of one's locale, from the entanglement of matters and meanings available in that present.

Grounding Agency: Locating Hope

The question of dark hope, if it's to perform any meaningful sort of role in the Anthropocene, is always wrapped up in the matter of agency. That is, what's possible? For whom? In what way? To what end?

Still more queries lurk at the edges: Is it possible to imagine a notion of hope that acknowledges the vastness of the present violence of the Anthropocene while simultaneously galvanizing one in the contextual ground of their present? Is it possible to conceive of an iteration of hope that tangibly animates without overlooking or eliding incurred and inherited traumas? In other words, can one envision hope in such a way that seriously remembers histories yet remains potent in the reimagination of the future?

The challenges that the Anthropocene poses are neither unilateral nor universal—*even as* they are shared planetarily. Put differently, the Anthropocene is not neutral. Kathryn Yusoff, theorist of inhuman geography, critiques this purported "neutrality" endemic to most practices of geology and climate science: "Seeking to monumentalize Anthropocene history is an attempt to reclaim an 'innocence' around this geohistory. The histories of the Anthropocene unfold a brutal experience for much of the world's racialized poor and without due attention to the historicity of those events. . . ."[5] As Yusoff reminds, "The Anthropocene might seem to offer a dystopic future that laments the end of the world, but imperialism and ongoing (settler) colonialisms *have been ending worlds for as long as they've been in existence.*"[6] In other words, one must admit to the gravity of anthropogenic climate change while resolutely recognizing that "the end of this world *has already happened* for some subjects."[7] Yusoff contends that one must account for the role of the grammar of geology in perpetuating extractive economics and colonial regimes exploiting persons of color particularly, delineating and classifying who or what can be deemed active or inert, human or property, and so forth.[8] There is an implicit connection between which matters and which bodies are marked for extraction—for the energy and labor that each provides. In Yusoff's words:

> The movement of energy between enslaved bodies in plantations, plants, long-dead fossilized plants, and industrialized labor is a geochemical equation of extraction in the conversion of surplus. But this racialized equation of energy is located in a larger field of production and semiotics of extraction.[9]

How does one take the woes of the Anthropocene seriously without perpetuating the "racial colorblindness" and class oversight Yusoff so poignantly identifies? What would it mean to mind the urgencies of this uncertain ecological present without forsaking those who have long endured the forces of injustice contributing to the Anthropocene? Can one responsibly think about the anthropogenic destruction of eco-interconnections without implying some sort of "general experience" or "shared lot?" Yusoff is rightly suspicious of these very concerns:

> If the imagination of planetary peril coerces an ideal of "we," *it only does so when the entrappings of late liberalism become threatened.* This "we" negates all responsibility for how the wealth of geology was built off the subtending strata of indigenous genocide and erasure, slavery and carceral labor, and evades what that accumulation *still makes possible in the present*—lest "we" forget that the economies of geology still largely regulate geopolitics and modes of naturalizing, formalizing, and operationalizing dispossession and ongoing settler colonialism.[10]

There is no general "we" to speak of in the Anthropocene—not if one wishes to take seriously the disproportionate nature of the violences of the past, present, and possible futures. And yet, this does not mean that one's location—eco-social, socio-ecological—is essentialized; nor does it imply that there is not a shared, transversal, earthen ground that carves space for negotiating across differences. How might hope spark the navigation of this tenuous terrain? Can it conceive of and redistribute, as it were, this ground as a commons in such a way that does not erase the colonial histories of land grabs, of supremacisms, of exploitation? Can it stitch together the potent tension between impending disasters of the so-called Anthropocene and the past and persistent catastrophes created by the evils of white heteropatriarchy and its related neoliberalism?

The Anthropocene does not occur outside of the structures of biopolitical governance but rather *through* them. To consider the calamities of anthropogenic climate change necessitates the question of agency as embedded in present modes of suppression, control, and surveillance. What sort of hope can stand in the face of all this? Here, Black critical theorists Fred Moten and Stefano Harney's notions of "policy" and "planning"—and their relation to "governance"—enrich the question of dark hope precisely by destabilizing it, by ensuring that one does not too quickly rush to, much less cling to, a decoy of hope planted by the apparatuses of the (neo)colonial state.

Moten and Harney argue that governance, which "should not be confused with government or governmentality," is "an instrumentalisation of policy, a set of protocols of deputisation, where one simultaneously auctions and bids on oneself, where the public and private submit themselves to post-fordist production."[11] It is, in other words, "the harvesting of the means of social reproduction *but it appears as the acts of will*, and therefore as the death drive, of the harvested."[12] Governance generates a façade pretending that individuals are bounded, impermeable subjects agentially making decisions between live choices and thus are "responsible for" that which happens to them; governance's insidiousness lies in its capacity to sell the narrative that one's decisions and therefore "lot" in life are "acts of the will," even as it generates inequitable power structures, imbalanced playing fields, disproportionate burdens.

Governance is the manifestation of "policy," according to Moten and Harney, wherein "policy's vision is to break it up then fix it, move it along by fixing it, manufacture ambition and give it to your children. Policy's hope is that there will be more policy, more participation, more change."[13] The interconnection between naïve hope and white reformist agendas of "progress" is thus apparent. Policy is the maintenance of "order," which it pretends is "neutral." Yet "order," unsurprisingly, has long benefited elite white folks, particularly. Policy maintains order under the guise of "helping": "After the diagnosis that something is deeply wrong . . . comes the prescription: help and correction. Policy will help."[14] The "help" that policy aims to provide is, of course, a farce, disguised as "hopeful" acts of will that solely aim to move one up the hierarchy of capitalist "productivity," white respectability politics, and the like: "Every utterance of policy, no matter its intent or content, is first and foremost a demonstration of one's ability to be close to the top in the hierarchy of the post-fordist economy."[15] One can sense policy as the ideological tie between governance, "international development," missionary work, and other forms of charity that offer surface-level assistance while failing to recognize these activities' complicity in constructing inequitable worlds.

Planning, on the other hand, promises something that policy never could nor would pretend to offer. Harney and Moten write, "Planning is self-sufficiency at the social level"[16] and aims to "invent the means in a common experiment launched from any kitchen, any back porch, any basement, any hall, any park bench. . . ."[17] In short, then, "planning . . . is not an activity, not fishing or dancing or teaching or loving, but the ceaseless experiment with the futurial presence of the forms of life that make such activities possible."[18] Planning, in other words, constitutes *the grounds for* political activities and communal life.

Policy stages itself as the correction of "planners," or those who resist, disrupt, or simply *refuse* the coercions of this managerial governance: "Policy is correction, forcing itself with mechanical violence upon the incorrect, the uncorrected, the ones who do not seek their own correction."[19] Planners are marked by the deputies of policy as "static, essential, just surviving," as those who "lack perspective" and "fail to see the complexity."[20] That is to say, "To the deputies [of policy], planners have no vision, no real hope for the future, just a plan here and now, an actually existing plan."[21] The deputies of policy envision "hope" solely as a generally white (or at least touting a tokenizing "diversity") phenomenon in the form of adherence to the status quo. The deputies of policy suggest that it proffers a supposedly impartial "law and order"—and thus figuring planners as lawless and disorderly—whereas planners keenly perceive that the "orderly" is amply violent; thus policy implements a vision of peace as orderly and violence as disorderly, thereby veiling the violences of "order," as such. Harney's explication of "policy" and "planning" in the interview that concludes *The Undercommons* offers a helpful conversational take:

> Think of the way we use *"policy,"* as something like thinking for others, both because you think others can't think and also because you somehow think that you can think, which is the other part of thinking that there's something wrong with someone else—thinking that you've fixed yourself somehow, and therefore that gives you the right to say someone else needs fixing. *Planning* is the opposite of that, it's to say, "look, it's not that people aren't thinking for themselves, acting for themselves together in concern in these different ways. It just appears that way for you because you've corrected yourself in this particular way in which they will always look wrong for you and where therefore you try to deploy policy against them."[22]

Because those who plan—and thereby *refuse* policy—supposedly "need hope" and "need vision" according to these deputies, they take it upon themselves to *impose* "hope" via the purported and perverted "help" they provide. In reality, "deputies fix others, not in an imposition upon but in the imposition of selves, as objects of control and command, whether one is posited as being capable of selfhood or not."[23] In this revealing sketch, policy forces "interest" in policy by claiming that "hope is an orientation toward this participation in change," meaning it maintains that it is *only* via governing policy—including, and ultimately *because of*, its attendant whiteness, capitalistic proclivities, and more—that hope is possible.

What should be clear—or, be becoming clear, anyway—is how hope is often staged as participation, as activity, within unjust systems that hold the possibility of justice as just-out-of-reach, maximizing the labor and profits that the elite extract from those upon whose backs that system of governance was, and continues to be, built. This system of governance occasionally offers a glint of success, at times accidentally, to a slim few who perform the necessary respectability politics and slip through the cracks in the walls meant to disenfranchise; but, as Jack Halberstam, in the introduction to *The Undercommons*, contends, "... we cannot be satisfied with the recognition and acknowledgement generated by the very system that denies a) that anything was ever broken and b) that we deserve to be that [broken] part."[24] The space-making space of the "undercommons" thus cannot be found in this system, and it refuses to take any part therein; in Halberstam's words, "... we refuse to ask for recognition and instead we want to take apart, dismantle, tear down the structure that, right now, limits our ability to find each other, to see beyond it and to access the places that we know lie outside its walls."[25]

This undercommon pathway is not one of repair—for existing structures may yet be beyond repair—but *refusal*. This "new" thing, this veiled place, is a "wild beyond" that can only be accessed by a path that is "paved with *refusal*."[26] Halberstam expounds, "Moten and Harney refuse the logic that stages refusal as inactivity, as the absence of a plan and as a mode of stalling real politics."[27] Their goal is instead "not to end the troubles but *to end the world that created those particular troubles*."[28] To inhabit the undercommons is not to actively participate in politics in any traditional sense (despite what the deputies of policy may wish); one is instead to "falsify the institution, to make politics incorrect...."[29] It is the abolition of the world of troubles created under the pretense of correction, charity, conversion. Harney and Moten exemplify, "What is, so to speak, the object of abolition? Not so much the abolition of prisons but the abolition of a society that could have prisons, that could have slavery ... and therefore *not abolition as the elimination of anything but abolition as the founding of a new society.*"[30] The undercommons is not a space for the elaboration of critique for the sake of some desire to be disruptive for disruption's sake alone. The space made by and as the undercommons is not necessarily aimed at a "what" (even as it stages refusal as a mode for Black liberation specifically) but a "where" and "with whom" and "how." They write, when it comes to "the building of any kind of partnership or collectivity: it's not the thing that you do; it's the thing that happens while you're doing it that becomes important, and the work itself is some combination of the two modes of being."[31] The activity of the undercommons predicates itself on movement, on *process*—not "forward" but among, amid, with. This movement is one of planning—conversational, improvisational, ongoing—as opposed to one of policy—monological, decreed, final. Dark hope endeavors to incarnate in concert with Moten and Harney's undercommons—neither programmatic nor purposeless, but opening space for activity and catalyzation. Dark hope does not dictate what must be done, but it makes room on and within one's contextual ground for communing and communicating, strategizing and organizing. Neither the undercommons nor dark hope necessitates particular forms of ethico-political action, even as they remain confidently resolute in their efforts against anti-Black violence, against environmental racism, against consumptive capitalist commodification.

Can one, much less a white philosophical theologian like this author, claim any meaningfully fecund iteration of hope that recognizes the precarity of this eco-social moment—undeniably disproportionately so for those marginalized by the structures of policy—yet still maintains some semblance of an unspeakably potent animating capacity? Is it possible to articulate a notion of hope that is capacious enough to carve space for anti-racist solidarity, not only across lines of critical difference but, further, even in the manifestation of conflicting interests? Can a dark hope compellingly hold these matters in tension, or will it be torn asunder under the weight of this paradox?

If dark hope is a kind of ground and assumes the critical features of ground—a matrix that preserves both interconnection and particularity—I believe, then, that dark hope might yet allow for a shareable sense of solidarity in response to and even *because of* multiplicitous positionalities and the differential work that follows. My aim is that this proposed hope would take on the anti-racist and anti-capitalist critiques made by these theorists and mobilize them within the context of the present environmental crisis. In other words, I intend to transmute and situate these critiques of anti-Black racism and capitalistic injustice in a strand of hope that can face the entangled woes of violence that the Anthropocene brings differentially across eco-social positionalities. To proffer an iteration of hope as a person of significant privilege carries the risk of replicating and reanimating the structural injustices that generated my privilege in the first place; dark hope thus strives to be in radical solidarity with these theorists, bringing the particularities of their anti-racist critique to the fore in this sketch of what hope might mean in times of potential planetary disaster. Dark hope holds that any such justice-seeking catalyst in the Anthropocene must regard anti-racist work as indispensable to its mission, not as an accessory thereto.

To equate hope with progress is to conflate hope and optimism. One of the central goals of scholar of religion Joseph R. Winters in his book *Hope Draped in Black* is to undo the false connections between hope and progress/optimism, granting particular attention to this oxymoronic connection in the experience of Black communities in the United States. Arguing forcefully that progress should be understood as "a triumphant category" and "a tool that helps to reinforce, affirm, and justify the order of things (and conceal the nasty aspects of the existing state of affairs)," especially for Black folks, Winters makes a case for a "melancholic hope"—or, a "hope draped in black"—that takes "remembrance, loss, and tragedy" seriously.[32] The paradoxical connection between melancholia and hope does not imply their opposition but their concomitance, according to Winters. Registering the unthinkable weight of "death, tragedy, and loss, including the losses, exclusions, and alienating effects of social existence" compels one to "refuse the tendency of progress to integrate past events, ideas, and possibilities into a coherent, status quo–affirming framework."[33] In other words, remembering, even amid the melancholia it engenders, serves as a hopeful impetus, refusing to allow the future to replicate the injustices of the present—racial, capitalist, and more. Ultimately, "This refusal potentially allows the past to disrupt, unsettle, and rework our sense of and relationship to the present."[34] "Progress" often forces one to reduce the traumas of the past, which ever flow into the present, minimizing their intensity by marking with fanfare "how far we've come." A dark, grounded hope would do well to learn from Winters here: If hope is to persist meaningfully in the present, it must necessarily carry and remember its contextual memories and inherited sufferings—many of which are on account of race, though not exclusively so. To remember the contextuality of dark hope would ensure that this iteration of hope is not purely an abstraction—untouched by the realities of the terrestrial. Nor would it be an imposition forced from the outside or from above for the sake of maintaining some façade of "order."

Any such hope must ensure that its aims subvert the forces that would otherwise suppress it—and it must refuse its cooptation and capture by the neocolonial state. Hope in the Anthropocene must not find definition in the rubrics of neoliberal architecture and white supremacist design. Here Jack Halberstam's "queer art of failure" uncovers a novel understanding of the agency performed in activities perceived as "failure" by any such heteronormative Powers that Be, thereby supplying dark hope with an illustration of agency that refuses to abide by the customs of the powerful. Halberstam's *The Queer Art of Failure* offers an unconventional optic for political engagement and activity predicated on the failure thereof—revealing important questions about the relationship between hope and failure. As Halberstam introduces, "Under certain circumstances, failing, losing, forgetting, unmaking, undoing, unbecoming, not knowing may in fact offer more creative, more cooperative, more surprising ways of being in the world."[35] Negativity and an embrace of inevitable failure "provides an opportunity to use these negative affects to poke holes in the toxic positivity of contemporary life."[36] It should be said, then, that this embrace of failure isn't just for the sake of some feel-good politics or some self-gratifying do-whatever-makes-you-happy-ness. It is the "punishing norms that discipline behavior and manage human development . . ." that demand a need for escape (particularly for queers)—which, for Halberstam, emerges through the failure to be held accountable to those norms.

Failure is a mode of resisting and refusing to make oneself "legible" to the violent forces of categorization, ordering, sorting, and dividing of things.[37] To fail to become legible is to refuse to abide, say, by gender norms, by performative expectations, by the demands for productivity, by the fixed and closed identity markers that are used to determine one's futures. What might dark hope learn from this sort of radical refusal made possible through intentional obfuscation? In contrast to this universalizing force of legibility, Halberstam strives for "more local practices of knowledge, practices . . . that may be less efficient, may yield less marketable results, but may also, in the long term, be more sustaining."[38] The ecological promise of this sort of approach is hard to miss.[39] A terrestrial perspectivalism engendered by critical attention to the ground—eco-social, socio-ecological—demands that one's praxes be bioregional, that one's activities materialize in response to the particularities of place. But the local cannot be discretely bounded or clearly delimited, even as its unique characteristics are still acknowledged. The former replicates nationalisms and their respective violent insularities; the latter extends keenly potent modes for attuning to place without discounting its porosity.

True to Halberstam's efforts to elude and to outright refuse legibility, Halberstam does not seek some simple dichotomous argument of activity or inactivity. Indeed, relatedly, could one render the depths of a dark hope clear, legible, or otherwise plain? Certainly not. "The queer art of failure"—from which the hope I propose draws wisdom—is about "alternative ways of knowing and being that are not unduly optimistic, but nor are they mired in nihilistic critical dead ends. It is . . . about failing well, failing often, and learning, in the words of Samuel Beckett, how to fail better."[40] "Failing better" shirks the idea of "improvement" or "progress" according to any sort of linear model, especially of the political sort; Halberstam pursues the idea of failure as a rupture, as an *opening*, in which such openness "means questioning, open to unpredictable outcomes, not fixed on a telos, unsure, adaptable, shifting, flexible, and adjustable."[41] Failure thus constitutes the potentiality for novelty; failure is the break in the rigid for the sake of the emergence of new life; failure is the burrowing critter, not eroding but carving space for the possibility of fecundity.

Failing better is not for the sake of "success" but for the sake of new opportunities that refuse to be accountable to the unwavering norms of an oppressor. To this end, Halberstam mobilizes James C. Scott's concept of "weapons of the weak"—or, modes of creative resistance to oppressive regimes that often appear in subtle or veiled ways. The idea of "weapons of the weak," Halberstam argues, "can be used to recategorize what looks like inaction, passivity, and lack of resistance in terms of the practice of stalling the business of the dominant."[42] Halberstam continues, "We can also recognize failure as a way of refusing to acquiesce to the dominant logics of power and discipline and as a form of critique. . . . Failure recognizes that alternatives are embedded already in the dominant and that power is never total or consistent. . . ."[43] These tools, these "weapons," undo the dominant without the need to engage those domineering actors directly. To fail is to elude, all the while delegitimizing the operative apparatus as presently configured.

Halberstam's vital queries probe the link between hope and agency: To take seriously the unutterable atrocities of the Anthropocene and its founding forces demands that one critically question the connection between hope and survival; if one can live without hope just as one can be killed with it, what meaningful difference does it make—if at all?[44] Just as dark hope is not synonymous with progress, neither can it be identified with success—that is, with a hoped-for outcome.

These queries, almost unthinkably, multiply as one complicates them further with the eco-social matters of contamination, pollution, and toxification. How might one more meaningfully think of hopeful change outside of the rubrics of linear "progress?" The Anthropocene makes apparent what was already the case: that "purity" has always been a fallacy, an impossibility. As cultural theorist Anna Lowenhaupt Tsing writes in her seminal monograph, *The Mushroom at the End of the World*, "We are contaminated by our encounters; they change who we are as we make way for others. As contamination changes world-making projects, mutual worlds—and new directions—may emerge.

Everyone carries a history of contamination; purity is not an option."[45] For Tsing, it seems, "contamination" is both ecological and ontological: pointing one toward the porous processes of the world, acknowledging the indeterminate, trans-corporeal, intra-relational flux that constitutes earthly becoming. Indeed, Tsing argues for the usefulness of the concept of "disturbance," pushing against the tendency to think of disturbance in purely destructive forms:

> Disturbance can renew ecologies as well as destroy them. How terrible a disturbance is depends on many things, including scale . . . disturbance, as used by ecologists, is not always bad—and not always human . . . as a beginning, disturbance is always in the middle of things: the term does not refer to a harmonious state before disturbance. Disturbances follow other disturbances. Thus all landscapes are disturbed; disturbance is ordinary.[46]

To be sure, Tsing qualifies this argument to recognize the disparities of toxic contamination as a result of and as a factor in social location; but, her point stands: one must "think" Earth (and human life therein) through the lens of shifting assemblages, muddied milieux, relational intra-activity. Disturbance, ecologically, yields heterogeneity: a necessary characteristic for wellness and flourishing.[47] This project's proposed ground—ontological, ecological, social—remains ever in-the-middle (hence, *milieu*), disturbed and disturbing. That is, the groundlessness of ground—or the porous disturbances necessary to its fecundity—prevents finality, instead prompting ongoing, processual activity. Disturbance, in other words, is that which ensures that this dark and grounded hope does not settle for the rigidities of the status quo. So, too, does disturbance prevent any articulation of hope as a return to or construction of some pure, utopian setting.

Here feminist philosopher of science Donna J. Haraway's *Staying with the Trouble: Making Kin in the Chthulucene* aids in the conceptualization of a counter-hope that does not rely on utopianisms, instead providing an alternative model for becoming "capable of response" in ways that do not prioritize or even require "a relationship to times called the future."[48] Haraway's arguments merit more than mere paraphrasing:

> In urgent times, many of us are tempted to address trouble in terms of making an imagined future safe, of stopping something from happening that looms in the future, of clearing away the present and the past in order to make futures. . . . Staying with the trouble does not require such a relationship to times called the future. In fact, staying with the trouble requires learning to be truly present, not as a vanishing pivot

between awful or edenic pasts and apocalyptic or salvific futures, but as mortal critters entwined in myriad unfinished configurations of places, times, matters, meanings.[49]

"Staying with the trouble" thus upends any meaningful relationship to abstract futurisms or otherwise unwavering lines of temporal flight, instead inviting a deeply present comportment of "becoming-with," of rendering capable.[50] This "staying with the trouble" serves as a two-pronged critique: (1) dismantling prevalent certainty in fixes of the religious (i.e., in an omniscient, omnipotent God who will "save us") *and* secular (i.e., in a techno-futurist solution that will "save us") sort, and (2) criticizing nihilistic fatalisms that suggest that there's "no use" in acting, seemingly implying "that only if things work do they matter."[51] Eliding conversations about "emergencies," which often connote "something approaching apocalypse and its mythologies," Haraway instead opts for temporal sketches of "urgencies," which "have other temporalities, and these times are ours."[52] It is this re-narrativization of the present moment that promises new frames that "reach into rich pasts to sustain thick presents to keep the story going for those who come after."[53] This careful spatiotemporal dance that Haraway performs aims toward a compassionate habitation of the present without sliding into some projected Harmony, while also remaining mindful of "those who come after" in such a way that avoids the privileging of anything other than the possibilities available in this thick present; it is precisely this liminal work that the critical lens of "narrative" accomplishes for Haraway, a centering of the "now" as always in-the-middle without veiling inherited pasts or forsaking potentially creative futures. Staying with the trouble as a narrativized ethic thus tends toward opportunities of "partial recuperation and getting on together" that ultimately cultivate "response-ability" in this or that subject—including and beyond the human.[54] Yet this "response-ability" is not general or undifferentiated, opposing any assumption of universal culpability for the state of things in favor of contextual possibilities of differing fecundities. With Tsing, Haraway tunes in to the troubling times of anthropogenic climate change to craft a collaborative ethic of abiding, not for the sake of any sort of fix, quick- or not, but for the fertile prospects of sympoietic remaining, of cobbling together, of gathering.

Dark hope takes on the resonances of Haraway's trouble-making presentism—neither "optimism" nor "despair"[55]—faithfully inhabiting the present precisely by *not* discounting the entangled inheritances of traumas, contaminations, and histories. To recall Winters here, this hope can only sprout from this contextual web, this eco-social ground. In other words, dark hope germinates *not in spite of but amid* the uncertainties of the present, bearing the full weight of its sensed narrative. In this way, this hope remains impure and conditional—and thus ever in-process.

Given that there is no pure or total salvation of nuclear fallout, of microplastic contamination, of lost topsoils, how would a dark hope make sense of any of this? How might dark hope contend with irreparability? To this end, Alexis Shotwell's *Against Purity* proves helpful. Shotwell rejects "the idea that we can access or recover a time and state before or without pollution, without impurity, before the fall from innocence. . . . "[56] In her forceful yet humorous words, "Being against purity means that there is no primordial state we might wish to get back to, no Eden we have desecrated, no pretoxic body we might uncover through enough chia seeds and kombucha."[57] In the vernacular of this present project, there is no primordial foundation that one might return to or reconstruct; there is only the in-process milieu of ground within which one emerges. Connecting the questions of toxicity and impurity to the concerns previously raised in this chapter by Yusoff, Harney, Moten, and Halberstam, Shotwell continues, "There is not a preracial state we could access, erasing histories of slavery, forced labor on railroads, colonialism, genocide, and their concomitant responsibilities and requirements."[58] If we inhabit "complex webs of suffering"—which we do, albeit ever differentially—Shotwell inquires, "What happens if we start *from there?*"[59] That is, what would it mean for one's concepts and activities to emerge from the soils of complexity, compromise, decomposition? Shotwell contends that this approach does not mean that one should settle for less, but that it instead offers a way to inhabit the contaminations of the present that do not pretend to be able to "heal," "solve," or "fix" problems even as they endeavor to mind, address, resolve, and *process* them. In a word, it would mean tending, salvaging, reclaiming, and recovering—not Saving! When hope so often connotes visions of absolute deliverance or unmitigated rescue, could an alternative, on-the-ground, remediating hope be possible?

Here the biomimetic—or, better, geomimetic—emerges as a liminal potentiality for recognizing wholesome change and the hope that becomes through it. Contaminated soils are not "saved," but, in some cases, they can be remediated and renewed. Through the processes of soil remediation, erosion prevention, and strategic planting (i.e., phytoremediation, agroforestry, etc.), degraded land can be made wholesome again through careful attention and nurture. But this does not "return" it to some imagined state of "purity." Nor does it necessarily undo the structures or end the world that caused that soil's contamination to begin with. But remediation is a strategy of way-making that is predicated on the principles of salvaging, of cobbling together, of maximizing agency with the tools, resources, and seeds on hand. What's more, remediation puts humans better in touch with the ecological and geological processes as they function prior to and outside of human-caused contamination. Black agrarian and activist Leah Penniman's work at the intersections of racial and ecological justice demonstrates just this:

> As our ancestors taught us, we learn about the Earth by observing and imitating her. The soil in the forest is never exposed; rather it is covered with humus, leaves, and growing plants. The forest does not stir up the earth; rather it enriches it from above. In restoring degraded soils, it is essential that we heed these lessons.[60]

Penniman thus links ecological lessons with social justice struggles, recognizing the wisdom necessary to steward degraded land—especially after one has been forced off of more fertile grounds by colonizers.[61] She reminds, "Because almost all wealth is inherited, and because our ancestors were among the dispossessed, many of us are not independently wealthy. This means that the land we are able to access may be contaminated with lead, eroded, or otherwise degraded."[62] The toil involved in reclaiming degraded land does not make it unpolluted, uncorrupted, or sinless: It is not saved by thoughts and prayers alone. But the eco-spiritual work of remediation and reclamation to renew "marginal land and bring back life where it has been banished" offers a fresh, here-and-now vision of hope that shirks optimism and pessimism, that sidesteps total deliverance and certain damnation.

Hope necessarily relates, somehow and someway, to futurity—the work that unfolds, the world that is sought. But what would it mean to conceptualize a contextualized hope that does not forsake the present even as it toils into the future? How might one theorize a dark hope that seeks the incarnation of something not yet present with solely the resources one has on hand? In what ways might dark hope open the edges of possibility without projecting any notion of linearity onto the futural? The question of hope's relation to time begs exploration.

Unfolding Temporalities: The Time of and for Hope

The crux of the Anthropocene—and the possibility of hope therein—is a matter of time. This, of course, means to suggest that some sort of dramatic civilizational overhaul, reduction of atmospheric CO_2, revitalization of more-than-human species, and so forth must come soon—really, now. But this matter of time is also *one of temporality itself*. Coalition-building, protest, revolution, and similar—not to conflate these distinct actions—all depend on their attention to the criticality of timing (e.g., "The time is nigh"; "This is our moment"; "We must ____ before it's too late"), and these sorts of hopeful political activities each reflect a particular understanding of temporality as such. It would seem that the question of what is possible always depends *not only* on how much time one has—or, "the time that remains"—*but also* on the ways in which one assumes that temporality operates.

As grounded in the present as one may wish to be, hope necessarily assumes some sort of relationship to the futural. One works *now* for justice to come. The primary goal here is to convey the inaccuracies of any form of linear gradualism or incremental progress—which Yusoff, Moten, Harney, and Halberstam have already initiated for us—instead, demonstrating the nonlinear spatio-temporality of hope simultaneously for the sake of biomimetic proximity as well as a commitment to a poietic apophasis that accompanies an on-the-ground perspective.

When it comes to time, my rather straightforward argument is this: One's understanding of temporality influences one's conception of hope, informing the modes of action one deems possible and, accordingly, one promotes—temporality as the ground of hope, in other words. Should things move about in foreseeable fashions, one need only anticipate what's to come in order to either promote or forestall such an event, depending on its degree of desirability; in other words, mechanistic timescapes are accompanied by a mechanistic "hope"—and thus mechanistic ethics. If Earth's processes follow straight trajectories, one need not account for phenomena such as feedback loops, amplifiers, tipping points, keystone species, and so forth; should the contrary be true (with which any reliable climate scientist would agree), dark hope and its attendant ethical actions may become a bit more complex. Moreover, if human social location is assumed to be universal or generic, then one need not account for terrestrial particularities, contextual disparities, and cultural diversities; should the contrary be true (with which most theorists of intersectionality would agree), then the matter of hope and its embodiment fold complexly.

I aim to theorize dark hope as contextually, eco-socially emergent and thus predicated on the possibilities eco-mimetically sensed in and through the nonlinear nature of nature—and the complexities accompanying the Anthropocene.[63] Aiding this effort, political theorist William E. Connolly mounts a compelling critique of what he terms the "doctrine of gradualism" in his book *Facing the Planetary*. Gradualism emerges from the projection of an Enlightenment-style mechanistic worldview onto planetary processes, organic and inorganic, generating an image of the world that changes with systematically machine-like predictability—neatly separable into subjects and objects, causes and effects, and so forth. By highlighting the principles of biological dynamism uncovered by Terrence Deacon, "symbiogenesis" as proffered by

Lynn Margulis, creativity as theorized by Alfred N. Whitehead, and contemporary findings made by climate scientists, Connolly offers a counternarrative: Earth cannot and should not be understood as a system of straight causes and effects, of tidy, uncomplicated, and mappable forces; this planet is instead a "series of interacting, partially self-organizing systems that often intersect."[64] Despite what neoliberal economists may think, Earth is not stably patterned or a steady context. Nor is it a standing reserve. To the contrary, Earth is composed of heterogeneous relations that overlap, crisscross, catalyze, deaden, amplify, and so on. There's nothing linear about Earth save hegemonic impositions upon it—of worldviews, of border walls. The more accurate and compelling alternative is to tune in to the "bumpy temporalities" composing Earth: the "bumpy history of climate, ocean currents, glacier flows, bacterial crossings, and species evolution" that are open-ended;[65] bumpy temporality might be imagined as a deep, borderless body of water across which currents and waves ripple, pull, amplify, cross over, drift, splash back, break—and not merely on the surface. Connolly expounds, bumpy temporality perceives "differential modes of temporal transition, each with its own degree of liveliness and real uncertainty," with entities and actors "whose liveliness at moments of criticality differ." He continues, "*Within each mode of activity* there are times when volatility is heightened during criticality and periods closer to equilibrium, when activity is more condensed into habit or automatism."[66] Earth, through this lens, becomes far more complicated, not merely complex but a *complicatio*—folding, multiplying, entangling.[67] What might this have to do with hope? For one, in connection with the work of Moten, Harney, Winters, and Halberstam, this attention to complication begins to subvert the common assumption that hope plays into linear progress narratives, so often a cipher for the preservation of the status quo. To the contrary, dark hope begins to take form as resolutely contextual way-making—including the refusal to capitulate to those forces that parade as Progress but in earnest were and are the progenitors of the Anthropocene.

If hope is neither universal nor linear, even as it is planetary and multiplex, how might it be possible for it to remain a present phenomenon even as it works toward better futures? The anonymous collective The Invisible Committee's 2017 book *Now* theorizes an anarchist political praxis predicated on a reconsideration of time as a purely present phenomenon, which will prove useful in tracing dark hope's relation to the present and its unfurling. The Invisible Committee contends that *"now"* is the time of the decision, and any deferral of the present or any step toward futurity is only ever to flee present decisions in their mind. This urgency of the now-moment—of the *jetztzeit*, if one wishes to be Benjaminian about it—demands of those who wish to heed its call a "*destituent*" logic that seeks a conception of the "political" as "that which bursts forth, which forms an event, which punches a hole in the orderly progression of disaster."[68]

With the echoes of Deleuze and Guattari (via Brian Massumi) palpable here,[69] one should begin to see a certain radical embrace of the present *for the sake of the present*, not purely or even obliquely for any imagined future, which The Invisible Committee likes to equate to a certain flavor of liberal hope. They argue forcefully, "No one has ever acted out of hope. Hope is of a piece with waiting . . . with the fear of breaking into the present—in short, with the fear of living."[70] Hope defers decisions, is cowardice-incarnate—in their estimation. They continue, "Hope, that very slight but constant *impetus toward tomorrow* that is communicated to us day by day, is the best agent of the maintenance of order."[71] Hope pacifies, suppresses, even debilitates, in their mind. And while The Invisible Committee in their uncompromising yet understandable secularity seem to conflate hope with what I think would be better termed "optimism,"[72] their point remains: beliefs, ideologies, or principles that stand *only* to benefit the future are effective tools of oppressive regimes that promise "something better" while using that "something better" as a false lure—a carrot eternally dangled in front of a cart-pulling horse, if you will.[73]

Instead, what's needed, the Committee proposes, is a radically reimagined present that neither succumbs to the temptations of wistful forward-gazing nor capitulates any sort of holism that pretends that the present can serve as some kind of grounds for undifferentiated "unity." As they contend, the present isn't ever anything remotely resembling a universal or an experience of unity; more accurately, the present is nothing if not *fragmentation*. To think seriously about political action of and for the present is to *accept fragmentation as the starting point*, which can "give rise to an intensification and pluralization of the bonds that constitute us. Then fragmentation doesn't signify separation but a shimmering of the world."[74] They thus turn to a communism capacious enough to account for the fragmented nature of *now*: "It's true that the world's fragmentation disorients and unsettles all the inherited certainties, that it defies all of our political and existential categories, that it removes the ground underlying the revolutionary tradition itself: it challenges us."[75] The present becomes a sort of groundless ground: relational fragmentation, fragmented relationality. This defiant act of refusing any imposed or imagined unity, simultaneously an insubordinate embrace of communal fragmentation, is, as they say, "what allows us to regain a serene presence in the world."[76]

Destituent—as opposed to "constituent"—potential is not at all about "countering" or even "pushing back," they argue; such counter-agentic modes of politics, they contend, are in fact products of liberal activism. This is where their anarchic method takes a radically negativist turn:

> Whereas constituent logic crashes against the power apparatus it means to take control of, a destituent potential is concerned instead with escaping from it, with removing any hold on it which the apparatus might have, as it increases its hold on the world in the separate space that it forms. Its characteristic gesture is *exiting*, just as the typical constituent gesture is taking by storm.[77]

To purely clash against the Powers that Be is to *reproduce* the logics of progress and development that undergird those very Powers; to revolt, according to The Invisible Committee, is not at all a matter of overthrowing the powerful but is instead a matter of *rejecting the frame of the decision* of liberal/conservative, progress/regression, or similar; it's a matter of ending the world that made these binaries *fundamental*[78] to its constitution, so to speak. Constituent logic, even at its most progressive, reinstills and reanimates the abstract futurisms that produced the extraordinarily ordinary injustices of the present; The Invisible Committee's basic objection is this: "We need to abandon the idea that there is politics only where there is vision, program, project, and perspective...."[79] Anarchism, for this reason, does not reside neatly within the parameters of "progressive" or otherwise "liberal" politics—neither of which adequately capture anarchism's rupture of attachments to future-oriented institutions: Any interaction with the political, as commonly conceived, corrupts the subject who takes part in it, even if only fighting against it; instead, they submit that the only responsible response is to desert, to exit, to refuse. Like Harney and Moten, The Invisible Committee seeks not a program but a plane of possibility, enacted *not* through engagement but through refusal, *not* by means of construction but via abolition. To lean in toward extant models of politics will generate nothing but the reproduction of the present, or so they claim.

I do not pretend to take on anarchism as my own political method, per se. Nor is it my express purpose in this chapter to reason for or against it as such; but, I do believe that The Invisible Committee's argument offers the question of hope an altogether affective lure toward "destituence," aiding one's capacity to envision a notion of hope that might plant itself firmly in the present and to refuse ties to futures that replicate the woes of the present.

Such concern about the reproduction of the present in the future—and, more specifically, the reification of the matters of injustice of the present in the future—is key to cultural theorist Lauren Berlant's argument in her 2011 book *Cruel Optimism*. Berlant's work effectively challenges any notion of naïve hope—or, better, optimism—that manifests as an unwavering attachment to the futural. Berlant describes optimism as an attachment, as a belief in "promise" or "possibility," as an affective structure that lures one beyond the impasse of the present. "Cruel optimism," then, is a relation or attachment to something outside of oneself that, despite the promise of flourishing that that relation or attachment bears for the subject, actually *inhibits* that subject's well-being. As Berlant claims, "A relation of cruel optimism exists when something you desire is actually an obstacle to your flourishing. . . . These kinds of optimistic relation are not inherently cruel. They become cruel only when the object that draws your attachment actively impedes the aim that brought you to it initially."[80] Cruel optimism describes a purportedly promising relation that generates far more negative consequences, catalyzing "a sense of possibility" that "actually makes it impossible to attain the expansive transformation for which a person or a people risks striving."[81] And yet, this cruel attachment is doubly so "insofar as the very pleasures of being inside a relation have become sustaining regardless of the content of the relation, such that a person or a world finds itself bound to a situation of profound threat that is, at the same time, profoundly confirming."[82] The desired object—which is really, in Berlant's words, "a cluster of promises we want someone or something to make to us and make possible for us"[83]—is effectively "an enabling object that is also disabling."[84] One could see how The Invisible Committee's use of "hope" effectively points to this reality of "cruel optimism"—not necessarily a robust conceptualization of hope. Hence my commitment to a dark hope that defies these abundant and abundantly damaging forms.

What's dangerous about cruelly optimistic relations is that they project into the future; they roll on and on; they persist despite whatever negative effects may come one's way. They're not a one-off sort of thing. They reproduce cycles that are repetitive and yet different: the "difference" here being the ever-renewed sense of optimism that one will finally be fully fulfilled, will finally win big, will finally put down the (*insert vice here*)—always next time! Berlant is clear: "Any object of optimism promises to guarantee the endurance of something, the survival of something, the flourishing of something, and above all the protection of the desire that made this object or scene powerful enough to have magnetized an attachment to it."[85] The attachments themselves, in addition to the eternally-just-out-of-reach promise they harbor, become part of that which is desired: One needs another pull of the slot-machine handle as much as one needs the promise of "surely inevitable" fortune, to use a trivial (but serious) analogy. When it comes to temporality and the question of ethico-political agency in these times of ecological crisis, Berlant identifies the potential (and, in many cases, actual) cruelties of politics as an attachment one seeks despite its ineffectiveness to do anything other than reproduce the present—simply magnifying the negative consequences of climate crisis, for example. What options are there, or are we left without any meaningful hope?

"Cruel optimism" can aptly name that which The Invisible Committee as well as Moten and Harney seek to not only avoid but to outright tear down. Both sets of authors limn alternative political modes that do not engage "the political," in its institutionalized connotation, for any engagement with the political affirms the system and its legitimacy. Cruel optimism is one of the reasons that one needs to "falsify the institution," in Moten and Harney's words.

How does dark hope toil for better futures without abandoning the present or mistaking it as some sort of futural abstraction? Black feminist cultural theorist Tina M. Campt may yet instill this sought hope with a renewed sense of intensified agency—albeit in subtle and perhaps unexpected ways. In her 2017 *Listening to Images*—which endeavors to "build a radical visual archive of the African Diaspora that grapples with the recalcitrant and the disaffected, the unruly and the dispossessed" and to discern "what modalities of perception, encounter, and engagement" by which that archive is constituted—Campt explores how "both quiet and the quotidian are mobilized as everyday practices of refusal" for "blacks in diaspora."[86] In Campt's work to generate this archive of the African Diaspora, she imagines the quiet and the quotidian "as instances of rupture and refusal."[87] Pointedly, ". . . contrary to what might seem common sense, quiet must not be conflated with silence. Quiet registers sonically, as a level of intensity that requires focused attention."[88] She writes later that her project aims to use "the conceptual frameworks of quiet, stasis, and refusal to reclaim the black quotidian as a signature idiom of diasporic culture and black futurity."[89] Yet refusal, even as a characteristic of the afro-futurities sought in her work, does not necessarily assume typically masculinist notions of outright confrontation or physical overthrow. Here is where Campt parts ways with The Invisible Committee as she centers quiet, counterintuitive modes of way-making:

> I theorize the practice of refusal as an extension of the range of creative responses black communities have marshalled in the face of racialized dispossession. In this context, refusal is not a response to a state of exception or extreme violence. I theorize it instead as practices honed in response to sustained, everyday encounters with exigency and duress that rupture a predictable trajectory of flight.[90]

This sort of refusal enacts—indeed, sets in motion—an entirely different future.

Campt interrogates the question of hope and its relation to the future explicitly, questioning, "What does it mean for a black feminist to think about, consider, or concede the concept of futurity?"[91] She responds to her own query later in an exceptional paragraph worth quoting at length:

> Futurity is, for me, not a question of "hope"—though it is certainly inescapably intertwined with the idea of aspiration. To me it is crucial to think about futurity through a notion of "tense." What is the "tense" of a black feminist future? It is a tense of anteriority, a tense relationship to an idea of possibility that is neither innocent nor naïve. Nor is it necessarily heroic or intentional. It is often humble and strategic, subtle and discriminating. It is devious and exacting. It's not always loud and demanding. It is frequently quiet and opportunistic, dogged and disruptive.[92]

Campt challenges the assumption that hope ineludibly is concerned with serving as some sort of oppositional force, taking on whomever or whatever head-on. Given that I am not yet ready to part with the term "hope," what might dark hope learn from an understanding of futurity as a matter of tense? Implied in Campt's notion of Black feminist futurity as a tense presents a certain obliqueness and nonlinearity: discrete but disruptive, indirect yet resolute. A Black feminist futurity "strives for the tense of possibility that grammarians refer to as the future real conditional or *that which will have had to happen*. The grammar of Black feminist futurity is a performance of a future that hasn't happened yet but must."[93] In other words, "It's a politics of prefiguration that involves living the future *now*—as an imperative rather than subjunctive—as a striving for the future you want to see, right now, in the present."[94] In theological terms, we might note how this prefiguration merits nothing short of the term *prophetic*. This prefigurative politics enacts refusal, but it does so "less by opposition or 'resistance,' and more by a refusal of the very premises that have reduced the lived experiences of blackness to pathology and irreconcilability in the logic of white supremacy."[95] Like Moten and Harney's "fugitivity," Campt argues that "refusal highlights the tense relations between *acts* of flight and escape, and creative *practices of refusal*—nimble and strategic that undermine the categories of the dominant."[96] To this end, to conceptualize a dark hope that heeds Campt's argument necessitates that it refuse the cruelly optimistic logics of progress within present regimes, instead practicing a future here-now by subverting the frame of the decision as defined by racist hegemonies. Put differently, hope shirks the optimism-pessimism binary in favor of contextual possibilities emerging from present grounds in all of their mystical irreducibility.

The present is not an undifferentiated plane of freedom but is the composition of competing affects, forces, powers. Instances of "stasis" are not motionless but are, in Campt's terms, "an effortful equilibrium achieved through a labored balancing opposing forces and flows."[97] Exploring an archive of photos of Black South African women from a collection stamped "Mariannhill-Sued-Africa 1894," Campt maintains, "These images require us to do more than just *see* stasis, for they capture unvisible forms of motion held in tense suspension. Their suspension registers beyond what we see, like the vibrations that form the fundamental basis of sonic frequency."[98] The portraits examined by Campt remind her to view tension as "a tense self-fashioning of/in stasis."[99] Self-fashioning refers to a sort of liminal capacity, a grounded agency—neither "agential intention" nor "autonomy."[100] She questions:

> What if we understand [self-fashioning] as a tense response that is not always intentional or liberatory, but often constituted by miniscule or even futile attempts in/as an effort to shift the grammar of black futurity to a temporality that both embraces and exceeds their present circumstances—a practice of *living the future they want to see, now*?[101]

Self-fashioning—encompassing quiet rejection, often appearing as stasis—registers as a mode of fugitivity by which one might be able to refuse "to accept the impossibility of blackness lived in dignity and with respect" even in the face of "the mounting disposability of black lives that don't seem to matter."[102] The question at hand is, "What constitutes futurity in the shadow of the persistent enactment of premature black death?"[103] Unthinkably, the gravity of this query multiplies when coupled with further racist and colonial violence looming and already materializing in the Anthropocene. How does one self-fashion amid this uncertainty? Campt argues for refusal as a means of "embracing a state of black fugitivity, albeit not as a 'fugitive' on the run or seeking escape. It is not a simple act of resistance. It is neither a relinquishing of possibility nor a capitulation to negation."[104] Instead, refusal is "a fundamental renunciation of the terms imposed upon black subjects that reduce black life to always already suspect by refusing to accept or deny these terms as their truth."[105] Refusal *creates possibilities amid undecidability*, "grappling with precarity, while maintaining an active commitment to the every [sic] labor of creating an alternative future."[106] Campt's politics of refusal, enacted via tense quotidian practices as "a responsibility to create one's own future as a practice of survival,"[107] exemplifies *negation* as a fecund response to undecidability. One does not rush to choose between available options in Campt's figuration but instead makes room for the possibility of *refusing the choice as presented*. Campt embodies the spirit of Moten and Harney's "rejection," thereby turning from reifying attachments of "cruel optimism" and embracing the present (cf. The Invisible Committee) to enact the imperative "what will *have had to* happen." What has this to do with dark hope? The goal of the remainder of this chapter is to make explicit these vital connections.

Dark Hope on the Ground

So, what exactly is dark hope? Or, perhaps better, how does it *become?* The aim of this dark and alluring iteration of "hope" is to offer an optic—if only a glass darkly—that might yet be sufficiently fertile in these contaminated times, muddied by the complexities of social and ecological location. What sort of hope might stand to mitigate or resist the ostensibly inevitable collapse of the planetary—the end of time, the end-time? And what might this dark hope look like if inimical to "Progress," conventionally conceived? As Anna Tsing confesses, and I concur with deep conviction, "I hardly know how to think about justice without progress."[108] But if the future is to be made more just, Progress will surely recapitulate the violences implicit in its constitution, reproducing the present in more insidious ways—as evidenced by state-sponsored surveillance, mass incarceration, exploitation of migrants, expansion of fossil fuel industries and their nest of subsidies, and so forth. If hope merely keeps one "progressing," moving forward, developing, industrializing, and more, then it replicates and reinforces these violences—enabling their multiplication in treacherously veiled (and often not-so-veiled) ways. That's not the kind of hope that I'm interested in arguing for.

Neither gradualisms of Progress (the left) nor passivities of Regression (the right) are apt to change the present. It's no longer exactly about making things "better" (liberal) nor making things "great again" (conservative)—though, to be sure, I do not mean to draw moral equivalencies where, I would argue emphatically, there are none.[109] Rather, it's a matter of undoing this world, of co-creating a new world—concurrently. I don't mean to suggest some sort of extra-planetary escapism but rather, upending these upwardly aimed sights, *a terrestrial revolution*—a rejection of the frame of the decision between action and inaction, interest and apathy. Dark hope, sparking this ethical impulse, seeks novel modes of world-making—ever requiring the deconstruction, if not destruction, of present worlds and their timescapes. Hope may catalyze, but this does not mean that it must do so according to liberal paradigms. Hope may (and should) catalyze rejection—the refusal to subordinate oneself to this world that allows, even encourages, injustice. Hope does not cry "Onward Christian soldiers!"—that is the optimistic anthem of the State, which parades in and as, in this case, the church. I'd like to suggest that this myopic understanding of "hope" as linked to Progress often comes from a tendency to cling tightly to whatever is considered Certain or Absolute—whether for the sake of security or for the preservation of power.

But what if hope were to be predicated *not* on certainty but, instead, on uncertainty? On undecidability? Perhaps, then, would it take on theological dimensions often forsaken—demanding some sort of measure of faith? But could an apophatic hope do anything at all, or would it recoil prior to any degree of embodied resoluteness?

This is one of the ways that the "dark" of dark hope comes in: as a way to think about hope as predicated not on certainty so much as uncertainty—a way-making in the dark.[110] Dark hope emerges from uncertainty, which is why it impels activity—faith seeking action, faith-seeking action. Dark hope is something like scooping water from a river: neither a fist nor spread-out fingers will suffice, only carefully cupped hands; there's a tenderness, precariousness, and sensitivity involved in dark hope, meaning that it must remain open, remain uncertain, remain in a cloud of unknowing. It would mean being open to becoming undone—surprised by novelty, moved by the unexpected, enamored with the wondrous. But this would not mean that it refrains from acting. Conversely, it would compel grounded responses that are fluid and not fixed, flexible and not linear: requiring improvisation, elasticity, inventiveness.

Drawing on the lessons of the previous chapters, dark hope sprouts forth from and at the edges of the articulable, unveiling possibilities heretofore unimagined. Yet—and this is the crucial lesson emerging from the negativisms as presented in their various forms in this chapter—dark hope does not limit itself to choosing A or B, One or Many, or the lesser of two evils. Instead, the apophatic underpinnings and negativist groundwork of dark hope extend the possibility of refusing the choice as offered, of abolishing the frame of the decision, of rejecting the world that pre-defined and pre-scripted that "choice." Dark hope is not linear but spirals—searching, at times apophatically. Such spiraling, breaking the undeviating straightness of present models of the political, is in concert with the call to "refuse the choice as offered," in Halberstam's terms.[111] Refusal is what breaks loops into spirals, not in the sense of spiraling out of control so much as fractal, emergent intensification.[112] In this way, this hope is resonant with and responsive to Harney and Moten's insistence on "the ceaseless experiment with the futurial presence of the forms of life" that make life-giving activities possible.[113] That is to say, that this variation of hope does not seek the reproduction of the present but the rupturing thereof for the sake of cultivating the undergirding matrices, the fertile grounds that generate potentialities for another world, for more just worlds.

And this hope, paradoxically perhaps, is harmonic with Berlant's concept of "cruel optimism," not in the sense that it replicates it or is otherwise another term for it. Instead, this hope, by means of apophatic folding, to whatever degree possible, intends to shirk the feedback loops of violence and slow death that accompany cruelly optimistic attachments. To undo or unsay one's relation to a particular thing, not necessarily permanently or even wholly, to reassess, reconvene, or reenergize faithfully promises prospects for the amplification, the regeneration, the reinvigoration of that active hope. This is not too divergent from Harney and Moten's emphasis on experimentation, whose processes of practicing, assessing, and re-hypothesizing necessarily fold through the twists of apophasis in pursuit of the creative grounds that prefigure experimentation. This is also not to negate the quasi-unavoidable critique that hope, even as (re)defined here, is still a form of attachment in Berlant's eyes. But this critical hope—drawing inspiration from, conspiring with, a theological spirit that still insists on the possibility of impossibility, the fecundity of faith, that may yet flash up as some sort of queer messianic promise inimical to linear progress—is an attachment to creativity itself, to the making and un-making of worlds toward the deferred ends of equity and wholesomeness. Some institutionalized religions are among the guiltiest when it comes to propping up cruelly optimistic forms of attachment that placate or otherwise uphold present hierarchies of power. The glinting theological spark sought here is the point of the needle joining patches, creating without ever doing so in any straightforward sense; any ostensible "progress" is only made by endless spirals of fabric and thread and toil that twist and turn and fold and unfold in each instant. Such a process is "sympoietic," in Donna Haraway's vernacular,[114] an unbounded system that changes and adapts—always partnered, never as separable units. The needle of hope only ever exists but in relation to its contextual work and only ever exists *among* its relations—not before.

Dark hope abides faithfully—not in the sense of submissive respectability politics or unreserved compliance, but seeking to create worlds that undermine the border walls erected not necessarily by tearing them down (except when/where possible) but by sowing seeds. Here I mean seed-sowing in both the literal and metaphoric sense: sowing as a prayerful activity that isn't exactly Progress even as it tenders the possibility of flourishing. The process of sowing seeds isn't linear, unilateral, unidirectional, or certain; it's oblique, multiplex, rhizomatic, committed.

In agricultural settings, there's plenty of math involved in calculating quantities of seed necessary to accurately sow a particular crop at a particular spacing in a particular bed for a particular amount of row-feet. And yet, all of this becomes ruptured in the event of seeding itself: All calculation is deconstructed by the un-anticipatable variables of rainfall, soil composition, heat waves, critter encounters, and beyond. Seeding is thus a relinquishing of all programmatic computation to a position of humility to Earth, of hospitality to what may come. Always, the decision of seeding is ungrounded even as seed meets soil, rending any linear certainties, instead only possible in the opening of an impossible horizon. Mary-Jane Rubenstein, though embedded deep in the realm of Derridean theory of "undecidability," unwittingly but superbly describes the emotion of seeding: "I must never be able to say 'I have decided,' much less 'I have decided well,' much less 'I am all square, and my duty is done.'"[115] There's nothing "all square" about an act of faith, including sowing.[116] The duty has only just begun to unfold—for a lifetime. Dark hope resists this closure or finality, especially as it toils in pursuit of nonlinear justice.

Sowing seeds is nothing less than disturbance, not merely a means to an end but an end in itself. Growth is not possible without sowing. Sowing resides and remains in the present, but always ever enacting that which "will *have had to* happen," in Campt's terms. To embody this hope, drawing on the wisdom of Tsing and Haraway, is to notice and to abide: finding cracks in the façades of present regimes that can be toppled *not (only)* by the swing of the hammer but by the planting of seeds in those cracks to render concrete rubble. In this way, this hope tiptoes between and among constructivist and negativist theories of action: that it need not be inhabited in solely activist forms that take on the regime directly but can also find materialization in the subtler and slower forms of refusal and rejection. All modes of this dark hope, though, reside firmly (yet tenderly) in and among the earth-ground, the terrestrial. As Haraway suggests, these times are "neither sacred nor secular; this earthly worlding is thoroughly terran, muddled, and mortal—and at stake now."[117] The urgency of these uncertain times must not cling to the machinic drives of present powers but must dismantle these apparatuses or spike their tires with "jack-rocks." Hope is necessarily a disruption of the political engines driving toward the cliff's edge; hope is an abandonment of Progress in preference to the stewardship of adaptation and novelty, which, perhaps paradoxically, includes processes of rejection and refusal.

"Dark" also modifies hope in another way: It reminds that hope is born out of lived experiences, out of ecological locations, which have histories and narratives. That is, dark hope takes seriously the ways in which hope is born from lament,[118] emerges from the scars of life, from experiences of trauma. I don't mean to suggest that these experiences are necessary for hope to exist (in no way am I interested in justifying this sort of violence!), but rather I name this to articulate how hope is always grounded in the particularities of our social locations, our identities, our ecologies, our landscapes. It's not "pure" or even "salvific," but it extends opportunities and carves space for creativity and resolution in the face of injustice. It sprouts forth from our locales, in other words. The "dark" of "dark hope" thus subverts paradigms that associate lightness with goodness and darkness with badness.[119] The "dark" of "dark hope" opens further semiotic registers that bolster the associations of darkness with richness, fullness, power, and vibrancy.

Dark hope does not promise any sort of purity or innocence, recalling Shotwell's work, but it *does* bear the potentiality of once more pulling the thread of hope through the contaminated patchworks of the present to create renewal that was not yet imaginable—even yesterday. While "total repair" or "salvation" may not be possible, *"mending"* perhaps is. So, too, *"remediation"* and *"regeneration."* This impossible novelty emerges only out of that which is, but it sparks new assemblages, formations, and experimentations that gather, coalesce, and collect into combinations that retool what is possible, that cultivate the growth of possibility itself. These processes are not straight lines but are complex ripples: intersecting and folding in movements of making and unmaking, building and destroying—all of which are pleats of creativity.

The Possibility of Dark Hope

To return one's perspective to the ground, to the terrestrial, challenges one to adapt one's understanding of hope as endemically emergent, materially dedicated, and immanently creative. Dark hope aims to refuse the binaries of optimism and pessimism in favor of crafty forms of dwelling that reject the choice as offered, that fold back not in hesitation but in apophasis, that sow seeds to rupture the concretized foundationalisms buttressing shifting forms of oppression. This hope maintains a robust sense of the possibility of novelty, even while safeguarding it against the temptation to assume that whatever is performing the hoped-for saving will come from outside, from above, from beyond. It impels activity, even as it recognizes the ecological and social contextuality of agency, capacity, and resources. Contamination of the scope and scale presented by the Anthropocene, compounded by the gravity of colonial exploitation, chattel slavery, gender-based violence, and so on, undo any notion of "hope" as unaffected, as unpolluted, as perfect; dark hope senses possibilities in the fog of uncertainty, creating amid, among, and within the eco-social and spatiotemporal milieu of the present. What exactly might these possibilities look like, and what sort of politics might this dark hope ground? The final chapter of this project will take on these matters.

Interlude

Seeds and the Subversive Act of Sowing

Octavia Butler's seminal novel *Parable of the Sower* (1993) portrays the efforts of sixteen-year-old Lauren Olamina to survive a world ravaged by climate change, racial injustice, unfettered neoliberal capitalism, and heteropatriarchy. It is, in other words, not a foreign world. As a young Black girl, these intersecting forces of oppression gravely impact Lauren, forcing impossible decisions and unimaginable ingenuity in her struggle northward after disaster strikes her neighborhood. But on this unbearably unjust journey, Lauren refuses the culturally prevalent and extant behavioral approaches of either total autonomy or uncritically accepting "relationality." That is, Lauren, early in her trek, recognizes that a lone wanderer is a "sitting duck" and that a blindly trusting person is equally at risk. Opting for a resolute third way, Lauren aims to form a coalitional collective by centering her discovered religion, Earthseed, as the transversal ground making unthinkable relationships possible. In this way, she implausibly develops relationships amid the insufferable landscapes across which she treads, forming a critically diverse community spanning old and young, Black and white, poor and slightly less poor.

While this novel merits a comprehensive excursus,[1] particularly the religio-ethical matters it presents, I wish to focus on just one element of the narrative: seeds. The symbolic and literal roles of seeds intertwine complexly—vitally matterphoric.[2] Early in the book, Lauren writes in her journal about her realization that her theological beliefs and praxes should be named "Earthseed":

> Well, today, I found the name, found it while I was weeding the back garden and thinking about the way plants seed themselves, windborne, animalborne, waterborne, far from their parent plants. They have no

ability at all to travel great distances under their own power, and yet, they do travel. Even they don't have to just sit in one place and wait to be wiped out. There are islands thousands of miles from anywhere—the Hawaiian Islands, for example, and Easter Island—where plants seeded themselves and grew long before any humans arrived.[3]

This novel lifeway offers itself to Lauren: She is not its progenitor but its disciple; it presents itself as a lure to be embodied, not as a dogma to be set in stone. Importantly, Lauren clarifies, "I've never felt that I was making any of this up—not the name, Earthseed, not any of it. I mean, I've never felt that it was anything other than real: *discovery rather than invention, exploration rather than creation*."[4] Her manner of religious construction is exploratory and in-process, not a creation *ex nihilo*. Later in the novel she exclaims in frustration at the accusation of having supposedly "made up" Earthseed: "Stumbling across the truth isn't the same as making things up."[5] What's apparent in this assertion is her understanding of Earthseed as perceiving, participating in, and exemplifying the lure she senses.

But seeds are far from just symbolic to Lauren; they're crucial in her preparations for survival, and she notes their vitality time and again throughout the novel. From her initial efforts to collect seeds for her "grab and run" pack to her using what little money she possessed to buy seeds on her trek north, Lauren's commitment to stewarding seeds could not be more clear. Near the end of the novel, when asked by a young member of her group, "What seed do you have?" she responds:

> Most of it is summer stuff—corn, peppers, sunflowers, eggplant, melons, tomatoes, beans, squash. But I have some winter things; peas, carrots, cabbage, broccoli, winter squash, onions, asparagus, herbs, several kinds of greens. . . . We can buy more, and we've got the stuff left in this garden plus what we can harvest from the local oak, pine, and citrus trees. I brought tree seeds too: more oak, citrus, peach, pear, nectarine, almond, walnut, a few others. They won't do us any good for a few years, but they're a hell of an investment in the future.[6]

The nourishment of seeds is simultaneously physical and spiritual—kernels of sustenance and hope. In right relation with ground, seeds extend futural possibility through their germination. Sowing is indeed, in theorist Tina M. Campt's words, what "will have had to happen" to enact a Black feminist futurity not just of survival but of flourishing. Lauren knows that much of these seeds will not produce hopeful nourishment for years—at minimum. And yet, their sowing is what will have had to happen.

Human history is predicated on this very process of saving seeds—the stewarding of desired strains and the fostering of interspecies relations. Seed-saving extends beyond the realm of the merely "agricultural," simultaneously undergirding the cultural and, crucially, the epistemological. Crops generate new possibilities for the alimentary, the culinary, the communal, the religious. Seeds carry stories, legacies of regeneration, threads of cultural memory.[7] That is to say, seed-saving is the stewarding and regenerating of possibility itself—which flows into just about every facet of human life. Drawing on the previous chapter's terminology, seed-saving is a potent "weapon of the weak."

But, given that seeds are the bearers of stories, seed-saving efforts are not immune from the particularities of history and social location. Seed-saving has largely been the work of rural women of color—work that is not registered as such.[8] This work is not factored into GDP (gross domestic product), for example, much like most of the work within the sphere of the domestic. What's more, seeds today—now overrun and overly modified by multinational corporations like Monsanto, Dow Chemical Company, Syngenta, and others—have become grossly commodified at the same time that they're stripped of their effectual essence: regenerative capacity; the mass production of hybridized seeds—or, seeds that, while often supposedly heartier and more disease-resistant, won't reproduce after just one growing season—ensures that growers remain financially indebted to these seed providers. This is nothing short of the eradication *not just* of life but of the *possibility for* life—at least not without supporting the wealthy elite who have colonized these markets. The commodification of seeds amounts to their reduction as inert "raw material" to be manipulated at will for the sake of shareholder pleasure.[9]

But seed-saving has always been—and in some small communities, despite agribusiness seed monopolies, continues to be—a form of creativity necessary to flourishing and wholesomeness. For most, this work is aimed solely at survival. Black farmer and activist Leah Penniman offers an example of this practice amid the transatlantic slave trade, sharing this family story:

> As insurance for an uncertain future, [West African women] began the practice of braiding rice, okra, and millet seeds into their hair. While there were no report-backs from the other side of the transatlantic slave trade, and rumors abounded that white people were capturing Africans to eat us, they still had the audacity of hope to imagine a future on soil.[10]

She continues, "Once sequestered in the bowels of the slave ships, they continued the practice of seed smuggling, picking up grains from the threshing floor and hiding the precious kernels in their braids."[11] Penniman goes on to state that anthropologists and historians have confirmed the veracity of these family stories.[12]

"Seed keeping"—to use the phrase of Owen Taylor and Chris Bolden-Newsome of Truelove Seeds and Sankofa Community Farm, respectively—stewards and safeguards the narratives that do not simply "accompany" seeds but that *constitute* them.[13] Seeds don't just "carry" stories; they *are storied*. As Penniman beautifully expresses, "In keeping the stories of our seeds alive, we keep the craft of our ancestors alive in our hearts."[14] Mass-produced, hybridized, and genetically modified seeds do not bear this promise, sterilized of any meaningful narrative. Culturally important seeds regenerate memories and, at the same time, unfold new possibilities for persistent lifeways. As Bolden-Newsome stated in an interview, ". . . for me, it is absolutely crucial to grow African American and African diasporic crops as a way to keep my people together. When we grow these foods and share these seeds, we ensure that important parts of our culture continue to live on."[15] Such activity of hopeful resistance is not aimed solely at some abstract future but plants itself in the present as a measure of "what will have had to happen" in order to realize a more just world.

In addition to the cultural value of seed-saving, the preservation of diverse seed varieties yields both economic and environmental advantages: simultaneously removing growers' burden of relying on agribusinesses for seed and the promotion of heterogeneous, biodiverse fields for the sake of ecological wellness. This is the aim of efforts like Taylor's Truelove Seeds and Penniman's Soul Fire Farm.[16] As ecofeminist Vandana Shiva writes of small-scale growers, ". . . we are losing our fundamental freedom to decide what seeds we will sow, how we will grow our food, and what we will eat. The seed is the first point of attack. But conversely, it is also our first line of defense. It is where we begin our fight for seed freedom."[17] The loss of seeds equates to the loss of futurity—economic, ecological, and beyond. But seed-saving proffers possibilities for "collective agency and community resilience," to use environmental sociologist Monica White's terms.[18] That is, seed-saving reconfigures seeds as neither property nor object but as commons.[19] Put differently, seed-keeping is an everyday strategy of resistance[20] that fosters a community's ability to "adjust, withstand, and absorb disturbance, and to reorganize while undergoing change."[21] This is not limited to the *anthro*- but transfuses across the *eco*-.

Uniform monocultures allow disturbances in one place to translate into disturbances in other parts of the system; while a blight can quickly spread across fields of not only a single crop but a single variety therein (which is the case of a large percentage of "conventional" agriculture), biodiversity resists this disturbance by virtue of its plurality. As Shiva notes, ". . . plurality . . . is ecologically necessary for survival in times of rapid change and accelerated breakdown."[22]

Seed-keeping strives toward resilience by prioritizing diversity as a principle of ecological health, rendering ecosystems less vulnerable to pests or disease.

It's not difficult to note the parallels here between agricultural and political monocultures. Each aims to achieve a homogeneous uniformity, a oneness that supposedly yields "efficiency," "streamlined processes," and integrated "chains of command." And yet both fail to account for—or, perhaps more accurately, choose to ignore or externalize—the pluralities of communities *written out of the equation* from the start. For this reason, Shiva has long drawn connections between the "monologics" of industrial agriculture and racism, sexism, and colonialism.

But returning to Lauren and *Parable of the Sower*, what might be learned from seed-keeping as an activity of subversive resistance, and in what ways might it characterize the imperfect yet resilient capacities of a dark hope embodied? Lauren's seed-saving forms the ground of possibility for the growth of a community—one that emerges not from the sterilized foundations of an imagined world but from the particular soils of this earthy world. Put differently, Lauren's community fashions itself terrestrially, sprouting forth from the terrain of the present, meaning that it does not, that it *cannot*, overlook its contextual features—traumas, potencies, harms, boons, contaminants, fecundities. Accordingly, the end of Lauren's journal entries read:

> ... today we remembered the friends and the family members we lost. We spoke our individual memories and quoted Bible passages, Earthseed verses, and bits of songs and poems that were favorites of the living or the dead. Then we buried our dead and we planted oak trees. Afterward, we sat together and talked and ate a meal and decided to call this place Acorn.[23]

In the face of anthropogenic climate change, of a world much like Lauren's, a terrestrial perspective absorbs the affects of its present milieu in search of creative modes of resistance, neither eliding past narratives flowing into the present nor relinquishing the present in some feigned struggle toward an unattainable futural utopia. A collective like Lauren's Acorn is imperfect, is muddied by its past, which does not strip it of its agency but instead leans into its extant resources in an effort to multiply its capacities to bring about wholesomeness.

What might a terrestrial collective, an earthy assemblage, of political actors look like, and what might its priorities be should it ground itself in and on the earth-ground? The following chapter explores the political consequences of a darkly hopeful perspectivalism, sketching the possibilities of multiplying capacities when reframing ethical decisions through the lens not of "progress" but of *(de)composition*.

4
Blooming
(De)Compositional Planetary Politics

> Inside rich histories of entangled becoming—without the aid of simplistic ideals like "wilderness," "the natural" or "ecosystem balance"—it is ultimately impossible to reach simple, black-and-white prescriptions about how ecologies "should be." *And so we are required to take a stand for some possible worlds and not others;* we are required to begin to take responsibility for the ways in which we help to tie and retie our knotted multispecies worlds.
>
> —THOM VAN DOOREN

On Political Grounds

If ground is not foundation, then what sort of politics might emerge from this ground? What's at stake here is not a matter of "constructing" some sort of ethico-political system, as one might do atop a calcified foundation. Rather, this political emergence is a matter of tuning into the contextuality of a location, minding particularities for aspects needing nurturing and for others ready to burst forth with life. This chapter explores one particular response to the question: If one assumes the slippage between philosophical ground and earth-ground, what sort of politics would follow? This chapter will not "answer" this question, unfortunately, as such an attempted answer would but reinforce the false idea of some sort of "universalizable" political project, utterly inattentive to its ground. But a response, I believe, nevertheless remains possible.

Central to this chapter's concerns are the inherent paradoxes of ground as earth-ground: drawing connections though never homogeneously, linking locales yet never flattening their differences, resolutely undergirding but never properly *firma*, materially entangling though ever fragmented. What sort of political activity does this ground then support, not as its abstracted foundation but *as its co-constitutive milieu*? What would it mean for the terrestrial to serve as not just a "factor" in the political landscape but its very ground? To begin to offer a response to these queries, it will be necessary initially to parse out some critical ecological features of soil and their usefulness for exploring what might be called a planetary politic. I will draw on recent scholarship on "soil organic matter," especially in the form of humus, to theorize ground as an integral, co-constitutive matrix catalyzing contextual collectives.

This chapter's main ethico-political interlocutors—Bruno Latour, with his particular use of the term "Terrestrial," and Eva Haifa Giraud, with her "ethics of exclusion"—will aid the present efforts to figure ground as a particularized yet connecting phenomenon for the sake of coalition-building. If the earth-ground is not a product but a process, not "progressing" even as its composting activities still yield fecundity, how might political activity reconfigure itself by rhizomatically relating to that cycling ground, rooting itself in the material-symbolic becomings of soil? Put differently, what might it mean to conceive of justice as an earthy process of *(de)composition*—making and unmaking, creating and abolishing, entangled? Not satisfied with purely constructive or deconstructive modes alone, might justice be envisaged as a concomitant process of composing and decomposing, of assembling and dismantling? Could it yet be possible, through the matterphoric inspiration of soil, to imagine efforts of justice *not* as "progress" but *instead* as transformation—refusing to be measured by extant structures that gave rise to whichever injustice one opposes and instead reframing the very metrics of justice as inimical to the forward-marching proclivities of the Global North? In other words, to use theological terms, could it yet be possible to imagine justice as terrestrially *resurrective*?

To signal the arc of this work and its central terms, Latour's attention to the three-pronged material interconnections between climate change, fascism, and globalized neoliberal capitalism will guide this chapter's articulation of (de)composition. Latour makes a case for a communitarian terrestrial politics that elides the tendencies toward the industrializing, externalizing, and colonizing inflections of "progress"—even as it advocates for tangible justice and radical equity. At the same time, Giraud's ethics of exclusion will draw our attention to the limits of "terrestriality." By focusing on exclusion, one can better mark the porous edges of particular contexts in an effort to indicate where location might compel intentional exclusion to foreground the inevitable erasures accompanying "relationality" or "entanglement." Sought here, then, is a twofold intention: a theorization of earth-ground as integral to political action—*not* as additive—and as an integral political actor. Thinking the earth-ground as a political force does not eradicate the necessity of remaining attentive to the particular nature of ground—relationally fragmented, differently entangled. This ground makes possible, makes space for, political activity while simultaneously offering a conceptual intervention for thinking justice *not* as progress but as a process of (de)composition.

Soiling Change: Humus, Compost, and (De)composition

Some clarifying remarks are warranted in this present experimental theorization—namely: How does soil—the matter, the metaphor, the metonym, the concept—inform any of the political questions at hand? And what is meant by "(de)composition"? For this, we'll need to dig into the vibrancies of "soil organic matter."

For the possibility of life in its many expressions, soil organic matter is vital, to say the least. And yet, this organic matter, as critical as it is, is not "one thing"—not in the slightest. It's not reducible to just carbon or nitrogen or leaf litter or microbes or heat energy or burrowing critters—it's the entanglement thereof. Taking, as an example, just the organic aspects of soil and their relation to the question of ground, one will begin to note inherent paradoxes that might lend themselves to terrestrially attuned political organizing.

Humus: Stable Substance or Organic Process?

Temporarily removing other elements of organic matter from the soil equation, let's just consider "one" of its aspects: humus.[1]

"Humus" is difficult to define, as it escapes taxonomic categories and evades the neat lines we often like to draw, especially in the West. Soil scientists Raymond Weil and Nyle C. Brady, representing a functional "majority opinion," define "humus" as "the portion of soil organic matter that is not alive or recognizable plant tissue, and is protected from rapid decomposition to some degree by the soil environment. It is generally colloidal in particle size and black in color."[2] This description has served as a general consensus, if one could call it that, concerning humus: In effect, humus is organic matter—dark, spongy, amorphous—that's been broken down into more stabilized forms over extremely long periods of time. Humus is colloidal—a nondiscriminant interspersion of matters that cannot be pinned down as any one thing. Weil and Brady note, "Humus colloids are not minerals, nor are they crystalline. Instead, they consist of a wide variety of partially decomposed cell walls and biomolecules derived mainly from microorganisms and bits of tissues derived mainly from plants."[3] Accordingly, humus remains mostly distinct from other parts of soil organic matter—such as detritus, or "plant litter," which is, first, far more separable in its composition and, second, far more accessible to breakdown for mineral and nutritional absorption by both soil's microbial community as well as by vegetation. This prevalent perspective seems to suggest that humus is distinguishable from other types of soil organic matter because of its purported "stability" and "longevity";[4] as Brady and Weil attempt to confirm: "The *more stable and well-protected portion* of the humus fraction is often referred to as passive organic matter because its carbon is not readily accessible to microbes and remains in the soil for hundreds or even thousands of years."[5] In contrast to "labile carbon," which is organic material subject to "rapid oxidation by soil organisms over periods of months to years," the carbon in humus appears to be *"stabilized* by various mechanisms that enable it to remain in the soil for relatively long periods (centuries or even millennia)."[6] Weil and Brady offer an unfortunately neoliberal vignette to explain their take:

> We can summarize the concept of two organic matter pools with a business analogy: the labile [carbon] largely serves as ready cash flow to pay the workers (feed the soil food web) while humus can be seen as the (carbon) capital of the system (accumulated organic matter), which builds important chemical and physical aspects of the soil.[7]

This common perspective of humus can be summarized in this way: Humus is stable, slow, and passive; labile carbon is unstable, fast, and active. Humus thus takes on an unstated role as a sort of foundation, relegated as a stage upon which the more interesting and energetic organic matters "do their thing."

But soil organic matter may not be as well understood as some may suggest. The past several years of research on soil organic matter have revealed inconsistencies in construal and modeling—primarily a result of overly mechanistic interpretations of decompositional processes. There is no satisfactory answer (yet) to the question posed by biochemist Selman Waksman in 1925: "Why does this take place, why does a part of the organic matter decompose rapidly and a part only very slowly?"[8] This is echoed in the 2011 article titled "Persistence of Soil Organic Matter as an Ecosystem Property," in which the authors ask the following: "Why, when organic matter is thermodynamically unstable, does it persist in soils, sometimes for thousands of years?"[9] To this day, the central problem is that ". . . it remains largely unknown why some [soil organic matter (SOM)] persists for millennia whereas other SOM decomposes readily. . . ."[10] What recent insights on soil organic matter seem to reveal is that soil is more thoroughly entangled in the processes of larger ecosystemic structures. What's more, these new insights foster critical attention to soil as process—as opposed to substance—including its components, long deemed "passive" and "stable." Waksman had this intuition early: "An attempt has first been made to learn not what 'humus' is, but *how it is formed* in the soil."[11] In William Bryant Logan's words, to understand the "processes of growth, decay, feeding, digestion, excretion, attack, and repulsion" integral to humus, one must "study the interconnections, not the essences."[12] To reiterate, soil, in general, is best understood as process, not substance. Waksman was well aware of this even in 1936: "Humus is not an intermediate product of decomposition. . . . Neither is humus a final product of decomposition. . . ."[13] In other words, one must conceptualize humus as a confluence of processes—not as a product of "things." This remains the contention of contemporary soil scientists Johannes Lehmann and Markus Kleber:

> Long-standing theory suggests that soil organic matter is composed of inherently stable and chemically unique compounds. Here we argue that the available evidence does not support the formation of large-molecular-size and persistent "humic substances" in soils. Instead, soil organic matter is *a continuum of progressively decomposing organic compounds.*[14]

Through this emergentist lens, one can see that there is no "final form" because we're dealing with open-ended processes and not bound things.[15]

While humus does indeed exist as an earthy phenomenon,[16] present conceptualizations of humus as stable and reliable—as things and not as processes—drastically affect soil carbon modeling in the Anthropocene. That is, reconfiguring one's understanding of humus reshapes how one understands soil's various capacities to store carbon before releasing it into the atmosphere—and thus altering possible responses to climate injustice.[17] To misunderstand the processes and characteristics of soil organic matter is to miss an opportunity to find better, more wholesome ways for carbon sequestration, sustainable agriculture, biodiversity restoration, and so on. To attend to humus as a steady "thing" as opposed to an ecosystem-entangled process yields a vastly differing *ground* for ethics. The dated view of SOM, in general, as a set of "things" and humus, in particular, as a subset thereof materializes into political activity that forsakes the terrestrial as actor and actant, as the very grounds for political mobilization. This processual optic of terrestrial milieux begins to signal the import of a reorientation of political milieux. The following sections aim to demonstrate the political vitalities of reconceiving the terrestrial through process-minded perspectives.

Compost: Recalcifying Ground as Foundation?

No matter where one lands when it comes to humus, what's apparent is this: Humus is commonly figured as slow and tepid in almost every respect, at least when compared to its seductive and hot counterpart "compost." This sort of mistake, albeit minor, reifies the tendency to foreground human political actors to the detriment of the grounding functions of Earth as political actor; in other words, I contend here that an overemphasis on the so-called active aspects of soil unintentionally reifies notions of Earth as a passive backdrop and obscures the integral, grounding functions of Earth in any robustly planetary politics.

Compost occupies considerable space in contemporary theorization—philosophically, politically, agriculturally, and beyond. My aim here is to present how solely focusing on compost, even as only a conceptual metaphor, reifies the error of reading ground as foundation and perpetuates the notion of the terrestrial as a mere additive to the political and not its very milieu. The problem is *not* using compost as a political metaphor; it is doing so *at the expense of* ground. And this oversight, I will soon argue, prevents one from contemplating that which grounds the possibility for planetary politics.

Composting, in the words of Brady and Weil, "is the practice of creating partially stabilized, useful organic decay products outside of the soil by mixing, piling, or otherwise storing organic materials under conditions conducive to aerobic decomposition and nutrient conservation."[18] This practice produces what's known as compost: organic matter that replenishes nutrients and serves as a slow-release fertilizer.[19] This process and its steamy upshot are most necessary to maintaining soil fertility, particularly in agricultural settings.[20] But even when made from on-site scraps, dry vegetation, and so forth, compost remains something of an additive, crucial to plant growth and microbial activity, but only in the relatively "short-term." The compost pile is "over there," and it must be brought "over here" and added to present soils. This is not to denigrate compost or to reduce its immense value to sustainable agriculture; my aim is not to denounce the ways in which compost has meaningfully served as a symbol for political activity but is instead to notice the consequences of doing so *without sufficient attention* to ground.[21] Instead, the question explored here is more concerned with the functional conceptual metaphor of *ground* and its associated political consequences as to the place of the terrestrial: Is it "within" one's politics or does it *ground* one's politics? Is it an accessory or is it *elemental*? Ground demonstrates an uncanny capacity for communicating transversality and contextuality, crucial to coalition-building, as well as evoking an understanding of change as (de)compositional. Compost illustrates the latter but not the former; ground may yet create space for theorizing both concomitantly.[22]

Both critical theorists and soil scientists seem to inadvertently reinforce the paradigmatic category of foundations in the lines drawn between humus and compost, if only implicitly. Both theorists and scientists seem to share the tendency to regard compost as active transformation and ground (humus) as utterly passive, as a selfsame foundation—whether theoretically or molecularly or both. To refrain from minding humus while at the same time granting one's attention to compost constructs an implicit assumption that ground is but the backdrop to be added to and to be *activated by* compost.[23] Taking seriously the challenges posed by Lehmann, Kleber, Schmidt et al., and even Waksman, such distinctions, or at least such an omission, may yet buttress a view of humus as sure, lasting, fixed. To think of humus as constant or effectively unchanging (at least on the timelines of supposedly "labile" carbon) is to return to a view of soil as substance and not process, thereby constructing a view of the terrestrial as once again the foundation for human activity.

Donna Haraway verges on this error when explaining her concept of "staying with the trouble": "Staying with the trouble requires making oddkin; that is, we require each other in unexpected collaborations and combinations, in hot compost piles. We become-with each other or not at all."[24] Amen! And yet, there is an oversight here: While Haraway's political arguments are deeply in line with this present project, her inattention to ground may perpetuate the assumption of humus as unchanging. To be sure, Haraway does write things like, "We are humus, not Homo, not anthropos; we are compost, not posthuman."[25] Indeed! Humus undoes the human timescapes of hope, making it understandable that Haraway might turn to compost as a temporally sensible matterphor. And yet, we can go further by asserting that one's politics of becoming-with must account for one's terrestrial context, one's ecological location, *not as additive but as the* grounding entanglement thereof; this is *precisely* the consequence of solely granting attention to compost as opposed to ground: One need not attend to particular locations, at least if one is only concerned with a conceptual metaphor and not necessarily with actual ecological fecundity. That is not to say that Haraway is ignorant of the need for contextuality as a constitutive factor in one's political theory—far from it! But it is to highlight the ease with which compost can become read as tantamount to a universal solution, even if one of heterogeneous composition and intra-active contribution, to be applied to any ground at all regardless of its conditions.[26] While composting may yet be a viable mode of remediation for contaminated soils,[27] it is not universally so. Nor is compost any one thing to begin with. More terrestrially attuned metaphors are necessary—or at least are helpful.

A fine example of mending and improving this lacuna—that is, the error of centering compost *at the expense of* the particularities of ground—can be found in ecopolitical theorists Sebastian Abrahamsson and Filippo Bertoni's brilliant article "Compost Politics: Experimenting with Togetherness in Vermicomposting." They introduce their project in this way:

> We argue that composting shifts what togetherness might come to be. In response to calls for new kinds of ethics, politics, and normativities for the time of the "Anthropocene," we thus attempt to rethink togetherness through vermicomposting. Vermicomposting is about doing togetherness in a way that is neither detached nor engaged.[28]

Their work, simultaneously a practical guide to vermicomposting and a political theorization informed by compost, acknowledges that vermicomposting unveils, both ecologically and politically, "the coexistence of heterogeneous and disparate processes and entities" that "may bring about problems."[29] Vermicomposting, as both ecological praxis and political matterphor, is open-ended experimentation: No single solution is universally fruitful. They expand on the ethical ramifications that follow: "To the vermicomposter, this begs the political and normative question 'what to do?' Through hands-on experience, we learn that there is no univocal answer to this question. There is no 'natural' answer, no moral guidelines 'out there.' Still, composting is possible."[30] A chorus of "amens!" are due yet again. Abrahamsson and Bertoni foreground the particularities of place, the contextual edges of agency, and the implicit connections between the ecological and epistemological. What's more, their article offers a "fluid recipe" for vermicomposting "that can be changed and modified to adjust to different contexts, problems and situations."[31] That is, they grant attention to compost as a local, organic process predicated on the relations (de)composing "it." It's apparent here that Abrahamsson and Bertoni are obviously committed to contributing to contextualizing, to grounding, eco-ethical engagement by acknowledging, for example, the following: "Tinkering with your bin, you are changing the conditions of the soil, and can try to make it more or less acidic, more or less moist, filled with this or that kind of food scrap."[32] In other words, their "compost politics" accepts the conditional and contextual nature of the work of composting. How might one supplement the dark brilliance of this compost politics with a revitalized attentiveness to the animating and vibrant activities of ground? This terrestrial politics, nourished by the rich fecundity of compost, could not be mistaken as merely the activation of that which one might assume to be passive or the extraction of energy to infuse one's foundation with temporary life. A politics of ground, a planetary politics, would be *suffused with* the terrestrial as its elemental matrix.

Don't get me wrong: As a person involved and invested in local organic agriculture, I would be remiss to denounce the value and vitality of compost to soil fertility and crop production. The rub is this: Humanity does not live by compost alone, but by the ground that undergirds not as unchanging foundation but as continual becoming. Heralding the (de)compositional properties of compost without adequate recognition of soil, broadly understood as (de)compositional, unfortunately, albeit inexorably, reifies the foundationalisms one may have hoped to avoid; this is the danger of misreading or misapplying kindred eco-theories. It should thus remain imperative that thinking about the processes of compost and humus—admittedly distinct phenomena—as wholly different, as inequitably active, or as unevenly necessary yields an image of ground not as a web of relations *but instead* as a severed sum of its individual and disjointed parts. This fallacy effectively, if only inadvertently, furthers an understanding of humus reinscribed as foundation, while compost becomes the zesty activator thereupon, despite any intended goal to deconstruct originary foundationalisms or persistent substance metaphysics. For this reason, compost presents itself as a convenient archetype: decomposition and transformation at a rate easily understood and thus palatable for thinkers of process; but predicating one's politics *exclusively* on the symbol of compost misunderstands and misrepresents ground as foundation, instead appealing to the very appealing "short term." Of course, most farmers invested in organic and regenerative agriculture understand that compost is a critical catalyst, often necessary *but certainly not sufficient* for the flourishing of crops. But the political theorization of compost—*at the expense of soil*—misses the point: That is, a politics modeled solely after compost, as disjointed from its earthy matrix, figures ground as passive backdrop, as inactive substance, which can only be rendered vibrant and fecund by means of the additive of compost. Unfortunately, it seems that compost as political symbol fails to reach beyond its limited range and application, accentuating processual transformation *at the expense of* tracing larger webs of relation beyond the heap. Compost can mistakenly be understood as the activating catalyst to convert "passive dirt" into "active soil," a universal solution to be "added," never mind the ground to which it is "applied." What should be clear, then, is how compost, as a theoretical political signifier, may yet unintentionally but inexcusably erase the crucial dimensions of particularity and contextuality integral to a terrestrial perspective.

(De)composition: Making or Unmaking?

Soil exists by and through (de)composition. I've chosen to intentionally notate "(de)composition" with the parenthetical prefix as a way of illuminating the constitutive paradoxes of soil—soon to argued as being relevant to the theorization of a viable planetary politics. That is, (de)composition *holds in tension* the ways in which organic life is rendered possible by and is *composed of decomposition*. Decomposition composes; composition decomposes. (De)composition thus limns the processual, transformative nature of soil, rejecting the notion of change as linear; instead, (de)composition fashions change in and as a nonlinear, transmutational milieu. This is becoming all the more clear in emerging understandings of decompositional processes of soil organic matter: Decomposition is not just the condensation reactions of plant litter broken down into more stable compounds, but, instead, decomposition is better understood as a folding network of plant litter, rhizospheric inputs, fire residues, microbial activity, sorption and desorption processes, deep soil carbon, freezing and thawing cycles, physical disconnections between decomposers and organic matter, and so forth.[33] In other words, decomposition is not an easily predictable process because it is an ecosystemic *complicatio*. As Schmidt et al. write, "Molecular structure alone does not control [soil organic matter] stability."[34] Put differently, "The persistence of soil organic carbon is primarily not a molecular property, but *an ecosystem property*."[35] The (de)compositional composition of soil is a function of its entanglement within wider networks, even as it itself remains a network.

It must be said that some ethical risks lurk here in the use of (de)composition as a symbol of meaningful change. Surely the associations between decomposition and death make this argument tenuous—and these associations only become all the more precarious when one considers the legacy of the surrogacy of suffering shouldered by those at the margins, not least women of color.[36] The preliminary question at hand concerns whether the use of the matterphor "(de)composition" unintentionally reifies the burdens of sacrifice, even martyrdom, forced upon the already heavily burdened, upon already suffering populations. This risk most certainly exists, and I do not take it lightly. While soil fecundity relies on this process of decomposition and decay, this does not mean that the same applies to human communities or that this matterphor should extend to the soteriological. Instead, (de)composition illustrates a novel optic for conceiving of justice outside of the ubiquitous lenses of "Progress." (De)composition opens new registers to imagine change that do not require some sort of forward-marching agenda, thereby ascribing some feigned meaning to death where utterly inappropriate.

(De)composition undoes the mechanisms of "Progress." As an alternative to "Progress," (de)composition offers an optic for conceiving of creativity and fecundity in ways that do not adhere to the paradigms of productivity, development, and so forth—all of which duplicitously prop up white supremacist and neoliberal capitalist regimes as but pipe dreams to those who've been written out of the equation from the start. In line with feminist eco-theorist Maria Puig de la Bellacasa's reflections on "conceptions of soil care" and their capacity to disrupt modes of "progressive and linear futurity" whose myopic obsession with "productivity" risks ecocide, (de)composition reimagines growth not according to capitalist paradigms of limitless expansion but in careful keeping with ecologically dynamic tension and interrelation.[37] That is, "The pace required by involved soil care poses the challenge of a relational encounter of different timelines that might affect the notions of the future that dominate in technoscience." As Puig de la Bellacasa argues incisively,

> In these temporalities of ecological care, growth is not necessarily exponential, nor extensive. This is not only because ecological growth involves cycles of living and dying, but also because what makes an ecology grow manifests itself in the intensification and teeming of involvements between members. Conceived as such, the time of soil is not 'one'; it exposes multifarious speeds of growth becoming ecologically significant to each other. To argue for a disruption of futuristic time through making care time is therefore not so much about a slowing or redirection of timelines but an invitation to rearrange and rebalance the relations between a diversity of coexisting temporalities that inhabit the worlds of soil and other interdependent ecologies.[38]

(De)composition can be understood as a refusal to capitulate to structures or conventions of "productivity," while still offering notions of creation, creativity, or generativity that remain hopeful for political engagement. In this way, we begin to see that (de)composition resists slipping into some sort of argument for the "necessity" of "sacrifice" or "death"—whether in the form of the production of labor, the losses disguised as "love," and so forth. Under the watch of "Progress," decay and death somehow "must" effect change—whether ascribed Purpose, written off, or externalized as a necessary loss to keep the wheels of Progress steadily rolling, no matter what or whom resides in its path. What counts as "Progress" often keeps hidden that which has been written out of the equation: the ways in which development erodes landscapes, industrialization bulldozes spheres of cultural creativity, and productivity obscures harms inflicted on the social and ecological.[39] (De)composition, even as it exposes the inherent violence implicit in "Progress," reveals ways of conceptualizing fecundity, growth, and betterment; in this way, one might be able to remain committed to the principles of "progressive politics"—including a hope for vast improvements across the registers of the socio-political—while also calling into question the regimes of violence that have long wreaked havoc under the purportedly innocent banner of "Progress."

(De)composition, as symbolized and metonymically materialized by soil, undoes imposed temporal expectations, as these organic processes, about which we know far less than we might have thought, can't be rushed or sped up in any considerable way. The open-ended processes of (de)composition open a novel and smudged lens through which we might be able to better think eco-social change and environmental justice—eluding persistent narratives of incremental reform in lieu of insurgent vivacity. Could (de)composition offer a darkly hopeful optic for theorizing sought-after political change and ecological wellness? In other words, what might it mean to consider (de)composition as both an ecological process and a conceptual metaphor for ethico-political engagement?

Terrestrial Politics: Latour and the Ground

If social change and environmental justice are to be reconceived through the concept of (de)composition, the question of "perspective" returns. Justice must always be located, always be locatable. Here, in Bruno Latour's *Down to Earth: Politics in the New Climatic Regime* (2019), the reconception of political action as a *terrestrial* rather than as a territorial mobilization offers a way to understand better the reorientation of perspective necessitated by and through (de)composition. Latour seeks a re-grounding of the ethical in the planetary, disorienting and reorienting the traditional poles of the local/global, left/right, and modern/premodern dichotomies in favor of directing politics toward the Earth (as opposed to the "global").[40] Latour—convinced that the world is at or near a tipping point not only ecologically but politically as well (symbolized by the 2016 election of Donald J. Trump, in Latour's opinion)—demands a dramatic paradigm shift: Humans, broadly, and the West, specifically, must return to a terrestrial, on-the-ground perspective that refuses to pretend that any sort of bird's-eye, objective, Archimedean, or otherwise at-a-distance viewpoint is in any way possible.

One initial critique is necessary here before continuing with Latour. While this present tipping point moment is indeed tense when it comes to impending climate catastrophe, rising neofascism, and so forth, by signaling these events as a quasi-implicit "start date" or, worse, "origin," it is possible to more sensitively attend to narratives of trauma on account of race, gender, or indigeneity than Latour. Here theorist Kathryn Yusoff's poignant intervention on discourse about climate change and colonialism (discussed in Chapters One and Three of this project) remains indispensable: "The Anthropocene might seem to offer a dystopic future that laments the end of the world, but imperialism and ongoing (settler) colonialisms *have been ending worlds for as long as they've been in existence*."[41] While tipping points themselves are not origins, to choose 2016 as the tipping point still aptly exemplifies Yusoff's argument about this violent, even if unintentional, oversight: 2016 merely heightened and exacerbated tensions, but it did not create them. In other words, Donald Trump is not an exception to the rule but is the *exemplification of the rule*—whether of white supremacy or heteropatriarchy or so on. While 2016 is a convenient tipping point to select for its confluence of grave political and ecological factors—the three most crucial ones Latour names as rampant economic inequality, vast deregulation, and globalization—doing so without attention to social location or reflection on the histories and systemic inequities of colonialism, slavery, racism, sexism, and so forth unintentionally reifies a perspective that generates a deceptive "universality" predicated on the experiences and proclivities of those who benefit from systems of oppression—white, elite, cisgender males especially.

With this critique in mind, Latour's notion of the "Terrestrial" still bears the promise of offering a reoriented perspective that may yet be compatible with the idea of (de)composition, though not without a bit of nuancing. In effect, Latour conveys the ways in which globalization assumes a "from-above" standpoint, leading to an evisceration of planetary ecological systems because "the planet is *much too narrow and limited* for the globe of globalization. . . ."[42] That is, the notion of the abstract "global" in globalization enables the externalization of Earth itself to achieve its desired neoliberal economic ends.[43] This Enlightenment-style farce imagines that humans can *see* and *know* in ways we really don't—imagining that we hover above, look over, oversee, or are otherwise detached from the planetary. This assumption leads to linear temporal projections, to externalized or otherwise "inconsequential" collateral damage,[44] to endless appeals for "limitless growth"; these illogical and ultimately ecocidal arguments are "possible" to make because one cannot see the intricacies of the ecological from the great heights of that imagined tower—Trumpian, ivory, Babelian, and so on. Latour argues that these matters are a result of utter *detachment* from the terrestrial, leading—"unthinkably," in the minds of neoliberals—to the disastrous reality that, *despite* ostensibly ever-growing knowledge, ". . . we have begun to see less and less of what is happening on Earth."[45] The abundant logics of capitalism have generated a gravely illogical circumstance: The eradication of the very matters that make life yet possible in the same moment that we purportedly "know" more than ever. The greater the distance between the knower and the known, between the indifferent observer and the Pale Blue Dot, the greater the ignorance to the material matters at hand. This great paradox of modernization—the increase of Knowledge as causing the decrease of noticing[46]—generates a bind, according to Latour. As a result, a revolution of one's experience of the eco-material is most necessary.

Latour thus offers the "Terrestrial" as the catalyzing principle and perspective of any hopeful future: a reattachment to the planetary for the sake of coalitional politics, all the while ensuring that such attachment does not concretize into nationalist, fascist, racist, or otherwise violent modes so often associated with what it means to attach oneself to land.[47] He claims, "Saying 'We are earthbound, we are terrestrials among terrestrials,' *does not lead to the same politics as saying* 'We are humans in nature.' The two are not of the same cloth—or rather of the same mud."[48] Paraphrasing, then: To conceive of humans as terrestrials suffused with the planetary, as opposed to as detached subjects among a world of natural or environmental objects, yields a vastly different understanding of political activity. But, returning to a question raised in the introduction to this project, wouldn't such an emphasis on grounding oneself in and on particular soils just reify nationalisms built upon (not least) the tenets of "blood and soil?" Is it possible to think terrestrially without (re)capitulating the violences of land-grabbing, xenophobic practices?

Terrestriality makes possible a paradoxical movement: "*attaching oneself to the soil on the one hand, becoming attached to the world* on the other."[49] A bit more straightforwardly, Latour writes, "The soil allows us to attach ourselves; the world allows detachment."[50] This is where the nuance of Latour excels: His "Terrestrial" ensures that one's thinking is grounded in place, yet he extends the possibilities of local connections to larger, planetary movements in a way that does not assume a globalizing universality. That is, maintaining the notion of "world as detachment" implicit in the "Terrestrial" ensures the potentiality for the earth-ground to serve as a transversal plane that does not erase the particularity of place even as it connects vastly distant and amply different locales. There is, as it were, a certain ungrounding function implicit in Latour's "Terrestrial." In a word, detachment here seems to signify something far more akin to "distance" than "divorce." The former implies the preserved possibility for connection; the latter suggests impassable disconnection. To illustrate this paradox, Latour helpfully explains, "It is in this very practical sense that the Terrestrial reorganizes politics. Each of the beings that participate in the composition of a dwelling place has *its own way* of identifying what is local and what is global, and of defining its entanglements with the others."[51] The Terrestrial is thus not an excuse to forsake larger webs of connection by myopically tending to one's own place—likely by erecting border walls around it.

The key, or at least *one* key, to this tenuous argument is Latour's longtime expansion of the political to nonhuman actants, agents, and forces.[52] Such a broadening of scope, drawing wider circles without succumbing to the temptation to reascend to some overlooking tower of Neutrality, refigures the ideas of animacy, capacity, affect, and agency to include more-than-human subjects and entities, all the while guarding against the tendency to anthropomorphize them for the sake of some imagined or desired "Harmony" or "Peace."[53] Terrestriality forces one to consider one's landscape—ecological, social, and so on—as constitutive of and intimately entangled with oneself. One's politics is shaped by one's landscapes, in short. Such an emphasis on location is not possible when gazing through the optics of Modernity.

Latour's expansion of the scope of actants also breaks open temporal schemes, as one now must consider agencies and forces written out of the equation by anthropocentric exceptionalisms. Resonant with William E. Connolly's "bumpy temporalities"[54] (discussed in Chapter Three), Latour's Terrestrial politics ebbs and flows in tune with the nonlinear and dynamic nature of planetary processes. Latour accentuates the perspectival nature of temporality— its pulsing and flowing, which moves us differently when we're embedded in the terrestrial and are no longer hovering above it.

With feet on the ground, with one's theories muddied with soil, the question of political activity becomes imbued with the phenomena of horizons as an effect of this proposed Terrestrial horizontality. One can no longer pretend that linear change is possible when one rejects the fallacy of a "from above" perspective; further, one cannot neglect the on-the-ground realities of particular communities when one is entangled with and in those communal narratives. "Progress," conventionally conceived, relies on the mistaken delusion that one can somehow assume a "from above" perspective. Succinctly, terrestriality unveils the misleading illusion of "Progress"—given that progress is almost always defined by the powerful, almost always delineated according to the schematics of the oppressor—all the while maintaining the possibility for transformational justice.

Here we might recall the integral roles of wonder and apophasis embedded in a terrestrial perspectivalism (as argued in Chapter Two): Can the aporetic character of (de)composition sufficiently break open the linear schemes of liberal politics to reveal more radically transformational political possibilities?

Placing (de)composition in conversation with Latour's "Terrestrial" discloses creative tactics and challenges pervasive models of inflexibly straight "change." This assemblage enables local praxis, drawing on extant resources without forsaking planetary connections. The planetarity invoked here is not a wider anthropocentric cosmopolitanism so much as a soiled inflection of the terrestrial as a politically grounding phenomenon. Terrestrial (de)composition, then, as both conceptual metaphor and material praxis may yet allow one to think with but also *beyond* the lenses of "asset-based community development": expanding the scope of "assets" past the borders of the anthropocentric, multiplying the span of "community" beyond the human, intensifying the potency of "development" to consider not just growth but fecundity. Terrestriality in concert with the proposed notion of (de)composition catalyzes possibilities for a more capacious perception of available assets not as things but *processes*: now encompassing nonhuman forces, proximate habitats, affects, weather systems, salvageable matters, and more.[55] Assets for political organizing and justice seeking thus transform from manipulable objects into fluent processes of formation, deformation, reclamation, and so forth.[56] "Grassroots" could yet take on entirely other terrestrial inflections in this sketch.

(De)compositional terrestriality sparks local, collective connections of *sympoietic* way-making, not "harnessing" but politically communing with earthworms, mycorrhizal fungi, scavengers, and so forth.[57] That is, one's political community broadens when considering the ground that renders political activity possible in the first place. While this is not an argument for the flattening of any sort of modes of valuation,[58] it is an acknowledgment of that which grounds human possibility. Using the optics of terrestrial (de)composition for guiding political organizing, we see that development would function not as the goals sought when measuring with the yardstick of "Progress" but, instead, according to the principles of transformative, organic possibility; that is, community development, in this view, could consider the affects and pleasures wrapped up in political toil[59] and could model its organizing in resonant concert with ecological processes.[60] In these ways, the (de)compositional earth-ground that constitutes the grounds for all possible political life functions as a transversal matrix—linking and stirring. As Catherine Keller relatedly notes,

> The planet *does not supersede . . . the multiple interhuman crises*—of race, migration, sexuality, economics—overheating at their own speeds of crashing immediacy. Instead, *it locates them all* in the same planetary oikos of our ecosociality. . . . To teach such earthen entanglement will not prevent great emergencies of climate change; but it fosters, *it grounds*, the emergence of a complex planetary public.[61]

Here I wish to accentuate the symbolic inspiration provided by earth-ground: reminding that political work, much like humus, is not a conglomeration of separable things but is an ecosystemic assemblage of processes that opens creatively in response to the milieu of forces—inherited, present, open-ended. But *this is only half the story*, after all.

Returning to some of the language put forth in Chapter One, if ground constantly ungrounds, if it is simultaneously groundless, not a universal thing so much as a *contextual event*, then the vision of politics emerging from it must account for fragmentation, for locality, even for exclusion. To this, we now turn.

Eco-Exclusion: Giraud and Terrestrial Decisions

Ground as earth-ground does not simply involve a pristine narrative of entanglement, of relationality. That is, while ground aims to convey a sense of planetarity, it is not a placid holism but entails local-centric, bioregional ethics.[62] In fact, ground simultaneously implies inherent fragmentation—inferred in both its groundlessness (or depth) and its location (or context)—as argued throughout this project.[63] The particularities of ground as earth-ground render it inimical to universal claims; ground reminds us that just as there is not a universal remedy to desertification or erosion or contamination or similar, neither is there a universal method for political engagement for the sake of radical justice. Here, critical theorist Eva Haifa Giraud's "ethics of exclusion," as articulated in her 2019 book *What Comes after Entanglement?*, will help shape the political implications of ground's inherent fragmentation, its irreducibly differential constitution, its cyclic processes of ungrounding. While Giraud is primarily concerned with anti-capitalist media activism and food justice, her theoretical illustration of the inevitability of exclusions in efforts to seek more compassionate entanglements helps elucidate this project's concern for a notion of ground that remains placed and particular, even as it is transversally planetary.

Giraud asks the vital query "What comes after entanglement?" not to "deny the entangled complexity of the world . . . but to explore the possibilities for action *amid and despite this complexity.*"[64] Her central concern is this: An ethics of "entanglement" always and inevitably exclude particular relations and foreclose unstated connections.[65] She argues, thus, "Exclusions . . . are not just created by systems and institutions in ways that foster marginalization or oppression . . . [I]t is important to recognize that all epistemologies or political and ethical approaches—even complex, pluralistic, and seemingly open ones—carry their own omissions."[66] A conceptual reorientation becomes necessary, according to Giraud, when one registers the inherent exclusionary and fragmented nature of principles and methods proffering entanglement—ground included! In her words, rather than developing "an ethics based on relationality and entanglement, it is important to more fully flesh out an ethics of exclusion, which pays attention to the entities, practices, and ways of being that are *foreclosed* when other entangled realities are materialized."[67] This is precisely what van Dooren means when arguing that "... we are required to take a stand for some possible worlds and not others."[68] This paradigm shift is necessary because, as Giraud argues, "Understanding exclusion not only as something that is inevitable and constitutive but also as a key site where agency is distributed, and where responsibility needs to be taken, necessarily shifts the types of questions that need to be addressed."[69] To dwell on exclusions and to center fragmentation in one's gaze opens new possibilities. After all, relations are always as much about what composes them as what does not.[70] Even if one understands exclusions as "relations of exclusion," the paradigm shift of focusing one's attention on that which has been excluded undeniably opens new ethical possibilities.[71] Giraud explicates,

> An emphasis on the entangled relations that compose a given situation is not enough to bring the equally critical exclusions that are forged by it into view. This emphasis can also obscure who bears the greatest burden of these relations. Centralizing exclusions, in contrast, holds potential for opening them to future contestation and the possibility of alternatives that could better spread these burdens.[72]

In other words, exclusions "play an equally constitutive role in materializing particular realities at the expense of others," meaning that rendering those exclusions visible opens creative modes of response.[73] This is not a matter of "relations vs. exclusions" but is an acknowledgment of their paradoxical co-constitution.[74] If exclusions are inevitable—indeed they are, according to Giraud—then one must not try to avoid them but should instead *foreground* them. By focusing on exclusions, one can more sensibly find ways of being accountable and responsible for what has been excluded. Exclusion directs one's attention to response-ability: "Exclusion can ... be a site where accountability is taken not just for who or what is classified as an actor worthy of moral consideration but—more fundamentally—for which worlds are materialized over others."[75] In this way, "the need to take responsibility for exclusions ... does not mean that they are a bad thing.... Certain exclusions, in certain situations, might be necessary in spreading the burden, resisting oppressions, and creating space for new ways of doing things to come into being."[76] Giraud's conceptual intervention recognizes how exclusions are an unavoidable reality, but, by foregrounding this reality, she argues that one can more meaningfully *take responsibility* for these constitutive exclusions.

The goal of Giraud's project is to render exclusions more visible—but *not* for the sake of overcoming those differences or tensions. Such a move would contradict the core of her argument; again, exclusions are unavoidable, so one cannot "overcome" them. Giraud's concern thus remains with what it means to develop an ethics *amid complexity*. If not seeking to overcome tensions, the project of centering exclusion then aims to foreground that ethical decisions must be made in light of and in responsibility to those tensions—*not in the erasure thereof*. An ethics of exclusion is fundamentally about "taking a stand for some worlds and not others" by acknowledging "the constitutive exclusions that underpin any form of ethical and political intervention, as any set of relations necessarily occurs at the expense of other possibilities."[77] Giraud notes, "In practice, it is vital to make purposive decisions about which relations need to be excluded in order to create space for less damaging relations to emerge."[78] Here we might think, for example, of the vital and vibrant political tactic of caucus spaces for gathering among folks of similar positionalities as a way of creating space for the sake of harm reduction.[79] But foregrounding exclusions *isn't just* to "notice" them or to "become aware" of their existence. The point here is not to simply "acknowledge" exclusions but to *politicize them*.[80] Exclusion isn't just something that inevitably "happens"; it is also "bound up with particular sociotechnical infrastructures and political decisions."[81] That is, exclusions are chosen explicitly and implicitly and are woven into the fabric of political matrices. "[B]y making exclusions visible and open to contestation by those who are most affected by them," new forms of responsibility can emerge, Giraud contends.[82]

The questions at hand, then, remain: In what ways does this ethics of exclusion shape the present notion of ground as earth-ground? What does this excursus on exclusion accentuate about ground as a possibility-producing matrix that remains particular? And, finally, how does exclusion further nuance planetary political activity?

As argued in the first chapter, ground as earth-ground—heterogeneously related *and* differently entangled—implies connection *and* fragmentation. Given that soil is not a selfsame or universal substance, even as it shares (de)compositional processes, emerging from it and relating to it can only ever occur contextually—indeed locally. Location thus simultaneously implies relations *and* exclusions. Even if one understands "exclusions" as "relations of exclusion," "relations" is rarely used to convey instances of exclusion but is instead primarily aimed at articulating that which is included, connected, communed. By foregrounding that exclusions inevitably persist, whether considered relations or not, (a) one becomes better attuned to the ethical modes that might better account for those exclusions, and (b) one can no longer ignore that exclusions are necessarily constitutive elements of any ethical decision.

To be located is to be located *somewhere*—to be in relation to a particular place. At the same time, and this seems to be too often omitted, to be located is precisely *not to be elsewhere*—to be out of immediate relation to any such elsewhere. Exclusion and fragmentation do not suggest that the effects of actions don't ripple outward beyond one's immediate locale—of course that is the case. But, somewhat paradoxically, to tend to a location means to acknowledge the porous limits of place, though not necessarily maliciously. The avoidance of malicious exclusions hinges on an awareness of that particular milieu. Thus, because one cannot tend to all places, to tend to a location means to foreground the exclusion of other locales, not that they don't remain ever related and even connected. Simply put, exclusion is the recognition of limits; exclusion is the acknowledgment of agency's constraints. This exclusionary process is at least twofold: (1) noting differences and marking exclusions *between* particular places, and (2) noting differences and marking exclusions *within* a particular place. I'll explain.

The first aspect of ground's exclusionary differences *between places* is fairly straightforward and was discussed in the first chapter of this project—namely, ground as a contextual process and a particular event (de)composed of the matters, minerals, climate, drainage capacity, and bacterial, rhizospheric, and fungal activity constitutive of a locale. Soils differ from one place to another, and especially so from one region to another. This reality mandates vastly differing ethical relations to one's contextual ground, meaning that which nurtures "here" may actually be destructive "there." This revelation is not new in ecological spheres. Nor is it in social spheres: Place, time, audience, and so forth are all necessarily entangled in the question of "What is right?" or "What is good?" But linking Giraud's argument with the socio-ecological thus entails the accentuation of the exclusions one draws by foregrounding the reality that one is acting *here and not elsewhere*. That is *not* to say that one is acting here *at the expense of* elsewhere, but it is to politicize the reality that one's activities are always already constituted by that which they exclude. To foreground these exclusions is not an erasure but an embrace of difference. Here the social notion of pluralism becomes infused with, even soiled by, the lessons of the ecological. To this end, Wendell Berry muses,

> A culture capable of preserving land and people can be made only within a relatively stable and enduring relationship between a local people and its place. Community cultures made in this way would necessarily differ, and sometimes radically so, from one place to another, because places differ. This is the true and necessary pluralism.[83]

Exclusions are necessary to difference, now taking on simultaneously ecological and social dimensions. Any politics emerging from this notion of ground hence takes on this not-exactly-revolutionary lesson that *here* is always already not "there."

But the other exclusionary aspect of ground—noting differences and marking exclusions *within* a particular place—presents further nuance that adds to, or should yet add to, the contextual emphasis explained above. A grounded ethic inspired by Giraud minds and politicizes the exclusions enacted *within* particular places. Organic agriculture is a premier and somewhat simple example of this: In the field, incessant decisions must be made as to which plants, which insects, which critters, and others *to exclude*. This is the function of the category of "weeds," which are simply plants that are "out of place" and thus must be excluded. Weeds do not exist as such, but they are, instead, a constructed set that the farmer or gardener defines as and deems excludable.

While, say, spinach (a "crop") and galinsoga (a persistent and pervasive "weed") can more or less "coexist," the presence of galinsoga renders the growth of a desired crop like spinach inadequate and inefficient. The spinach gets shaded out or choked—lacking sufficient light and space for root-growth. Those involved in agriculture, especially of the organic and sustainable sort, are amply aware of this reality of choosing particular worlds over others. That is the central kernel of what it means to "cultivate." Those not involved in agriculture tend to misuse the term "cultivate": While the more positive connotations of "cultivation"—such as promotion, nurturing, or fostering—are indeed valid, these inflections tend to prioritize the *result* of the action of cultivation and *not* the activity itself. "Cultivation" is really just a fancy term for "weeding," which is really just a palatable term for "destroying certain plants while preserving others." To cultivate is to exclude some life for the sake of others. Here we can begin to tangibly encounter how exclusion is constitutive of the process of decision-making and the manner by which *one must foreground* the exclusions that always already persist in one's present milieu.

This example is rather simplistic, but it demonstrates the practice of foregrounding decisions for some worlds and not others. This, of course, does not yet even begin to address the reality of malicious exclusions—not least the violent exclusion of Black bodies as a function of whiteness. But a terrestrial perspective is constituted by the aporias of horizontality, thus making the porous processes of exclusion advocated here certainly more nuanced and organic with regard to more complex eco-social matters.

So what exactly does any of this mean? This brief reflection on the exclusions that take place *within* particular places is meant to convey the following: While ground is a principle of transversal connection, it does not imply the flattening of difference or the erasure of contextuality. Instead, ground—and the phenomenon of relating to it—entails an *amplified acknowledgment* of difference and the *vital disclosure* of the constitutive exclusions (de)composing it. Differential exclusions constitute the conditions of possibility of and for ground without erasing the persistence of interconnectivity. To wholesomely relate to ground as earth-ground does not imply selfsame, changeless actions so much as open-ended, in-tune communions—ever *in touch* with the (de)compositional composition of place, of community.

On the Grounds of Politics

This chapter has been asking: What does political activity look like when one assumes the metonymic materialization of ground as earth-ground? Here, to close, I offer brief, constructive claims in response to such a query. Returning to the principle named in the introduction of this project, I am concerned here primarily *not* with the question of "What?" so much as the query of "What processes make possible?" or "What processes lend possibility?" In a word, what's at stake here is not the question of "what sort" of politics but, alternatively, "What are the processes that ground planetary politics?"

One cannot claim universal truths in the wake of these terrestrial reflections, but veritably one *can* root oneself in adamant political resolutions that are placed, particular, and precise. Yet a predication of these resolutions on porous process as opposed to static substance upends the calcification of grounded-ness into some other, if only disguised, iteration of "blood and soil." Ground—simultaneously connecting *and* fragmenting, transversal *and* disruptive—reveals itself as a matrix of change—*not* linear or reformist change but *(de)compositional, transformative change.* Ground prompts the imagination of possibilities for change that are neither straight nor straightforward, shirking the timelines and metrics of operative systems of mechanistic thinking. A politics prefigured by ground would aim to embody (de)composition as the theoretical lens to imagine change, thinking and acting creatively with attention to processual events, not separable things.[84] Relatedly, Jack Halberstam, reflecting on the radical change imagined by Fred Moten and Stefano Harney's theorization of the "undercommons" (discussed in Chapter Three), pointedly maintains, "We must change all the things that are fucked up and change cannot come in the form that we think of as 'revolutionary'—not as a masculinist surge or an armed confrontation. *Revolution will come in a form we cannot yet imagine.*"[85] (De)composition precipitates apophatic folding amid political work for the sake of opening new possibilities yet to be imagined. Grounded political engagement does not adhere to the notion of "progress" as measured by the systems—white supremacist, militaristic, colonial, heterosexist, capitalist, and so forth—that created the very woes justice-seeking communities intend to undo.

A grounded planetary politics is fundamentally about taking a stand for some worlds and not others. It necessitates clarity about one's priorities and transparency about one's criteria for decision-making; in other words, it requires foregrounding the conditions of possibility for decision-making. This prioritization of criteria is crucial here, drawing lines of relation and marking points of exclusionary rupture that undergird a community's intentions; in other words, it foregrounds and politicizes the exclusions inevitably made in the process of decision-making. A grounded politics means clarifying which relations are excluded and acknowledging that that's the case; a planetary politics of this sort is thus *profoundly not* a space-making process for the relativistic free-play of ideas or the free-for-all's of fake news and alternative facts. A grounded politics concerns itself with carving space in a particular place for the communal discernment as to which worlds must be stood for and which ones must be rejected—and *why*. The apophatic inclinations of this project ensure that this process of decision-making remains open-ended without stripping this politics of its capacity for resolute way-making. This terrestrial politics thereby foregrounds which worlds are excluded for the sake of that for which a particular justice-seeking community strives. Planetary politics concerns the ecological matters that make political activity possible, that which renders political life a potentiality, recognizing the intersecting webs that simultaneously compose and cut across entangled places. The ecological concern of this present argument thus implies that planetary politics would tend to the matters crucial to the play of politics as the constitutive matrix thereof; that is, it would mind these eco-materialities in such a way that does not leave them as some additive, natural resource, standing reserve, or background upon which this play materializes, but rather to plant and pleat them within the understanding of political life as always ever eco-material. Not only does the earth-ground ground one's socio-political concerns, but it is also *intimately constitutive of them*. By making politics possible, the terrestrial participates therein as a grounding actor, not as a peripheral or partisan issue. Planetary politics is, thus, marked by its eco-pluralities, a robustly pluralistic effort to generate bioregional coalitions that aim to act in concert, which is not to say "the same," in recognition of and in service of their critical differences.

Conclusion

> ... what if, upon contemplation, every edge, every *eschatos* of space or time, appears as a fold or a tangle of further relation?
> —CATHERINE KELLER

An Ending, On Endings

How does one end something that remains in-process, ever unfolding? How does one mark an ending in such a way as not to foreclose that which inevitably comes—after? If endings do not mark finality or closure, then is it feasible to conceive of ends as open, as ongoing?

Ends function as the fissuring ground of new beginnings. Ends, in other words, decompose into new life—becoming beginnings.[1] The *eschaton* does not actually conclude but instead marks another world made possible, as Catherine Keller limns. The question here in this end, therefore, is not what is left behind so much as what knots of relation persist, what new tapestries might yet be woven.

On the Ground has aimed to offer conceptual tools and theoretical interventions for the sake of the planetary and its most vulnerable inhabitants. Conceiving of ground as earth-ground reorients one's sense of perspective, folding together the matters of social and ecological location, thereby producing a more radically contextual location from which to begin the work of theopoetic and ethico-political activity. Ground proposes an earthy poetics that opens creative modes for theorizing and embodying dark hope amid the Anthropocene—neither futurally escapist nor abandoning the futural as such. The paradoxical constitution of ground—as that which is interconnectedly placed and contextually entangled—generates new forms for coalition-building and political activity in the face of most hopeless circumstances. Does any of this guarantee that "it'll all work out"? Not in the least.

Ground does not guarantee life or its flourishing, but it does harbor the promise that it may yet be possible. It bears the messianic spark that new beginnings may emerge from endless ends without the erasure or disremembering of anguishing ends—past and impending. The agony and tenderness of ends fold into beginnings, neither "made new" nor "born again," but *transformed*, all the same.[2] Their persistence and remembrance in the unfolding present catalyze the hope that the world can and should be made otherwise.

Ground gives us something not just to stand on but to move on. It opens new space for collective actions that might have otherwise remained disparate and distant. The Anthropocene demands such a transversal ground—at least if we wish to mitigate already-underway travesties threatening the destruction of most webs of life. Any legitimately powerful response to anthropogenic climate change requires such a grounding matrix upon which political coalitions might begin to assemble in vibrant and compelling ways. What better ground, what other ground, than the earth-ground?

Yet this ground cannot be reduced to what is usually meant by "common ground." To be tuned into ground is to know well the contextual intricacies entailed in the work of environmental justice, regenerative agriculture, soil remediation, community development, and so forth. Ground necessarily undermines any futile attempt to calcify it into a selfsame artifact, destabilizing any view of it as one or universal or total. Its (de)compositional processes subvert conventional conceptions of change as straight, straightforward, or sure. Ground remains groundless in that it cannot be reduced to anything other than the milieu of complex processes perpetually producing it. Hence this ground is not the erasure of difference but the entanglement thereof. What is shared then, what makes this ground a differential commons that refuses the flattening tendencies often accompanying the label "common ground," are the mysteries of terrestrial interconnection, the sacred experience of planetarity amid and because of vast differences. That which is shared does not override that which differs, to be sure. They are held in an irresolvable paradoxical tension. In other words, this sense of terrestrial transversality does not undo, expunge, or otherwise atone for the violences that have long separated peoples from their lands, their families, their religions, and their cultures. Not in the least. But it does cede ground for reparative action, resource redistribution, and regenerative community-building.

It is the reconfiguration and reclamation of ground that grants the possibility of relations across critical difference, decomposing the orthodoxies of identitarian essentialisms without succumbing to the temptation to overlook differences. In this way, it opens a terrain for place-based intersectional approaches to environmental justice, folding the nuanced particularities of ecological location into movements already contending well with those of social location and vice versa. There's a concomitant and reciprocal drift: ecological diversity and socio-political pluralism flowing, one into the other.

The prefiguration of ground implies a degree of vulnerability, of openness to, that grounds all human experience: What possibilities persist without Earth, without the fecundity of the earth-ground? Surely none—save the few who might participate in the escapist, technocratic, extra-planetary fantasies of the ultra-rich. We necessarily remain exposed to the planetary in our relations to it. Vulnerability, while a shared condition, is not uniformly experienced. This vulnerability is, of course, the same vulnerability that is exploited and abused by those with inordinate power. But this violence does not eliminate the reality by which we as a species can only persist *because of* the earth-ground—the ground to which we remain vulnerable and which remains vulnerable to us. Judith Butler's poetic queries on vulnerability, discussed in Chapter Two, point to the inescapable nature of vulnerability: "Who 'am' I, without you? When we lose some of these ties by which we are constituted, we do not know who we are or what to do. . . ."[3] Translated for this context, we might ask: Who am I, who are "we," without Earth? This seems to be the most obvious point, but it's a necessary admission if one is to remember the earth-ground as the ground of eco-political activity, not as a supplementary accessory that remains merely a "part" of one's political position or social positionality.

There's nothing optional about the urgency and necessity of environmental justice; there's nothing debatable about the need for planetary wellness. This does not mean that these terrestrial threats supersede the urgencies of other necessary matters of justice on issues of race, gender, sexual orientation, immigration status, ability, class, and so on. Rather, these terrestrial threats *ground them all*. The risks of anthropogenic climate change, menacing the irreparable fraying of ecological webs, constitute *the very location of our social injustices*. But the ground proposed in this project insists that these social concerns remain folded into environmental ones: neither transcending them nor forsaking them, nor just complementing or supplementing them, but *composing* their relational milieu. That anthropogenic climate change threatens human civilization in unprecedented ways does not, remembering Kathryn Yusoff's crucial intervention, erase the histories of those whose worlds have already ended. The unthinkable scale of climate catastrophe does not negate the inconceivable pain of genocide, enslavement, or similar—but it does mark new urgencies to incite the assemblage of collectives toiling as a radical counterpower to those pushing the species off the edge of biodiversity collapse, of ecocide.

The introduction to this project was framed as an invitation to engage in an earthy experiment, opening this work as a ritual exercise in poetic theorization and eco-social imagination. This conclusion, however, is not a terminus so much as a benediction, a lure at the unfolding edge of this project. Should the arguments made heretofore be found compelling, in what sort of ways do we both, you and I, emerge new and different from this text? What sort of work might we now perceive as necessary? Ultimately, I understand this end as another invitation, as it were, into grounded practices of environmental justice, as I attempt to do the same: by minding the particularities of eco-social place, nurturing local webs of wholesome relation, foregrounding exclusions and their criteria. This is not a commissioning, per se, in that I hold no legitimate right to "authorize" some particular ethico-political praxis, for praxis is always entangled in a particular location; what works here may not work there. Still, tuning in to earthy, theopoetic intuition, we may yet find transversal tactics to be shared.

In this unfurling end, I hope that *On the Ground* has prompted the consideration of not exactly "what" needs to happen but, digging deeper, *the grounds* for what needs to happen. Without sufficient care for these grounds, we are all the more likely to witness the irreversible erosion of our collective futures—futures that remain differential yet shared. Perhaps a downward glance at the soily matrix so often taken for granted might remind us how vastly different and vastly interconnected our efforts are toward environmental justice. Maybe then we might uncover evermore creative and robust modes of engagement, even at the brink of collapse, catalyzing sacred earth-work not necessarily because of transcendent revelation so much as earthen meditation. The mysteries of horizons remain—and ever will. But with a muddied faith, I remain darkly hopeful in matters of holy resistance and terrestrial resilience.

Acknowledgments

This project would not have been possible without the rich relational soils out of which it has emerged. This book has only materialized because of vast multitudes of peoples and places—and the possibilities they have extended. There are countless folks to thank for the support they have provided over the years during which this work materialized, only some of which are named here.

Catherine Keller, my teacher, has offered endless support, critical guidance, and poetic wisdom. It was not only her "Talking Dirty" chapter that inspired this book but her critical theological imagination that kept me inspired to teach and write. Few have shepherded me like my dear mentor Laurel Kearns, who has taught me to seek the wondrous and has embodied faithful resistance longer than most could. Without her, I would have given up on all this long ago. To Traci West and Andrea White, for holding this work accountable in its pursuit of intersectional environmental justice, I am filled with gratitude. And to the muse Jesse Mann, whose boundless curiosity is unparalleled, I owe many thanks for years of supporting this research. Many colleagues have been there to challenge me and care for me; I extend my deep appreciation, particularly to Gabe Crooks, Michael Anderson, Hunter Bragg, Lauren Sawyer, Kelsey Wallace, Hilary Floyd, Christina Walling, Marcus Mescher, Ashley Theuring, and Bill Madges. Tess Dankoski's research assistance and indexing enriched this project in untold ways; I cannot thank her enough. This book would not have materialized without the steadfast advocacy of John Garza and the unparalleled editing of Mildred Sanchez.

I am exceedingly grateful to the men of Northern State Prison, at once students and teachers, for teaching me how to teach and for holding my work accountable as a witness to their testimonies.

My dear friends and mentors at the Community Supported Garden at Genesis Farm, who sustained me in both body and spirit and whose faithful work stewards land and nourishes neighbors, have given more to this work than they could ever know. And to Eileen Gebbie and Aram Mitchell, whose keen questions and critical guidance have enriched not just the spirit of this work but my own spirit, I know not how to convey the depth of my gratefulness.

To the companions who have shaped *not just* the sprouts of this work but this author in invaluable ways, I am simply, unspeakably thankful. To Carly Lynch, Emma Lietz-Bilecky, Tyler Lietz-Bilecky, Nathan Mather, Tanner Affleck, and so many others, I am indebted. To my friends and companions in Norwood—not least Lyric Morris-Latchaw, Matt Latchaw, Jacob Taylor, Sam Overkamp, Alyssa Overkamp, Marykate Glenn, Grace Marshall, Doug Walker, Robert Lockridge, Erin Tuttle-Lockridge—who have kept me nourished by compassionate community and with good food in the latter stages of this project, I would be lost without you. Special thanks to Megan Suttman, not only for her generosity in sharing her artwork for the cover of this book but also for the ways she has taught me to craft thoughtfully.

To my Mom and Dad, who have shown me love in the most relentless of ways, I haven't the words to even begin to express my gratitude. I wouldn't know where to begin. To Sydney, I owe my thanks for her unfailing encouragement, without which none of this would have been possible. To my grandfather, "Rudy" Van Horn, for witnessing to a life of love and companionship, I hardly know a better man.

And, as ever, to my partner, Jennifer, for her boundless passion, keen mind, and inspiring faithfulness, I owe everything. It is her love that grounds me.

Notes

Epigraph

Tess Taylor, "Apocalypto for a Small Planet" in *Work & Days* (Pasadena, CA: Red Hen Press, 2016), 49.

Introduction

Epigraph: Wendell Berry, "The Body and the Earth," in *The Art of the Commonplace: The Agrarian Essays of Wendell Berry*, ed. Norman Wirzba (Berkeley, CA: Counterpoint, 2002), 284–285.

1. Cf. Karmen MacKendrick, "Remember—When?" in *Sexual Disorientations: Queer Temporalities, Affects, Theologies*, ed. Kent L. Brintnall, Joseph A. Marchal, and Stephen D. Moore (New York: Fordham University Press, 2017), 277–291.

2. Contemplation implies a space-making "borrowed from Latin *contemplātus*, past participle of *contemplāre, contemplārī* 'to look at fixedly, observe, notice, ponder,' from *con-* + *-templāre, -templārī*, the verbal derivative of *templum*, meaning 'space of sky or land delimited orally by an augur, sacred precinct, building consecrated to a deity.'" "Contemplate," *Merriam Webster*, https://www.merriam-webster.com/dictionary/contemplate.

3. See Jesse Ribot, "Cause and Response: Vulnerability and Climate in the Anthropocene," in *New Directions in Agrarian Political Economy: Global Agrarian Transformations*, vol. 1, ed. Madeleine Fairbairn et al. (New York: Routledge, 2016), 667–705.

4. A couple of matters: First, I draw an important line of distinction between liberal and progressive/revolutionary, as the former has become, at least in U.S. politics, quite centrist, concerned solely with reforming the establishment, at best, so to speak. Second, this caricature is to draw the reader's attention to the linear

"progress" narratives characteristic of many white liberals who have made their political activism unwittingly akin to offering spare room for "others" to join them on their already-moving train with an already-chosen destination. A thorough critique of these approaches will feature in Chapter Four. White progressive political theories, of course, have been done in better and worse fashions. Fortunately, those like Catherine Keller, Bruno Latour, and William Connolly have generated meaningful conceptions of dynamic, pluralistic publics seeking more just worlds; their works will indeed fertilize the ground of this project. But, often, it seems that, at least in popular rhetoric, "common ground" connects *at the expense of* recognizing and embracing critical difference; put differently, "common ground" can easily perpetuate narratives like "racial colorblindness" or "post-racial approaches" that do little, if anything at all, to challenge systemic racial injustices that persist in arguably more *insidious* ways today. The ground sought here is one that might further anti-racist solidarity, which identifies disparities of effects and incongruences of labor, in pursuit of radical equity.

5. All discursive practice is, to some degree, performative. I merely mean to accentuate here that there may yet be other fashions by which an argument might materialize other than *just* being "stated."

6. On the distinctions between theopoetics and "theopoetry," see David L. Miller, "Theopoetry or Theopoetics," *Cross Currents* 60, no. 1 (March 2010): 6–23.

7. The particularities of these phenomena of experience will receive robust explication in Chapter Two.

8. This builds on the arguments made by John B. Cobb Jr. and Herman E. Daly in their 1994 book *For the Common Good*. See John B. Cobb Jr. and Herman E. Daly, *For the Common Good: Redirecting the Economy Toward Community, the Environment, and a Sustainable Future* (Boston: Beacon Press, 1994).

9. This cloudiness does not aim to reintroduce the hierarchies pervading dichotomies such as transcendence/immanence. Rather, this cloud is more akin to a fog, disorienting and reorienting the very axes accompanying these hierarchical concepts. The rich traditions of mystical negative theology, long accused of otherworldly myopia, do, indeed, offer precedence for this sort of claim. For example, Pseudo-Dionysius wrote in his *Mystical Theology*, "the more our words are confined to the ideas we are capable of forming; so that now as we plunge into that darkness which is beyond intellect, we shall find ourselves not simply running short of words but actually speechless and unknowing." In other words, as Catherine Keller puts it, "The ascent is actually a plunge: the cloud circulates in an atmosphere that *undoes the very axis of up and down*." See, respectively, Pseudo-Dionysius, *Mystical Theology*, in *Pseudo-Dionysius: The Complete Works*, trans. Colm Luibheid (New York: Paulist Press, 1987), 139; Catherine Keller, *Cloud of the Impossible: Negative Theology and Planetary Entanglement* (New York: Columbia University Press, 2015), 73.

10. Catherine Keller, who brought my attention to the term *tiqvah*, notes its potential fecundity for theorizing "hope" in the Anthropocene. See Catherine Keller, *Political Theology of the Earth: Our Planetary Emergency and the Struggle for a New Public* (New York: Columbia University Press, 2018), 173–174. For more, see

O'neil Van Horn, "On the Matter of Hope: Weaving Threads of Jewish Wisdom for the Sake of the Planetary," in *Earthly Things: Immanence, New Materialisms, and Planetary Thinking*, ed. Karen Bray, Heather Eaton, and Whitney Bauman, 111–122 (New York: Fordham University Press, 2023).

11. That is, the Jewish (and specifically Kabbalistic) notion of world-mending.

12. For a theological extension prioritizing survival, resistance, and quality of life over against ostensibly abstract notions of salvation, see Delores Williams, *Sisters in the Wilderness: The Challenge of Womanist God-Talk* (Maryknoll, NY: Orbis Books, 1993), esp. 19–26, 127–157. For womanist, process theological reflection on the dangers of prioritizing salvation over against way-making, see Monica A. Coleman, *Making a Way Out of No Way: A Womanist Theology* (Minneapolis, MN: Fortress Press, 2008), esp. 11–84.

13. For more on the connection between (dark) hope, apophasis, and political mobilizing, see Keller, *Political Theology of the Earth*.

14. The role of China and India in global emissions should not be discounted. I foreground the West here, given my own context and intended audience.

15. Again, it is worth noting the resonances here with the epigraph which began this introduction: Berry's reflections on soil as "the great connector of lives" that demands our "proper care for it," because without it "we can have no community," and "because without proper care for it we can have no life." Berry's reflections on soil-care disclose the paradox named here—that is, the concomitance of contextuality and interconnectivity, the simultaneity of particularity and planetarity. These matters will take shape in Chapter Four through engagement with Giraud, especially.

16. See, for example, the following (which is by no means an exhaustive list): Karen Baker-Fletcher, *Sisters of Dust, Sisters of Spirit: Womanist Wordings on God and Creation* (Minneapolis, MN: Augsburg Fortress Press, 1998); Rosemary Radford Ruether, ed., *Women Healing Earth: Third World Women on Ecology, Feminism, and Religion* (Maryknoll, NY: Orbis Books, 1996); Greta Gaard, "Ecofeminism Revisited: Rejecting Essentialism and Re-Placing Species in a Material Feminist Environmentalism," *Feminist Formations* 23, no. 2 (Summer 2011): 26–53; Ivone Gebara, *Longing for Running Water: Ecofeminism and Liberation* (Minneapolis, MN: Fortress Press, 1999); Melanie L. Harris, *Ecowomanism: African American Women and Earth-Honoring Faiths* (Maryknoll, NY: Orbis Books, 2017); Carolyn Merchant, "Reinventing Eden: Western Culture as Recovery Narrative," in *Uncommon Ground: Toward Reinventing Nature*, ed. William Cronon (New York: W.W. Norton, 1995), 132–159; Martha Mies and Vandana Shiva, *Ecofeminism* (London: Zed Books, 2014); Shamara Shantu Riley, "Ecology Is a Sistah's Issue Too: The Politics of Emergent Afrocentric Ecowomanism," in *This Sacred Earth: Religion, Nature, Environment*, 2nd ed., ed. Roger S. Gottlieb (New York: Routledge, 2004), 368–381; Alice Walker, "The Only Reason You Want to Go to Heaven Is That You Have Been Driven Out of Your Mind (Off Your Land and Out of Your Lover's Arms)," *On the Issues* VI, no. 2 (Spring 1997): 16–23, 54–59; Delores Williams, "Sin, Nature, and Black Women's Bodies," in *Ecofeminism and the Sacred*, ed. Carol J. Adams (New York: Continuum, 1993), 24–30.

17. It must be noted that this work represents only but a minute sliver of the toil necessary to dismantle white supremacy and its many insidious forms; to this end, I must acknowledge that the lands on which I write this text here-now is stolen land of the Shawnee and Miami peoples, and earlier drafts of this work were penned on the lands of the Lenape. To the extent possible, then, this research focuses on contemporary questions of anti-Black racism and environmental injustice, not to ignore histories and realities of indigenous peoples displaced through white settler colonialism but simply to direct the scope of this work in other directions for the sake of specificity and focus. This focus does not mean to suggest that attention should not be given to indigenous concerns regarding environmental justice.

18. Christopher Carter, "Blood in the Soil: The Racial, Racist, and Religious Dimensions of Environmentalism," in *The Bloomsbury Handbook of Religion and Nature: The Elements*, ed. Laura Hobgood and Whitney Bauman (New York: Bloomsbury, 2018), 47.

19. Carter, "Blood in the Soil," 46–47.

20. For a study on the question of race, trauma, relation to Earth, and the reclamation of Black ecological wisdom, see Dianne Glave, *Rooted in the Earth: Reclaiming the Relationship of African American Environmental Heritage* (Chicago: Lawrence Hill Books, 2010).

21. Elonda Clay, "How Does It Feel to Be an Environmental Problem? Studying Religion and Ecology in the African Diaspora," in *Inherited Land: The Changing Grounds of Religion and Ecology*, ed. Whitney Bauman, Richard Bohannon, and Kevin O'Brien (Eugene, OR: Wipf & Stock, 2011), 149; emphasis mine.

22. Clay, "How Does It Feel," 150.

23. Clay, 162.

24. See Monica M. White, *Freedom Farmers: Agricultural Resistance and the Black Freedom Movement* (Raleigh: University of North Carolina Press, 2019).

25. Willie James Jennings, *The Christian Imagination: Theology and the Origins of Race* (New Haven, CT: Yale University Press, 2011), 87.

26. See Jennings, *The Christian Imagination*, 207–249, esp. 226.

27. Jennings, 248.

28. Jennings; emphasis mine.

29. Jennings; emphasis mine.

30. These terms will receive robust explication in the central chapters of this work.

31. Jennings, *The Christian Imagination*, 294; emphasis mine.

32. adrienne maree brown, ed., *Pleasure Activism: The Politics of Feeling Good* (Chico, CA: AK Press, 2019), 18.

Interlude. The Differences of Our Soils, the Soils of Our Differences

1. For the sake of clarity, a city by the name of Guaitil in the Guanacaste province of Costa Rica is well known for its pottery and other *artesanías*. The Guaitil that I resided in, however, is a little-known town near San Ignacio de Acosta in the state of San José.

1. Planting: Ground Is Not Foundation

Epigraph: Jenny O'Dell, *How to Do Nothing: Resisting the Attention Economy* (Brooklyn: Melville House, 2019), 21.

1. This argument is resonant with, yet distinct from, Edmund Husserl's notion of "earth-ground" (*Erdboden*). It shares with Husserl's concept, as phenomenologist Anthony Steinbock puts it, the reality that "the earth-ground is constitutive of our experience of space and movement" (113). Husserl's earth-ground functions modally as the grounds of human experience, revealing the fallacy that any human could ever be "above" this grounding principle, and it is in this way that my inflection of ground concurs with his. So, too, do our notions share—whether implicitly or explicitly—a commitment to decolonization and deterritorialization, as it were, for, in Steinbock's words, the "earth-ground is not something that belongs to us; it does not function as a 'resource' or 'possession'" (121). Where the two differ is in emphasis and intention: Husserl's *Erdboden* is primarily focused, it would seem, on phenomenological experience of spatiality, movement, and rest, as suggested by Steinbock; my focus is on eco-social matters. In a word, as will, I hope, become apparent, the particular variation of ground in this present project suggests that any notion of (earth-)ground must take on a more overt ethico-political commitment to the terrestrial—that is, to soil. See Anthony Steinbock, *Home and Beyond: Generative Phenomenology After Husserl* (Evanston, IL: Northwestern University Press, 1995), esp. 97–122. For Husserl's own explication, see Edmund Husserl, "Grundlegende Untersuchungen Zum Phänomenologischen Ursprung Der Räumlichkeit Der Natur," in *Philosophical Essays in Memory of Edmund Husserl*, ed. Marvin Farber (Cambridge, MA: Harvard University Press, 1940), 307–325.

2. Thus, this project draws inspiration from yet seeks to further texts like Manuel Tironi, et al., "Soil Theories: Relational, Decolonial, Inhuman," in *Thinking with Soils: Material Politics and Social Theory*, ed. Juan Francisco Salazar et al. (New York: Bloomsbury, 2020), 15–38, esp. 26–28, as well as Kristina M. Lyons, *Vital Decomposition: Soil Practitioners and Life Politics* (Durham, NC: Duke University Press, 2020). That is, I argue that the notion of "ground" is a crucial element that must be foregrounded in any soil-centric material politics. The conceptualization of ground as soil is what I understand to be the crucial contribution of this present project.

3. Catherine Keller, "Talking Dirty: Ground Is Not Foundation," in *Ecospirit: Religions and Philosophies for the Earth*, ed. Laurel Kearns and Catherine Keller (New York: Fordham University Press, 2007), 65.

4. Keller, "Talking Dirty."

5. David Macauley, *Elemental Philosophy: Earth, Air, Fire, and Water as Elemental Ideas* (Albany: State University of New York Press, 2010), 5.

6. As Lowell Duckert and Jeffrey Jerome Cohen write, "These words of wind, whorl, and water yearn to be metaphors, linguistic conveyance devices. The elements might be described as metaphor magnets, but their ability to bond materiality and narrative is deeper than mere impress or gravitational trajectory. Through their action metaphor becomes *matterphor*, a tropic-material coil, word and substance together

transported: of language but not reducible to linguistic terms, agentic and thick." Jeffrey Jerome Cohen and Lowell Duckert, "Eleven Principles of the Elements," in *Elemental Ecocriticisms: Thinking with Earth, Air, Water, and Fire*, ed. Jeffrey Jerome Cohen and Lowell Duckert (Minneapolis: University of Minnesota Press, 2015), 10–11; emphasis in original. In his book, *Stone*, Cohen elaborates, "A conveyance device that is at once linguistic, story-laden, thingly, and agentic, a metaphor is an ontological sliding, a tectonic veer, materiality coming in and out of figure, 'matterphor.'" Jeffrey Jerome Cohen, *Stone: An Ecology of the Inhuman* (Minneapolis: University of Minnesota Press, 2015), 4.

7. Jacques Derrida, *Of Grammatology*, trans. Gayatri Chakravorty Spivak (Baltimore, MD: Johns Hopkins University Press, 1976), 48.

8. It should be noted, as will become apparent, that Deleuze will reclaim a fecund notion of the transcendental—as exemplified in his "plane of immanence"— though not in any typical sense.

9. Derrida, *Of Grammatology*, 61. For an excellent extension of Derrida's concepts of *différance*, bottomlessness, trace, khora, etc., in relation to related concerns, see Catherine Keller, *Face of the Deep: A Theology of Becoming* (New York: Routledge, 2003), 157–167.

10. Jacques Derrida, *Positions*, trans. Alan Bass (Chicago: University of Chicago Press, 1981), 52.

11. Derrida, *Of Grammatology*, 23. In *Margins of Philosophy*, Derrida expands on the ways in which foundations prop up a metaphysics of Being, of substantive presence: "Since Being has never had a 'meaning,' has never been thought or said as such, except by dissimultating itself in beings, then *différance*, in a certain and very strange way, (is) 'older' than the ontological difference or than the truth of Being. When it has this age it can be called the play of the trace. The play of a trace which no longer belongs to the horizon of Being, but whose play transports and encloses the meaning of Being: the play of the trace, or the *différance*, which has no meaning and is not. Which does not belong. There is no maintaining, and no depth to, this bottomless chessboard on which Being is put into play." Jacques Derrida, *Margins of Philosophy*, trans. Alan Bass (Chicago: University of Chicago Press, 1982), 22. While I will later use the term "depth" constructively (despite Derrida's aversion thereto), Derrida's point stands: Depth as an invocation of hierarchy, of relation between signifier and signified, of meaning and condition should be undone, deconstructed.

12. *Fond*, of course, means "foundation" in French. But, somewhat problematically, as will become apparent later in this section, it can also mean "ground"; the consequences of these blurred connotations may explain Derrida's equating of foundation and ground.

13. For further details, see Edward W. Said, *Beginnings: Intention and Method* (New York: Basic, 1975).

14. Kathryn Yusoff, *A Billion Black Anthropocenes or None* (Minneapolis: University of Minnesota Press, 2018), 24. More to come on Yusoff in Chapter Three.

15. Yusoff, *Black Anthropocenes*, 25–26.

16. Said, *Beginnings*, 373. Said also suggests that origins are "theological" and beginnings are "secular," with which I would not disagree with one small revision: origins are "*onto*-theological." Much of this project hopes to disentangle "ground" from the foundational theological dogmatisms that not only proffer unhelpful visions of God but, further, anti-ecological (which is to say, ecologically destructive) praxes. Material feminist philosopher Stacy Alaimo suggests that even in light of the poststructuralist aversion to origins, it is still worth exploring how beginnings or "origin stories can provoke an environmental ethics. . . ." Stacy Alaimo, *Exposed: Environmental Politics and Pleasures in Posthuman Times* (Minneapolis: University of Minnesota Press, 2016), 114. Robin Wall Kimmerer makes a similar argument in relation to the difference between the Judeo-Christian creation myth and the Haudenosaunee creation myth. See Robin Wall Kimmerer, *Braiding Sweetgrass: Indigenous Wisdom, Scientific Knowledge, and the Teachings of Plants* (Minneapolis, MN: Milkweed Editions, 2013), 3–10. Of course, to this end, Lynn White Jr.'s early diagnosis of Christian anti-ecological concerns is most relevant; see Lynn White Jr., "The Historical Roots of Our Ecologic Crisis," *Science* 155.3767 (March 10, 1967): 1203–1207.

17. Said, *Beginnings*, 5.

18. Said, xvii.

19. . . . that is, if one translates the *bet* of *b'reshit* in Genesis' opening stanza capaciously. See Catherine Keller, *Face of the Deep*, 157–171.

20. Keller, 161.

21. Said, *Beginnings*, 6.

22. Said, xvii.

23. Jacques Derrida, *Rogues: Two Essays on Reason*, trans. Pascale-Anne Brault and Michael Naas, (Stanford, CA: Stanford University Press, 2005), 122. He goes on to differentiate the event of "running aground" from "ground" or "grounding": "As for grounding [*échouage*], this is not the same as *running aground*. Grounding is the moment when, this time intentionally, freely, deliberately, in a calculable and calculated, autonomous manner, the captain of a ship, failing to keep his heading, takes responsibility for touching bottom and this decision too resembles an event. And yet the accident of running aground, as we said, is also an event." Derrida, *Rogues*, 122.

24. Catherine Keller, "Introduction: The Process of Difference, the Difference of Process," in *Process and Difference: Between Cosmological and Poststructuralist Postmodernisms*, ed. Catherine Keller and Anne Daniell (Albany, NY: State University of New York Press, 2002), 12.

25. Keller, "Talking Dirty," 68.

26. This *New York Times Magazine* article explores this curious and curiously frightening phenomenon: Ava Kofman, "Bruno Latour, the Post-Truth Philosopher, Mounts a Defense of Science," *New York Times Magazine*, 25 October 2018, https://www.nytimes.com/2018/10/25/magazine/bruno-latour-post-truth-philosopher-science.html?searchResultPosition=1.

27. The gendered dynamics of "groundless ground" and its associated "abyss" (and similar) are vital to note. This finds expression rather lucidly, for example, in the works of Grace Jantzen and Catherine Keller. Jantzen traces the associations of abyss with a "chaotic" femininity—through womb-like imagery in medieval mystics, for instance—that is juxtaposed to the solid "foundations" upon modern knowledge is "built"; in her words, whereas the abyss is figured as unstable watery depths, "the solidity of foundations is, metonymically, manly reliability." See Grace Jantzen, "Eros and the Abyss: Reading Medieval Mystics in Postmodernity," *Literature and Theology* 17, no. 3 (September 2003): 244. Keller offers an extended meditation on the gendered depths of the watery biblical abyss—Genesis's *tehom*—conveying the relationship between, in her words, "tehomophobia" and "gynophobia"; see Keller, *Face of the Deep*, 1–99. Further, Keller makes a resonant case for the proposed "groundless ground" through her reading of Luce Irigaray's rereading of Heidegger. Irigaray's *The Forgetting of Air in Martin Heidegger* deconstructs his *Grund* by means of, in Keller's words, "an elemental play of sexual difference," instead proposing a "'groundless ground' comprising a 'relation between . . .'"; Keller, "Talking Dirty," 68. See Luce Irigaray, *The Forgetting of Air in Martin Heidegger*, trans. Mary Beth Mader (Austin: University of Texas Press, 1999), 85.

28. *Ungrund* is attributable to the seventeenth-century German mystic Jakob Boehme. For some contemporary reflections on Boehme's *Ungrund*, see Kathryn Wood Madden, "Images of the Abyss," *Journal of Religion and Health* 42, no. 2 (Summer 2003): 117–131; Jon Mills, "Retracing the *Ungrund*," in *The Unconscious Abyss: Hegel's Anticipation of Psychoanalysis* (Albany: State University of New York Press, 2002), 21–52; Ernest B. Koenker, "Potentiality in God: *Grund* and *Ungrund* in Jacob Boehme," *Philosophy Today* 15, no. 1 (2001): 44–51. The apophatic functions of this theopoetic musing will emerge in Chapter Two.

29. See Jacques Derrida, *On the Name*, ed. Thomas Dutoit, trans. David Wood, John P. Leavey, and Ian McLeod (Stanford, CA: Stanford University Press, 1995), 89.

30. Keller, "Talking Dirty," 69.

31. More nuanced understandings of trees' capacity to communicate challenges this simplification. Trees form rhizomic assemblages readily, not least with mycorrhizal fungi. The philosophical demonization of "roots" over against "rhizomes" feels a bit passé in this time of eco-crisis; this sort of language can ultimately, if only implicitly, detract from or discourage eco-activisms. Deleuze and Guattari are quick to remind about the ways in which concepts haunt insidiously from surprising places and can make surprising, heterogenous connections; this disparaging of "roots," then, should be no exception, for the planetary needs all the help it can get these days.

32. Gilles Deleuze and Felix Guattari, *A Thousand Plateaus: Capitalism and Schizophrenia*, trans. Brian Massumi (Minneapolis: University of Minnesota Press, 1987), 90.

33. Deleuze and Guattari, *A Thousand Plateaus*, 237–238.

34. This, to be sure, is also Alfred N. Whitehead's argument concerning becoming. His "philosophy of organism" contends "that the notion of an actual entity as the unchanging subject of change is completely abandoned." See Alfred North Whitehead, *Process and Reality: An Essay in Cosmology*, corrected ed., ed. David Ray Griffin and Donald Sherburne (New York: The Free Press, 1978), 29. That is, any suggestion that an actual entity/occasion (a unit of becoming, of process, of flux) could be conceived "as the unchanging subject of change" is false and a misreading. Whitehead is ultimately concerned, no Tillichian pun intended, with pure change and *not* a theory of background matter/substance through which change moves. Whitehead expressly eschews this sort of understanding of process: "The actual occasions are the creatures which become, and they constitute a continuously extensive world. In other words, extensiveness becomes, but 'becoming' itself is not extensive" (35). In other words, "There is a prevalent misconception that 'becoming' involves the notion of a unique seriality for its advance into novelty. This is the classic notion of 'time,' which philosophy took over from common sense" (35). For this reason, Whitehead claims that we cannot adequately speak in terms of "subjects" but that "'subject' is always to be construed as an abbreviation to subject-superject'" (29). Even though, according to him, "The ultimate metaphysical truth is atomism," Whitehead qualifies this claim by stating, "But atomism does not exclude complexity and universal relativity. *Each atom is a system of all things*" (35–36). He'll later go on to explain that "every actual entity is present in every other actual entity. The philosophy of organism is mainly devoted to the task of making clear the notion of 'being present in another entity'" (50). The microscopic and macroscopic entangle, according to Whitehead. Of course, this process ontology will need to answer to critical race theory's challenge thereto, and it will also need to deconstruct the neoliberal valuation of global interconnection. I offer critiques to these ends in Chapters Two and Three.

Further, Édouard Glissant makes a very similar argument in his *Poetics of Relation*. I wish to note this resonance here and to signal to the reader that Glissant's "Relation" will figure prominently in the following chapter. See Édouard Glissant, *Poetics of Relation*, trans. Betsy Wing (Ann Arbor: University of Michigan Press, 1997), esp. 159–188.

35. Deleuze and Guattari, *A Thousand Plateaus*, 90.

36. See Gilles Deleuze and Felix Guattari, *What Is Philosophy?*, trans. Hugh Tomlinson and Graham Burchell (New York: Columbia University Press, 1994), esp. 35–42.

37. Deleuze and Guattari, *What Is Philosophy?*, 36.

38. Gilles Deleuze, *Difference and Repetition*, trans. Paul Patton (New York: Columbia University Press, 1994 [1968]), 229.

39. Deleuze, *Difference and Repetition*.

40. Keller, *Face of the Deep*, 168; for more on Deleuze's understanding of depth (and its relation to process theology), see Keller, *Face of the Deep*, 161–171.

41. Deleuze and Guattari, *What Is Philosophy?*, 42.

42. I will later contest present forms of injustice predicated on constructing violent hierarchies of power; what I mean to suggest here, though, is that this concept of ground does not come with (or such is my hope) the same harm associated with foundations—forceful, unyielding, oppressive.

43. The grammar here is a bit ambiguous, but it is intentionally so. I aim to use "connecting" here in reference to the ways in which a deep ground, a groundless ground, interconnects; yet I intend for this verb to be, in a sense, intransitive—objectless, in a word—in an attempt to exemplify how process destabilizes static, substantive objects.

44. As Deleuze and Guattari note, "Immanence is immanent only to itself and consequently captures everything, absorbs All-One, and leaves nothing remaining to which it could be immanent. In any case, whenever immanence is interpreted as immanent *to* Something, we can be sure that this Something reintroduces the transcendent." Deleuze and Guattari, *What Is Philosophy?*, 45.

45. See Deleuze and Guattari, *A Thousand Plateaus*, 344.

46. Deleuze and Guattari, 293; emphasis mine.

47. Cf. Henri Bergson, *The Creative Mind: An Introduction to Metaphysics*, trans. Mabelle L. Andison (Citadel Press, 1992), 153–186; Henri Bergson, *Creative Evolution*, trans. Arthur Mitchell (New York: Dover, 1998), 296–373; Gilles Deleuze, *Bergsonism*, trans. Hugh Tomlinson and Barbara Habberjam (New York: Zone Books, 1988), 37–90.

48. Bergson, *The Creative Mind*, 172; emphasis mine.

49. Karen Barad, *Meeting the Universe Halfway: Quantum Physics and the Entanglement of Matter and Meaning* (Durham, NC: Duke University Press, 2007), 39–70.

50. Barad states, "I introduce the term 'intra-action' in recognition of [entities'] ontological inseparability, in contrast to the usual 'interaction,' which relies on a metaphysics of individualism (in particular, the prior existence of separately determinate entities)." Barad, *Meeting the Universe Halfway*, 128.

51. Karen Barad, "Posthumanist Performativity: Toward an Understanding of How Matter Comes to Matter," in *Material Feminisms*, ed. Stacy Alaimo and Susan Hekman (Bloomington: Indiana University Press, 2008), 139; emphasis mine.

52. Barad, "Posthumanist Performativity, 139.

53. Barad, *Meeting the Universe Halfway*, 316–317.

54. Marjolein Oele, "E-Co-Affectivity beyond the Anthropocene: On Soil and Soil Pores," in *E-Co-Affectivity: Exploring Pathos at Life's Material Interfaces* (Albany: State University of New York Press, 2020), 142.

55. This tendency to abstract "the environment" as if it weren't all that is but is somehow instead only the so-called pure thing that exists without human influence pervades much of eco-discourse of the colloquial sort. For the damaging effects of this abstraction, see William Cronon, "The Trouble with Wilderness; or, Getting Back to the Wrong Nature," in *Uncommon Ground: Rethinking the Human Place in Nature*, ed. William Cronon (New York: W. W. Norton, 1995), 69–90; for further

reflections on the gendered impacts of this perspective, see Carolyn Merchant, "Reinventing Eden: Western Culture as Recovery Narrative," in *Uncommon Ground: Rethinking the Human Place in Nature*, ed. William Cronon (New York: W. W. Norton, 1995), 132–159.

56. Stacy Alaimo, *Bodily Natures: Science, Environment, and the Material Self* (Bloomington: University of Indiana Press, 2010), 14.

57. Linda Lorraine Nash, *Inescapable Ecologies: A History of Environment, Disease, and Knowledge* (Berkeley: University of California Press, 2006), 8; emphasis mine.

58. Alaimo, *Bodily Natures*, 2.

59. Alaimo, 4.

60. See "Toxic Wastes and Race in the United States: A National Report on the Racial and Socio-Economic Characteristics of Communities with Hazardous Waste Sites," *United Church of Christ (UCC)*, 1987. For an update, see Robert D. Bullard, Paul Mohai, Robin Saha, and Beverly Wright, "Toxic Wastes and Race at Twenty 1987–2007: A Report Prepared for the United Church of Christ Justice & Witness Ministries," *United Church of Christ (UCC)*, March 2007.

61. Nancy Tuana, "Viscous Porosity: Witnessing Katrina" in *Material Feminisms*, ed. Stacy Alaimo and Susan Hekman, (Bloomington: Indiana University Press, 2008), 188–213.

62. For a comprehensive analysis of soil classification and soil types, see Nyle C. Brady and Raymond R. Weil, *The Nature and Properties of Soils*, 15th edition (New York: Pearson, 2017), 101–147.

63. For a complex chart demonstrating the many ways to classify soil *just by texture*, see "Soil Texture Calculator," *United States Department of Agriculture: Natural Resources Conservation Service*, accessed 13 May 2020, https://www.nrcs.usda.gov/wps/portal/nrcs/detail/soils/survey/?cid=nrcs142p2_054167.

64. Brady and Weil, *The Nature and Properties of Soils*, 1085.

65. Of course, ecological processes are often indifferent to human conceptualizations of ethics. For an argument regarding the possible ethical risks of highlighting, if not lauding, decomposition and decay as symbols of meaningful change—and particularly the ways in which these processes hold the potential to reify violence, martyrdom, or surrogacy, especially for persons pushed to the margins—see Chapter Four.

66. Humus is soil organic matter that is amorphous and heterogeneous in nature. It will be the subject of discussion in Chapter Four.

67. William Bryant Logan, *Dirt: The Ecstatic Skin of the Earth* (New York: W. W. Norton, 1995), 16.

68. Logan, *Dirt*, 64–65.

69. Logan, 76.

70. Logan, 115.

71. Logan, 63.

72. Bergson, *The Creative Mind*, 170.

73. Bergson, *Creative Evolution*, 296–373.

74. Cf. Bergson, *The Creative Mind*, 213.

75. Bergson, 168.

76. Bergson, 176; emphasis mine.

77. Deleuze and Guattari, *A Thousand Plateaus*, 361; emphasis mine.

78. Wendell Berry diagnoses this relation between hubris and exploitative agricultural practices as a larger, cultural problem (at least for a great number of white folks in the U.S.). He's not wrong: "We became viewers of 'views.' And because we no longer traveled in the wilderness as a matter of course, we forgot that wilderness still circumscribed civilization and persisted in domesticity. We forgot, indeed, that the civilized and the domestic continued to depend upon wilderness—that is, upon natural forces within the climate and within the soil that have never in any meaningful sense been controlled or conquered. Modern civilization has been built largely in this forgetfulness." Wendell Berry, "The Body and the Earth," in *The Art of the Commonplace: The Agrarian Essays of Wendell Berry*, ed. Norman Wirzba (Berkeley, CA: Counterpoint, 2002), 96.

79. See, for example, Chris Arsenault, "Only 60 Years of Farming Left if Soil Degradation Continues," *Scientific American*, 5 Dec 2014, accessed 29 Feb 2020, https://www.scientificamerican.com/article/only-60-years-of-farming-left-if-soil-degradation-continues/. See also, H. Eswaran, R. Lal, and P.F. Reich, "Land Degradation: An Overview," *Natural Resources Conservation Service Soils*, 2001, accessed 29 Feb 2020, https://www.nrcs.usda.gov/wps/portal/nrcs/detail/soils/use/?cid=nrcs142p2_054028.

80. As Whitehead states, "There is an error; but it is merely the accidental error of mistaking the abstract for the concrete." He later expands, ". . . if we desired to obtain a more fundamental expression of the concrete character of natural fact, the element in this scheme which we should first criticise is the concept of simple location . . . among the primary elements of nature as apprehended in our immediate experience, there is no element whatever which possesses this character of *simple location* . . . I hold that by a process of constructive abstraction we can arrive at abstractions which are the simply located bits of material, and at other abstractions which are the minds included in the scientific scheme. Accordingly, the real error is an example of what I have termed: The Fallacy of Misplaced Concreteness." In other words, to mistake an abstraction for material reality is to commit this fallacy. Alfred N. Whitehead, *Science and the Modern World* (New York: The Free Press, 1925), 52, 58.

81. Brady and Weil, *The Nature and Properties of Soils*, 1085.

82. Aldo Leopold, *A Sand County Almanac: And Sketches Here and There* (Oxford: Oxford University Press, 1966), 253.

83. For an approachable, narrativized work on the functions of underground life and its effects not only on soil but on the Earth, broadly, see Yvonn Baskin, *Under Ground: How Creatures of Mud and Dirt Shape Our World* (Washington, D.C.: Island Press, 2005); for a critical reflection on the roles of micro- and mesofauna in soil ecology, see David C. Coleman, D. A. Crossley, and Paul F.

Hendrix, *Fundamentals of Soil Ecology*, 2nd ed. (Cambridge, MA: Elsevier Academic Press, 2004).

84. For a more robust extension of this argument, including a useful bibliography on this topic, see Brady and Weil, *The Nature and Properties of Soils*, 482–543.

85. For a comprehensive analysis of root functions, see Amram Eshel and Tom Beeckman, eds., *Plant Roots: The Hidden Half* (Boca Raton, FL: CRC Press, 2013); Zoe G. Cardon and Julie Lynn Whitbeck, *The Rhizosphere: An Ecological Perspective* (Cambridge, MA: Elsevier Academic Press, 2007).

86. Brady and Weil, *The Nature and Properties of Soils*, 508; emphasis mine. For more, see Brady and Weil, 508–512; D. H. McNear Jr., "The Rhizosphere—Roots, Soil, and Everything in Between," *Nature Education Knowledge* 4, no. 3 (2013): 1–7.

87. Brady and Weil, *The Nature and Properties of Soils*, 510.

88. Brady and Weil.

89. Brady and Weil; emphasis mine.

90. Brady and Weil, 498–500.

91. Brady and Weil, 497–498. See also M. Blouin, M. E. Hodson, E. A. Delgado, et al., "A Review of Earthworm Impact on Soil Function and Ecosystem Services," *European Journal of Soil Science* 64 (2013): 161–182; C. A. Edwards and N. Q. Arancon, "Interactions Among Organic Matter, Earthworms, and Microorganisms in Promoting Plant Growth," in *Soil Organic Matter in Sustainable Agriculture*, ed. F. Magdoff and R. R. Weil (Boca Raton, FL: CRC Press, 2004), 327–376; J. A. Amador and J. H. Görres, "Role of the Anecic Earthworm *Lumbricus terrestris* L. in the Distribution of Plant Residue Nitrogen in a Corn (*Zea mays*)—Soil System," *Applied Soil Ecology* 30 (2005): 203–214. For a helpful visual aid, a chart illustrating earthworms' role in distributing nitrogen, a critical element aiding the process of photosynthesis, in a soil system can be found in Amador and J. H. Görres's study. Brady and Weil offer the following comments on this chart: "Data from soil columns (called mesocosms) in which corn litter labeled with 15N (isotope of nitrogen) was incubated for 3 weeks with or without an earthworm (*Lumbricus terrestris*). After the incubation, the earthworms and remaining litter were removed, and corn plants were grown for 30 days. Without earthworms, most of the N remained in the litter. In contrast, the earthworms made nearly all the N available for biological processes, including plant uptake (which nearly doubled) and gaseous losses (which increased fivefold). . . . Such studies demonstrate that earthworms dramatically hasten the cycling of nutrients in the soil–plant system."; Brady and Weil, *The Nature and Properties of Soils*, 497.

92. Fungi are legion. As Brady and Weil write, "Tens of thousands of species have been identified in soils, representing some 170 genera. As many as 2500 species have been reported to occur in a single location. Scientists, using DNA and fatty acids extracted from soils, estimate that there are at least 1 million fungal species in the soil still awaiting discovery." Brady and Weil, 512–513. For all things fungal, see Paul Stamets, *Mycelium Running: How Mushrooms Can Help Save the World* (Berkeley, CA: Ten Speed Press, 2005).

93. For more, see Brady and Weil, *The Nature and Properties of Soils*, 512–520. See also, Richard Karban, *Plant Sensing and Communication* (Chicago: University of Chicago Press, 2015). For an artistic but ever meaningful extension of this phenomenon, see Richard Powers, *The Overstory* (New York: W. W. Norton, 2018).

94. A thorough study of the processes of mycorrhizal symbiotic relations can be found here: Sally Smith and David Read, *Mycorrhizal Symbiosis*, 3rd ed. (Cambridge, MA: Elsevier Academic Press, 2008).

95. Brady and Weil, *The Nature and Properties of Soils*, 516; emphasis mine.

96. Berry notes, "A culture capable of preserving land and people can be made only within a relatively stable and enduring relationship between a local people and its place. Community cultures made in this way would necessarily differ, and sometimes radically so, from one place to another, because places differ. This is the true and necessary pluralism." Berry, *The Art of the Commonplace*, 180. It's crucial to emphasize here, though, how one should not essentialize such relations, thereby foreclosing transversal and transcultural relations made possible by porosity. It is also vital to mention how Berry, at least in this bit of writing here, does not acknowledge the barriers between peoples and places through violent phenomena such as settler colonialism, redlining, occupation, or otherwise.

97. Berry, *The Art of the Commonplace*, 303; emphasis mine.

98. For Wendell Berry's use of "exploitation" and "nurture" as the paradigmatic models of agriculture, see Wendell Berry, *The Unsettling of America: Culture and Agriculture* (Berkeley, CA: Counterpoint, 1977), 5–17.

99. Logan, *Dirt*, 19.

100. Berry, *The Art of the Commonplace, Art of the Commonplace*, 225.

101. Berry, 226; emphasis mine.

102. Berry, 228.

103. The functions of the aporetic—namely, its role in and fecundity for inviting apophatic theopoiesis, for meditating on the unsayable, the mysterious—will find explication in Chapter Two.

104. Berry, *The Unsettling of America*, 35; emphasis mine.

105. This same phenomenon is present in, say, acts of charity or missionary assistance that fail to listen to and respond to the articulated needs of the directly-impacted, never mind how these acts are routinely accompanied by a gross indifference to the roles capitalism, colonialism, and so on have played in creating these global inequities.

106. For example, Brady and Weil are sure to illustrate soil as integral to globalized neoliberal economics, failing to question how that very system contributes to, if not outright *causes*, the tragedies of erosion, compaction, and so forth, that they are ostensibly concerned about: "Scientists now recognize that the world's ecosystems provide goods and services estimated to be worth tens of trillions of dollars every year—as much as the gross national products (GNP) of all the world's economies. . . . Ecosystem services can be thought of as:

—*provisioning* (providing goods such as water, food, medicines, lumber, etc.),
—*regulating* (processes that purify water, decompose wastes, control pests, or modify atmospheric gases)
—*supportive* (assisting with nutrient cycling, seed dispersal, primary biomass production, etc.) and
—*cultural* (providing spiritual uplift, scenic views, and outdoor recreation opportunities)" (Brady and Weil, *The Nature and Properties of Soils*, 20).

While they're not wrong about these vital "services" that soil provides (which, while not possible here, deserves both a Marxist and intersectional feminist reflection on the unacknowledged "labor" of soil), they *are* wrong in their desire to make soil more appreciated in, even more integral to, neoliberal economic calculus—which is, if nothing else, the systematic erasure of any meaningful earth-ground, relinquishing it as a mere background or stage upon which the wealthy can have their way.

107. Wendell Berry suggests just this: "Soil loss, for example, is a problem that embarrasses all of our technological pretensions. If soil were all being lost in a huge slab somewhere, that would appeal to the would-be heroes of 'science and technology,' who might conceivably engineer a glamorous, large, and speedy solution—however many new problems they might cause in doing so. But soil is not usually lost in slabs or heaps of magnificent tonnage. It is lost a little at a time over millions of acres by the careless acts of millions of people. It cannot be saved by heroic feats of gigantic technology but only by millions of small acts and restraints, conditioned by small fidelities, skills, and desires. Soil loss is ultimately a cultural problem; it will be corrected only by cultural solutions." Berry, *The Art of the Commonplace*, 202.

108. Cf. Masanobu Fukuoka, *The One-Straw Revolution: An Introduction to Natural Farming*, trans. Chris Pearce, Tsune Kurosawa, and Larry Korn (Emmaus, PA: Rodale Press, 1978).

109. Cf. Kimmerer, *Braiding Sweetgrass*.

110. See Amanda David, "Rootwork Herbals," *Rootwork Herbals*, accessed 13 May 2020, https://www.rootworkherbals.com/about-the-herbalist-amanda-david.

111. Leah Penniman, *Farming While Black: Soul Fire Farm's Practical Guide to Liberation on the Land* (White River Junction, VT: Chelsea Green Publishing, 2018), 8.

112. Ibid., 7. For further on the history of Black farming in the United States, see Monica M. White, *Freedom Farmers: Agricultural Resistance and the Black Freedom Movement* (Raleigh, NC: University of North Carolina Press, 2019); Katrina Quisumbing King, Spencer D. Wood, Jess Gilbert, and Marilyn Sinkewicz, "Black Agrarianism: The Significance of African American Landownership in the Rural South." *Rural Sociology* 83, no. 3 (2018): 677–699; and Chris Carter, "Blood in the Soil: The Racial, Racist, and Religious Dimensions of Environmentalism," in *The Bloomsbury Handbook of Religion and Nature: The Elements*, ed. Laura Hobgood and Whitney Bauman (New York: Bloomsbury, 2018), 45–61.

113. O'Dell, *How to Do Nothing*, 21.

114. Berry, *The Art of the Commonplace*, 183.

115. This, of course, is the very lesson Audre Lorde provides in arguing that "the master's tools will never dismantle the master's house." Audre Lorde, *Sister Outsider* (Trumansburg, NY: Crossing Press, 1984), 110.

Interlude. Poetics at the Edge

1. This is an allusion to Gloria Anzaldúa's indispensable articulation of "borderlands" (as opposed to "borders"): "Borders are set up to define the places that are safe and unsafe, to distinguish *us* from *them*. A border is a dividing line, a narrow strip along a steep edge. A borderland is a vague and undetermined place created by the emotional residue of an unnatural boundary. It is in a constant state of transition. The prohibited and forbidden are its inhabitants. *Los atravesados* live here...." Gloria Anzaldúa, *Borderlands/La Frontera: The New Mestiza* (San Francisco: Aunt Lute Books, 1987), 3; emphasis in original.

2. Cf. Timothy Morton, *Dark Ecology: For a Logic of Future Coexistence* (New York: Columbia University Press, 2016), 71–77.

3. This is, after all, fairly faithful to the early definition and method of theology: *fides quaerens intellectum*.

4. Catherine Keller, *Face of the Deep: A Theology of Becoming* (New York: Routledge, 2003), xviii.

5. Cf. Bruno Latour, *We Have Never Been Modern*, trans. Catherine Porter (Cambridge, MA: Harvard University Press, 1993); Karen Barad, *Meeting the Universe Halfway: Quantum Physics and the Entanglement of Matter and Meaning* (Durham, NC: Duke University Press, 2007).

6. Rainer Maria Rilke, *Letters to a Young Poet*, trans. Stephen Mitchell (New York: Vintage Books, 1986), 34–35.

2. Rooting: Terrestrial Theopoetics of and for the Planetary

Epigraph: Édouard Glissant, *Poetics of Relation*, trans. Betsy Wing (Ann Arbor: University of Michigan Press, 1997), 1.

1. While this language emerges from Glissant, who will guide much of this chapter, the resonance of my rhetoric with the Lurianic Kabbalistic notion of *sh'virat ha-kelim* ("breaking of the vessels") is not accidental.

2. *Poiesis*, with its lengthy history stemming back into the depths of ancient Greek philosophy, implies the process of the "making" or "constructing" of novelty. While the terms "poetic" and "poietic" are not exact synonyms, I use them often interchangeably here to emphasize the material nature of poetics and the aesthetic character of *poiesis*. That is, I will use the terms in such a way as to convey the way-making nature of each—spoken or acted, heard or felt. Both engender *creativity*: imagining and making the world—differently.

3. The resonance here with Alfred N. Whitehead's concept of God as dipolar—primordial and consequent, luring and saving—is also not accidental. As Roland Faber and Jeremy Fackenthal relatedly muse, "God is not in any way a force that can be confounded with earthly powers or coercive measures, be they only verbally suppressing and oppressively directing; the poetic understanding of creation is that of the divine not as an effective cause but as an attractor, suggestive of a seducer of beauty." Roland Faber and Jeremy Fackenthal, "Introduction: The Manifold of Theopoetics," in *Theopoetic Folds: Philosophizing Multifariousness*, ed. Roland Faber and Jeremy Fackenthal (New York: Fordham University Press, 2013), 4.

4. The meaning of "holy" is "set apart," after all.

5. Glissant, 199.

6. Catherine Keller, *Face of the Deep: A Theology of Becoming* (New York: Routledge, 2003), xviii.

7. The premier political theorist on these matters whose work informs my own, if only tangentially in this setting, is Jasbir Puar. See, for example, Jasbir Puar, *The Right to Maim: Debility, Capacity, Disability* (Durham, NC: Duke University Press, 2017).

8. For a reflection on the *theo*poetic implications of Caribbean poetics, see Mayra Rivera, "Poetics Ashore," *Literature and Theology* 33, no. 3 (September 2019): 241–247.

9. Mayra Rivera, *Poetics of the Flesh* (Durham, NC: Duke University Press, 2015), 2–3.

10. For a terse reflection on the status of climate refugees with a helpful bibliography from various governmental organizations and think-tanks, see, for example, John Podesta, "The Climate Crisis, Migration, and Refugees," *Brookings*, 25 July 2020, accessed 22 April 2020, https://www.brookings.edu/research/the-climate-crisis-migration-and-refugees/.

11. See, for example, Tom Philpott, *Perilous Bounty: The Looming Collapse of American Farming and How We Can Prevent It* (New York: Bloomsbury, 2020); H. Eswaran, R. Lal, and P. F. Reich, "Land Degradation: An Overview," *Natural Resources Conservation Service Soils*, 2001, accessed 29 Feb 2020, https://www.nrcs.usda.gov/wps/portal/nrcs/detail/soils/use/?cid=nrcs142p2_054028; Chris Arsenault, "Only 60 Years of Farming Left if Soil Degradation Continues," *Scientific American*, 5 Dec 2014, accessed 29 Feb 2020, https://www.scientificamerican.com/article/only-60-years-of-farming-left-if-soil-degradation-continues/; "Climate Change and Agriculture: A Perfect Storm in Farm Country," *Union of Concerned Scientists*, 20 March 2019, accessed 21 April 2020, https://ucsusa.org/resources/climate-change-and-agriculture. For a popular, brief (neoliberal) economic assessment, see Linh Anh Cat, "Soil Erosion Washes Away $8 Billion Annually," *Forbes*, 21 May 2019, accessed 21 April 2020, https://www.forbes.com/sites/linhanhcat/2019/05/21/soil-erosion-washes-away-8-billion/#66c3f4fb5b6c.

12. Rivera, *Poetics of the Flesh*, 3.

13. Rivera.

14. I wish to signal here that this will be the topic of conversation in Chapter Three, meaning that these brief musings will materialize in far more substantial ways—soon.

15. My gratitude to my friend and colleague Carly Lynch for her articulation of trauma's resistance to, indeed rupturing of, the dualisms often pervading biomedical models of "healing." See also, Sharon Betcher, *Spirit and the Politics of Disablement* (Minneapolis, MN: Fortress Press, 2007), esp. vii–24.

16. Derek Walcott, "The Antilles," in *What the Twilight Says: Essays* (New York: Farrar, Straus and Giroux, 1998), 69.

17. Walcott, "The Antilles," 70.

18. Rivera, *Poetics of the Flesh*, 3.

19. Walcott, "The Antilles," 69.

20. Glissant, *Poetics of Relation*, 33; emphasis mine.

21. Glissant, 32; emphasis mine.

22. As Herman Daly and John Cobb write, "Whenever the abstracted-from elements of reality become too insistently evident in our experience, their existence is admitted by the category 'externality.' Externalities are ad hoc corrections introduced as needed to save appearances. . . . *Externalities do represent a recognition of neglected aspects of concrete experience, but in such a way as to minimize restructuring of the basic theory.* As long as externalities involve minor details, this is perhaps a reasonable procedure. But when vital issues (e.g., the capacity of the earth to support life) have to be classed as externalities, it is time to restructure basic concepts and start with a different set of abstractions that can embrace what was previously external." John B. Cobb Jr. and Herman E. Daly, *For the Common Good: Redirecting the Economy Toward Community, the Environment, and a Sustainable Future* (Boston: Beacon Press, 1994), 37; emphasis mine.

23. Rivera, "Poetics Ashore," 242.

24. Glissant, *Poetics of Relation*, 151.

25. Glissant.

26. Glissant, 144; emphasis mine. On a similar point concerning the enactment of colonial, hegemonic territoriality via a contortion of theological imagination, see Willie James Jennings, *The Christian Imagination: Theology and the Origins of Race* (New Haven, CT: Yale University Press, 2010), esp. 207–249.

27. Glissant, *Poetics of Relation*, 151.

28. Glissant writes, "To the extent that our consciousness of Relation is total, that is, immediate and focusing directly upon the realizable totality of the world, when we speak of a poetics of Relation, we no longer need to add: relation between what and what? This is why the French word *Relation*, which functions somewhat like an intransitive verb, could not correspond, for example, to the English term *relationship*." Glissant, 27. Cf. Barad's use of the term "intra-active" to define a similar phenomenon. Karen Barad, *Meeting the Universe Halfway: Quantum Physics and the Entanglement of Matter and Meaning* (Durham, NC: Duke University Press, 2007), 128.

29. See, for example, Naomi Klein, *This Changes Everything: Capitalism vs the Climate* (New York: Simon and Schuster, 2014). For a theological extension, see Catherine Keller, *A Political Theology of the Earth: Our Planetary Emergency and the Struggle for a New Public* (New York: Columbia University Press, 2018).

30. See William Connolly, *Climate Machines, Fascist Drives, and Truth* (Durham, NC: Duke University Press, 2019).

31. Erica Burt, Peter Orris, and Susan Buchanan, "Scientific Evidence of Health Effects from Coal Use in Energy Generation," *Healthcare Research Collaborative*, University of Illinois at Chicago School of Public Health, April 2013, https://www.groundwork.org.za/archives/2012/ClimateHealthRoundtables/Health%20effects%20from%20coal%20use%204-10-2013.pdf; Susan Buchanan, Erica Burt, and Peter Orris, "Beyond Black Lung: Scientific Evidence of Health Effects from Coal Use in Electricity Generation," *Journal of Public Health* Policy 35, no. 3 (2014): 266–77; for a great virtual bibliography of health concerns related to coal, generally, see "Health Impacts," *Coal River Mountain Watch*, accessed 5 May 2020, https://www.crmw.net/resources/health-impacts.php; L. Fazzo, F. Minichilli, M. Santoro, et al., "Hazardous Waste and Health Impact: A Systematic Review of the Scientific Literature," *Environmental Health* 16, no. 107 (2017): 1–11; William J. Ripple and Robert L. Beschta, "Wolves and the Ecology of Fear: Can Predation Risk Structure Ecosystems?" *BioScience* 54, no. 8 (August 2004): 755–766.

32. Plato, *Theaetetus*, ed. Bernard Williams and Myles Burnyeat, trans. M. J. Levett (Indianapolis, IN: Hackett Publishing Company, 1992), 155d.

33. Mary-Jane Rubenstein, *Strange Wonder: The Closure of Metaphysics and the Opening of Awe* (New York: Columbia University Press, 2008), 4.

34. Cf. Rubenstein, *Strange Wonder*, 7. Indeed, remembering the lessons from Edward Said in the previous chapter, wonder is the *beginning* of philosophy—*not* its origin.

35. Rubenstein, 5.

36. Rubenstein, 8; emphasis in original.

37. Rubenstein, 10–11.

38. Rubenstein, 9; emphasis in original.

39. Informing these musings are the following works: Gilles Deleuze, *The Fold: Leibniz and the Baroque*, trans. Tom Conley (Minneapolis: University of Minnesota Press, 1993), esp. 3–13; Catherine Keller, *Cloud of the Impossible: Negative Theology and Planetary Entanglement* (New York: Columbia University Press, 2015), esp. 1–14, 168–195.

40. Rubenstein, *Strange Wonder*, 8.

41. See Deleuze, *The Fold*; see also, Gilles Deleuze, *Difference and Repetition*, trans. Paul Patton (New York: Columbia University Press, 1994 [1968]).

42. Glissant, *Poetics of Relation*, 138–139; emphasis mine.

43. Rubenstein, *Strange Wonder*, 16; emphasis original.

44. Rubenstein.

45. Rubenstein, 23.

46. adrienne maree brown, *Emergent Strategy: Shaping Change, Changing Worlds* (Chico, CA: AK Press, 2017), esp. 41–50, 67–82, 103–150.

47. Rubenstein, *Strange Wonder*, 60.

48. These concerns will receive greater treatment in Chapters Three and Four as I articulate some of the larger ethical and political consequences of this project.

49. Cf. Donna J. Haraway, *Staying with the Trouble: Making Kin in the Chthulucene* (Durham, NC: Duke University Press, 2016), 1–4.

50. Rubenstein skillfully conveys the exemplary failure of Heidegger to remain with wonder by examining his shifting understanding of *thaumazein* in conjunction with his multiple readings of Plato's "Allegory of the Cave"; see Rubenstein, *Strange Wonder*, 25–60.

51. Keller offers this stunning portrait of the open(-ended) nature of poiesis: "No facts will bring closure; no apokalypsis will trump its own apophasis. . . . There is no God-guarantee on the outcome; but there is the lure. To come forth, to come out, to come again, and, further, to encounter the knowingness of nonknowing whatever comes. It may have never left, and never left off multiplying." Keller, *Cloud of the Impossible*, 315–316.

52. One may be, oddly enough, reminded of Nicholas of Cusa here: Cusa's notion of *complicans* and *explicans* do indeed inform these musings; as Cusa writes, "God therefore, is the enfolding (*complicans*) of all in the sense that all are in God" and ". . . God is the unfolding (*explicans*) of all in the sense that God is in all." He concludes, "It follows, then, that all are in all and each is in each." Nicholas of Cusa, *De docta ignorantia*, in *Nicholas of Cusa: Selected Spiritual Writings*, trans. H. Lawrence Bond (New York: Paulist, 1997), 135, 140. Catherine Keller treats these Cusan matters in a robust manner in *Cloud of the Impossible*, esp. 87–123.

53. Cf. Glissant, *Poetics of Relation*, 144.

54. Stacy Alaimo, *Bodily Natures: Science, Environment, and the Material Self* (Bloomington: University of Indiana Press, 2010), 2.

55. Alaimo, *Bodily Natures*, 20.

56. Alaimo, 63.

57. These poets are not invoked accidentally nor haphazardly but because they occupy a vital role in this author's inspiring cloud of witnesses. Relevant to this project, if only loosely, include the following works: Claudia Rankine, *Citizen: An American Lyric* (Minneapolis: Grey Wolf Press, 2014); Pablo Neruda, *Stones of the Sky/Las Piedras del Cielo*, trans. James Nolan (Port Townsend, WA: Copper Canyon Press, 1987 [1970]); Ernesto Cardenal, *Psalms* (New York: Crossroad, 1981); Mark Strand, *Reasons for Moving, Darker and the Sargentville Notebook: Poems* (New York: Knopf, 1992); bell hooks, *Appalachian Elegy: Poetry and Place* (Lexington: University of Kentucky Press, 2012).

58. In Whiteheadian terms, without either the accounted for, inherited past of the actual occasion (an openness to the particularities grounding and making possible an event) or the sensed data prehended in the subject-superject's initial aim (an openness toward the alluring possibilities yet unfolding), there could be no

becoming whatsoever. It is only porosity that enables these phenomena—again, not in the sense that there are separable subjects who inter-act but as processes of becoming that are *intra-active*.

59. Judith Butler, *Precarious Life: The Powers of Mourning and Violence* (London: Verso, 2004), 28.

60. Butler, *Precarious Life*, 22.

61. It's worth noting that this argument runs the risk of being read as glorifying grief. While the risk is there, I believe that the dismissal of loss as a central human experience, particularly as it demonstrates our manifold interconnections, is far riskier, given the ways in which we are constituted, albeit *ever differentially*, by vulnerability and precarity simply as a consequence of our natures.

62. Aimé Césaire, "Poetry and Knowledge," in *Lyric and Dramatic Poetry: 1946–1982* (Charlottesville: The University of Virginia Press, 1990), xlviii; emphasis in original.

63. For an approachable take written by astrophysicists on the elemental interrelations between the human and cosmic, see Karel Schrijver and Iris Schrijver, *Living with the Stars: How the Human Body Is Connected to the Life Cycles of the Earth, the Planets, and the Stars* (Oxford: Oxford University Press, 2015).

64. Césaire, "Poetry and Knowledge," xlii.

65. Césaire.

66. Butler, *Precarious Life*, 22; emphasis in original.

67. Butler, 20.

68. Wendell Berry, *The Unsettling of America: Culture and Agriculture* (Berkeley, CA: Counterpoint, 2015), 135.

69. For Calvin Warren's case concerning anti-Black violence at an ontological level, see Calvin Warren, *Ontological Terror: Blackness, Nihilism, and Emancipation* (Durham, NC: Duke University Press, 2018).

70. Butler acknowledges the tenuousness of a similar circumstance as they mind the ways in which their argument for a relational ontology could well be read as undercutting the liberative work happening through, in their specific case, LGBTQ+ activism: ". . . essential to so many political movements is the claim of bodily integrity and self-determination. It is important to claim that our bodies are in a sense *our own* and that we are entitled to claim rights of autonomy over our bodies. . . . *I am not suggesting that we cease to make these claims. We have to, we must.* . . . But is there *another* normative aspiration that we must also seek to articulate and to defend? Is there a way in which the place of the body, and the way in which it *disposes us outside ourselves or sets us beside ourselves*, opens up *another* kind of normative aspiration within the field of politics?" Butler, *Precarious Life*, 25–26; emphasis mine.

71. Butler, 22–23; emphasis mine.

72. Butler, 29; emphasis mine.

73. Butler, 46.

74. Cf. Butler, 31.

75. Here Whitehead's notion of "prehensions"—positive and negative—might be assistive in absorbing this paradox.

76. Keller, *Cloud of the Impossible*, 229.

77. Here the work of Jane Bennett and Mel Chen (in addition to the already-cited work of Stacy Alaimo) is absolutely indispensable. See Jane Bennett, *Vibrant Matter: A Political Ecology of Things* (Durham, NC: Duke University Press, 2010); Stacy Alaimo, *Exposed: Environmental Politics and Pleasures in Posthuman Times* (Minneapolis: University of Minnesota Press, 2016); Mel Y. Chen, *Animacies: Biopolitics, Racial Mattering, and Queer Affect* (Durham, NC: Duke University Press, 2012).

78. See, for example, Glissant, *Poetics of Relation*, 32. Cf. Rubenstein, *Strange Wonder*, 1–24.

79. See Keller, *Cloud of the Impossible*, 233.

80. See Mayra Rivera, *The Touch of Transcendence: A Postcolonial Theology of God* (Louisville, KY: Westminster John Knox, 2007), esp. 1–16.

81. Mayra Rivera, *The Touch of Transcendence*, 127–140.

82. Édouard Glissant and Manthia Diawara, "One World in Relation: Édouard Glissant in Conversation with Manthia Diawara," *Nka Journal of Contemporary Aftrican Art* 28 (2011): 9.

83. Chapter Three takes up this very task—that is, the explication of how this sort of revelation might inspire and inform human collectives, how this catalytic ground might undergird political activity.

Interlude. Mountaintop Removal and the Impossibility of Hope

1. An aerial video of this coal impoundment can be found courtesy of Coal River Mountain Watch's own Junior Walk here: Coal River Mountain Watch, "Brushy Fork Impoundment," YouTube video, March 30, 2017, https://www.youtube.com/watch?v=Oej3runt_-A; the Brushy Fork Impoundment's coordinates are: 37°55′08″ N, 81°29′10″ W.

2. The Buffalo Creek disaster of 1972 is an example of this. The Pittstown Coal Company's dam #3, just four days after being declared "satisfactory" by inspectors, burst, unleashing over 130 million gallons, killing 125 persons, injuring 1,121, and leaving over 4,000 homeless—out of a population of only 5,000! See "The Buffalo Creek Flood and Disaster: Official Report from the Governor's Ad Hoc Commission of Inquiry," *West Virginia Archives & History*, 1973, http://www.wvculture.org/history/disasters/buffcreekgovreport.html; Kai Erikson, *Everything in its Path: Destruction of Community in the Buffalo Creek Flood* (New York: Simon and Schuster, 1976); Gerald Stern, *The Buffalo Creek Disaster: How the Survivors of One of the Worst Disasters in Coal-Mining History Brought Suit Against the Coal Company—And Won* (New York: Vintage Books, 2008). More recently, in Roane County, Tennessee, the Kingston Fossil Plant coal fly ash slurry spill released 1.1

billion gallons of coal ash slurry on December 22, 2008. For all records of the Kingston spill, see: "Records Collection: TVA Kingston Fossil Plant Fly Ash," *United States Environmental Protection Agency (EPA)*, accessed 5 May 2020, https://semspub.epa.gov/src/collection/04/AR61117.

3. More aerial footage of the school, preparation plant, and coal impoundment can be found courtesy of Junior Walk here: Coal River Mountain Watch, "Marsh Fork Elementary," YouTube video, March 30, 2017, https://www.youtube.com/watch?v=pCw1BtgnGM4; the impoundment's coordinates are: 37°52′03″ N, 81°31′02″ W.

4. See "Panther Creek Mining, LLC," *Blackhawk Mining*, 2020, https://www.blackhawkmining.com/panther_creek_mining_llc.php.

5. The "Surface Mining Control and Reclamation Act of 1977," which oversees "reclamation" efforts carried out by mining operations after abandoning their mine site, stipulates that the company must "(19) establish on the regraded areas, and all other lands affected, a diverse, effective, and permanent vegetative cover of the same seasonal variety native to the area of land to be affected and capable of self-regeneration and plant succession at least equal in extent of cover to the natural vegetation of the area; *except, that introduced species may be used in the revegetation process where desirable and necessary to achieve the approved postmining land use plan.* . . ." It is this latter clause, it seems, that gives corporations a loophole to sow what they wish. In any case, one need only see what qualifies as a "reclaimed" site to know what a farce this law is. See Surface Mining Control and Reclamation Act of 1977, 30 U.S.C. 1201 (1977). For an example of a "reclaimed" site, one can examine Kayford Mountain via Google Earth or similar digital mapping programs at the following coordinates: 37°58′22.5″ N, 81°22′21.4″ W. Further, mining operations can refrain from adequate, holistic restoration if a proposal is made to "convert" the destroyed land into space "suitable for an industrial, commercial, residential, or public use," granting them the privilege to throw down their sod seed and walk away. While some mountaintop removal sites have been used for commercial activity, there are several instances of using the land to build federal prisons (Belcher Mountain, WV) and golf courses (Glen Alum Mountain, WV; Compton Mountain, WV)—*hardly* just (let alone sustainable) forms of economic development. For more, see Ross Geredien, "Post-Mountaintop Removal Reclamation of Mountain Summits for Economic Development in Appalachia," 7 December 2009, accessed 7 May 2020, http://ilovemountains.org/reclamation-fail/mining-reclamation-2010/MTR_Economic_Reclamation_Report_for_NRDC_V7.pdf; for a useful, interactive online database concerning surface mine reclamation in Appalachia, see "Mountaintop Removal Reclamation FAIL," *ilovemountains.org*, accessed 7 May 2020, http://ilovemountains.org/reclamation-fail/?lat=38.5062&lon=-80.521&zoom=15#map.

6. Cf. Anna Tsing's use of the term "blasted landscapes"; see Anna Lowenhaupt Tsing, *The Mushroom at the End of the World: On the Possibility of Life in Capitalist Ruins* (Princeton, NJ: Princeton University Press, 2015), 3, 181, 282.

3. Sprouting: Dark Hope in Undecidable Times

Epigraph: Catherine Keller, *Political Theology of the Earth: Our Planetary Emergency and the Struggle for a New Public* (New York: Columbia University Press, 2018), 90.

1. Microplastics can be found, for example, unthinkably, in deep-sea sediments. See Lisbeth Van Cauwenberghe, Ann Vanreusel, Jan Mees, Colin R. Janssen, "Microplastic Pollution in Deep-Sea Sediments," *Environmental Pollution* 182 (2013): 495–499.

2. Laura Poppick, "The Ocean Is Running Out of Breath, Scientists Warn," *Scientific American*, 25 Feb 2019, accessed 29 Feb 2020, https://www.scientificamerican.com/article/the-ocean-is-running-out-of-breath-scientists-warn/; Peter Brannen, "When a Killer Climate Catastrophe Struck the World's Oceans," *The Atlantic*, 6 Dec 2018, accessed 29 Feb 2020, https://www.theatlantic.com/science/archive/2018/12/oxygen-loss-during-mass-extinction/577537/.

3. For one, the "disappearance" of insects bodes collapse of unthinkable proportions: Brooke Jarvis, "The Insect Apocalypse Is Here: What Does It Mean for the Rest Of Life on Earth?," *New York Times Magazine*, 27 November 2018. https://www.nytimes.com/2018/11/27/magazine/insect-apocalypse.html?fbclid=IwAR1giFvMYWLJuhW8A7gLmKToppP_RQVnn7oU6RWoswWctsXJcboF9X5Tmds.

4. One of the Hebrew terms for "hope" is *tiqvah*, meaning both "cord" and "hope." Catherine Keller, who brought my attention to the term *tiqvah*, notes its potential fecundity for theorizing "hope" in the Anthropocene. See Keller, *Political Theology of the Earth*, 173–174. For my own reflections on the term and its promise as a mode for theorizing a livable hope in the wake of disaster, see O'neil Van Horn, "On the Matter of Hope: Weaving Threads of Jewish Wisdom for the Sake of the Planetary," in *Earthly Things: Immanence, New Materialisms, and Planetary Thinking*, ed. Karen Bray, Heather Eaton, and Whitney Bauman, 111–122 (New York: Fordham University Press, 2023).

5. Kathryn Yusoff, *A Billion Black Anthropocenes or None* (Minneapolis: University of Minnesota Press, 2018), 11–12.

6. Yusoff, *Black Anthropocenes*, xiii; emphasis mine.

7. Yusoff, 12; emphasis mine.

8. Yusoff writes, "Geologic principles are used to establish a biocentrism that delineates from the human to subhuman to inhuman, as a property relation and as a mark of agentic properties. It is not that geology is productive of race per se but that empirical processes mesh across geological propositions and propositions of racial identity to produce an equation of inhuman property as racially coded." Yusoff, 73. See also, Yusoff, 1–19.

9. Yusoff, 16.

10. Yusoff, 106; emphasis mine. This is where I depart ways with theorists like Marjolein Oele; despite Oele's critical contributions to eco-discourse through her concept of "e-co-affectivity," as theorized in response to soil and its porous properties,

I am wary of an over-emphasis on the theorization of a "new" "we" and "us," as Oele proposes. For example, she writes, "In sum, focusing on soil as mediating interface for a new 'us' is effective in that it offers us a way to imagine a joint, participatory material body that connects—weaves snares—between all of us, yet does so in a way that does not homogenize and overpower. Rather, it empowers invention, resourcefulness, and creativity through that which moves, while being itself non-firm, unstable, and liminal. It may thus allow for the formation of a non-anthropocentric 'us,' whose name and being is yet to be determined. This would be a Latourian 'us' where human agency is not only part of a larger constellation, but mediated and transformed in such a way that we may no longer call such agency by the current name of 'human.'" I am more interested in a more explicitly pluralistic conception of any such notion of planetarity—one that grounds the possibility of a speakable "we" without verging on, if not committing, the erasures articulated by Yusoff. Nevertheless, Oele's does indeed catalyze more robust commitments to nonhuman matters, agencies, minerals, and beyond. See Marjolein Oele, "E-Co-Affectivity beyond the Anthropocene: On Soil and Soil Pores," in *E-Co-Affectivity: Exploring Pathos at Life's Material Interfaces* (Albany: State University of New York Press, 2020), 139–164.

11. Stefano Harney and Fred Moten, *The Undercommons: Fugitive Planning and Black Study* (New York: Autonomedia, 2013), 80.

12. Harney and Moten, *The Undercommons*; emphasis mine.

13. Harney and Moten, 81.

14. Harney and Moten, 78.

15. Harney and Moten, 77.

16. Harney and Moten, 76.

17. Harney and Moten, 74.

18. Harney and Moten, 74–75.

19. Harney and Moten, 78.

20. Harney and Moten, 79.

21. Harney and Moten.

22. Harney and Moten, 112; emphasis original.

23. Harney and Moten, 79

24. Harney and Moten, 6.

25. Harney and Moten.

26. Harney and Moten, 8.

27. Harney and Moten, 9.

28. Harney and Moten; emphasis mine.

29. Harney and Moten, 20.

30. Harney and Moten, 42; emphasis mine.

31. Harney and Moten, 104.

32. Joseph R. Winters, *Hope Draped in Black: Race, Melancholy, and the Agony of Progress* (Durham, NC: Duke University Press, 2016), 15, 16.

33. Winters, *Hope Draped in Black*, 20, 21.

34. Winters, 21.

35. J. Jack Halberstam, *The Queer Art of Failure* (Durham, NC: Duke University Press, 2011), 2–3.
36. Halberstam, *The Queer Art of Failure*, 3.
37. Halberstam here is not far from Moten and Harney's reflections on "fugitivity." See, for example, Harney and Moten, *The Undercommons*, 22–43.
38. Halberstam, *The Queer Art of Failure*, 9.
39. Cf. The latter portion of Chapter One of this project concerns the fallacy of "general use" over against the promise of local, bioregional eco-wisdom, as discussed by Wendell Berry.
40. Halberstam, *The Queer Art of Failure*, 24.
41. Halberstam, 16.
42. Halberstam, 88.
43. Halberstam.
44. For more on this question in relation to particularly Jewish conceptions of hope, especially in the wake of disaster, see Van Horn, "On the Matter of Hope."
45. Anna Lowenhaupt Tsing, *The Mushroom at the End of the World: On the Possibility of Life in Capitalist Ruins* (Princeton, NJ: Princeton University Press, 2015), 27.
46. Tsing, *The Mushroom*.
47. Cf. Tsing, 27–34, 160–163.
48. Donna J. Haraway, *Staying with the Trouble: Making Kin in the Chthulucene* (Durham, NC: Duke University Press, 2016), 1.
49. Haraway, *Staying with the Trouble*.
50. Haraway, 12. The similarities here to Glissant's notion of "give-on-and-with" as discussed in Chapter Two are worth noting.
51. Haraway, 4.
52. Haraway, 37.
53. Haraway, 125.
54. Haraway, 11.
55. Cf. Haraway, 3–4. Haraway does specifically argue that her "staying with the trouble" is neither "hope" nor "despair," both of which represent the two common strands of response to anthropogenic climate change in her estimation. But I would like to suggest that Haraway's use of the term "hope," while her critique is vitally important, is closer to "optimism," in my opinion. Haraway's use of the term hope fixes it as solely future-gazing, thereby forsaking opportunities for interrelational engagement in the present. In her words, "Neither despair nor hope is tuned to the senses, to mindful matter, to material semiotics, to mortal earthlings in think copresence." (4). The nuances of my own position will emerge later in this chapter in my engagement with The Invisible Committee and Lauren Berlant, in particular.
56. Alexis Shotwell, *Against Purity: Living Ethically in Compromised Times* (Minneapolis: University of Minnesota Press, 2016), 3.
57. Shotwell, *Against Purity*, 4.
58. Shotwell.

59. Shotwell, 5; emphasis mine.

60. Leah Penniman, *Farming While Black: Soul Fire Farm's Practical Guide to Liberation on the Land* (White River Junction, VT: Chelsea Green Publishing, 2018), 86.

61. Cf. Penniman, *Farming While Black*, 72.

62. Penniman.

63. To anticipate the potential threat of this argument's undoing of itself, I wish to offer a bit of a caveat here. Danger lurks near; the danger at hand is, as is often the case, a matter of essentialism: Is the modeling of one's ethic on one's principles of temporality a form of "naturalizing" or "essentializing" the bio-, eco-, or geo-? Or, is it an attunement to and an attempt to harmonize with the relational and contextual nature of nature? These queries cannot be answered adequately here, and they constitute the possibility of an entirely different and an entirely massive project. I raise these questions, instead, to simply acknowledge and admit the danger of essentializing the patterns of the ecological in anthropo-focused political activities, all the while reminding that nature and culture are adamantly not separate, despite what the Enlightenment taught. I am willing to risk this danger in an effort to reintegrate politics and ecology, economics and the environment, ethics and ecosystems—which are never actually separate but are too often simply imagined so.

64. William E. Connolly, *Facing the Planetary: Entangled Humanism and the Politics of Swarming* (Durham, NC: Duke University Press, 2017), 92.

65. Connolly, *Facing the Planetary*, 32. In the first essay of his 2019 book *Climate Machines, Fascist Drives, and Truth*, Connolly contends that earth and social sciences would look quite different now had they taken up the "minor" tradition of philosophy (i.e., that of Sophocles, Heraclitus, Lucretius, Spinoza, Nietzsche, etc.) as opposed to the now "major" tradition (i.e., that of Plato, Aristotle, Aquinas, Kant, Hegel, etc.); in the second essay, he applies this argument to the situation of the Anthropocene, relating Deleuze and Guattari's concept of the "abstract machine" as a way of understanding the agencies, forces, and amplifiers affecting our contemporary planetary crisis. See William Connolly, *Climate Machines, Fascist Drives, and Truth* (Durham, NC: Duke University Press, 2019), 17–71.

66. Connolly, *Facing the Planetary*, 106–107.

67. For a theo-philosophical extension of this, see Catherine Keller, *Cloud of the Impossible: Negative Theology and Planetary Entanglement* (New York: Columbia University Press, 2015), 87–126, 168–195.

68. The Invisible Committee, *Now* (Los Angeles: Semiotext(e), 2017), 61.

69. As Brian Massumi, in the translator's foreword to Deleuze and Guattari's *A Thousand Plateaus*, writes, "A concept is a brick. It can be used to build the courthouse of reason. Or it can be thrown through the window. What is the subject of the brick? The arm that throws it? The body connected to the arm? The brain encased in the body? The situation that brought brain and body to such a juncture? All and none of the above. What is its object? The window? The edifice? The laws the edifice shelters?" Gilles Deleuze and Felix Guattari, *A Thousand Plateaus: Capitalism*

and Schizophrenia, trans. Brian Massumi (Minneapolis: University of Minnesota Press, 1987), xii.

70. The Invisible Committee, 16.

71. The Invisible Committee.

72. To direct the reader to my own work and an explication of the distinctions between hope and optimism (and even between distinct notions of hope), see O'neil Van Horn, "Dark Hope: Notes on Uncertain Futures," *Literature and Theology* 33, no. 3 (September 2019): 278–291.

73. The Invisible Committee thus would likely have much to say about popular theologies that are only concerned with the so-called heavenly. For this reason, liberation theologian and biblical scholar Miguel De La Torre argues that "hope" is a tool of oppression—encouraging passivity, apathy, inactivity—contending instead that those who are concerned with justice should *embrace hopelessness*. See Miguel A. De La Torre, *Embracing Hopelessness* (Minneapolis, MN: Fortress Press, 2017).

74. The Invisible Committee, 43.

75. The Invisible Committee, 45.

76. The Invisible Committee, 46.

77. The Invisible Committee, 79.

78. The implied relation between "fundamental" and its *"fond"*—or, foundation—is not accidental here.

79. The Invisible Committee, 65.

80. Lauren Berlant, *Cruel Optimism* (Durham, NC: Duke University Press, 2011), 1.

81. Berlant, *Cruel Optimism*, 2.

82. Berlant.

83. Berlant, 23.

84. Berlant, 25.

85. Berlant, 48.

86. Tina M. Campt, *Listening to Images* (Durham, NC: Duke University Press, 2017), 3, 4.

87. Campt, 5.

88. Campt, 6.

89. Campt, 9.

90. Campt, 10.

91. Campt, 15.

92. Campt, 17.

93. Campt; emphasis original.

94. Campt; emphasis original.

95. Campt, 32.

96. Campt; emphasis original.

97. Campt, 51–52; here Campt is drawing on Darieck Scott's notion of "muscular tension" to theorize a black feminist concept and practice of futurity. For more, see Darieck Scott, *Extravagant Abjection: Blackness, Power, and Sexuality in the African*

American Literary Imagination (New York: New York University Press, 2010), 38–39, 58, 64.

98. Campt, 52.
99. Campt, 57.
100. Campt, 59.
101. Campt.
102. Campt, 65, 107.
103. Campt, 107.
104. Campt, 109.
105. Campt, 109, 113.
106. Campt, 116.
107. Campt, 114.
108. Tsing, *The Mushroom*, 24–25.
109. That is, it is a gross injustice to draw moral equivalencies between liberalism and conservatism, broadly speaking, in the United States. Despite the left's general complicity in many injustices and its ineptitude to enact meaningful social change, the left pales in comparison to the right on these fronts, undeniably so in the wake of Donald Trump.
110. One should not miss the allusion to Rebecca Solnit's important "hope in the dark." See Rebecca Solnit, *Hope in the Dark: Untold Histories, Wild Possibilities*, 3rd edition (Chicago: Haymarket Books, 2016).
111. Harney and Moten, *The Undercommons*, 8.
112. See adrienne maree brown, *Emergent Strategy: Shaping Change, Changing Worlds* (Chico, CA: AK Press, 2017), esp. 51–66.
113. brown, *Emergent Strategy*, 74–75.
114. See Haraway, *Staying with the Trouble*, 58–98.
115. Mary-Jane Rubenstein, *Strange Wonder: The Closure of Metaphysics and the Opening of Awe* (New York: Columbia University Press, 2008), 166.
116. Rubenstein agrees, offering this same argument in her deconstruction of Derrida's (mis)reading of Kierkegaard's *Fear and Trembling*. See especially Rubenstein, *Strange Wonder*, 168.
117. Haraway, *Staying with the Trouble*, 55.
118. See Emmanuel Katongole, *Born from Lament: The Theology and Politics of Hope in Africa* (Grand Rapids, MI: Wm. B. Eerdmans, 2017).
119. For an excursus on "light supremacy" and issues concerning theological notions of "light," "lightness," "darkness," and "blackness," see, Catherine Keller, *Face of the Deep: A Theology of Becoming* (New York: Routledge, 2003), 200–212.

Interlude. Seeds and the Subversive Act of Sowing

1. There are ample theorists and activists committed to Butler's literary corpus as a site for the emergence of novel concepts and ethics. See, for example, adrienne maree brown and Walidah Imarisha, ed., *Octavia's Brood: Science Fiction Stories*

from Social Justice Movements (Oakland, CA: AK Press, 2015); Monica A. Coleman, *Making a Way Out of No Way: A Womanist Theology* (Minneapolis, MN: Fortress Press, 2008), 126–131.

2. See Jeffrey Jerome Cohen and Lowell Duckert, "Eleven Principles of the Elements," in *Elemental Ecocriticisms: Thinking with Earth, Air, Water, and Fire*, ed. Jeffrey Jerome Cohen and Lowell Duckert (Minneapolis: University of Minnesota Press, 2015), 10–11; Jeffrey Jerome Cohen, *Stone: An Ecology of the Inhuman* (Minneapolis, MN: University of Minnesota Press, 2015), 4.

3. Octavia Butler, *Parable of the Sower* (New York: Grand Central Publishing, 1993), 77–78.

4. Butler, *Parable of the Sower*, 78; emphasis mine.

5. Butler, 261.

6. Butler, 321–322.

7. My gratitude is owed to the kind folks of the Community Supported Garden at Genesis Farm in Blairstown, New Jersey, for their exemplification of this work, with whom I've been fortunate to partner in very small ways; my gratitude is due particularly to farmer Judy Von Handorf—from whom I've learned many of these lessons about seeds and seed-saving, thanks to her generous spirit and caring manner.

8. See Vandana Shiva, *Who Really Feeds the World? The Failures of Agribusiness and the Promise of Agroecology* (Berkeley, CA: North Atlantic Books, 2016), esp. 111–124.

9. On the patriarchal habit of figuring nature as passive, receptive material awaiting transformation at and by the hands of masculine activity, see Carolyn Merchant, "Reinventing Eden: Western Culture as Recovery Narrative," in *Uncommon Ground: Toward Reinventing Nature*, ed. William Cronon (New York: W.W. Norton, 1995), 132–159.

10. Leah Penniman, *Farming While Black: Soul Fire Farm's Practical Guide to Liberation on the Land* (White River Junction, VT: Chelsea Green Publishing, 2018), 149.

11. Penniman, *Farming While Black*.

12. Penniman. See also, for example, Judith Carney, *Black Rice: The African Origins of Rice Cultivation in the Americas* (Cambridge, MA: Harvard University Press, 2009).

13. As cited in Penniman, *Farming While Black*, 151. See, "Truelove Seeds," *Truelove Seeds*, https://trueloveseeds.com/; "The Sankofa Community Farm at Bartram's Garden," *Bartram's Garden*, https://bartramsgarden.org/explore-bartrams/the-farm/.

14. Penniman, *Farming While Black*, 152.

15. See, for example, Owen Taylor, "Landscapes of Resistance," *Heirloom Gardener*, Fall 2019, 70–71.

16. See "Soul Fire Farm," *Soul Fire Farm*, http://www.soulfirefarm.org/.

17. Shiva, *Who Really Feeds the World?*, 79.

18. See Monica White, *Freedom Farmers: Agricultural Resistance and the Black Freedom Movement* (Chapel Hill: University of North Carolina Press, 2018), esp. 3–27.

19. See Shiva, *Who Really Feeds the World?*, esp. 67–84.

NOTES TO PAGES 99–105   161

20. Cf. White, *Freedom Farmers*, 6.
21. White, 8.
22. Vandana Shiva, *Biopiracy: The Plunder of Nature and Knowledge* (Berkeley, CA: North Atlantic Books, 1999), 123.
23. Butler, *Parable of the Sower*, 328.

4. Blooming: (De)Compositional Planetary Politics

Epigraph: Thom van Dooren, *Flight Ways: Life and Loss at the Edge of Extinction* (New York: Columbia University Press, 2016), 60–61; emphasis mine.

1. For a most comprehensive review of the changes in understanding of humus, see Markus Kleber and Mark G. Johnson, "Advances in Understanding the Molecular Structure of Soil Organic Matter: Implications for Interactions in the Environment," in *Advances in Agronomy* (London: Academic Press, 2010), 106: 77–142. For an approachable analysis of the complications and contestations concerning soil organic matter, see Johannes Lehmann and Markus Kleber, "The Contentious Nature of Soil Organic Matter," *Nature* 528 (2015): 60–68; Michael W. Schmidt, et al., "Persistence of Soil Organic Matter as an Ecosystem Property," *Nature* 478 (2011): 49–56.

2. Nyle C. Brady and Raymond R. Weil, *The Nature and Properties of Soils*, 15th edition (New York: Pearson, 2017), 1077.

3. Brady and Weil, *Properties of Soils*, 349.

4. For further reading on the fallacies of this line of thinking, see Lehmann and Kleber, "Soil Organic Matter."

5. Brady and Weil, *Properties of Soils*, 573; emphasis mine.

6. Brady and Weil, 561; emphasis mine.

7. Brady and Weil.

8. Selman Waksman, "What Is Humus?" *Chemistry* 11 (July 7, 1925): 464.

9. Schmidt et al., 49. Here the authors are echoing the query raised earlier in this article: John I. Hedges, et al., "The Molecularly-Uncharacterized Component of Nonliving Organic Matter in Natural Environments," *Organic Geochemistry* 31 (2000): 945–958.

10. Schmidt et al., 49.

11. Waksman, "What Is Humus?," 465; emphasis mine.

12. William Bryant Logan, *Dirt: The Ecstatic Skin of the Earth* (New York: W. W. Norton, 1995), 15.

13. Selman Waksman, *Humus: Origin, Chemical Composition and Importance in Nature* (Baltimore, MD: Williams and Wilkins, 1936), 88.

14. Lehmann and Kleber, "Soil Organic Matter," 60.

15. Cf. Lehmann and Kleber, 60. For an ontological extension of this principle based on theoretical quantum physics, see Karen Barad, *Meeting the Universe Halfway: Quantum Physics and the Entanglement of Matter and Meaning* (Durham, NC: Duke University Press, 2007).

16. . . . though the use of the term "humic substances" as a scientific and taxonomic category remains questionable; see Lehmann and Kleber, "Soil Organic Matter," esp. 62, 65–66.

17. See Kleber and Johnson, 78–79, 126–129. Also, Schmidt et al., 53–55.

18. Brady and Weil, *Properties of Soils*, 593.

19. See Brady and Weil.

20. It should be noted that one of the earliest agricultural researchers of compost in the United States was Black scientist and agrarian George Washington Carver. That is, Carver preceded the supposed "father" of U.S. sustainable agriculture, J. J. Rodale, who depended on Carver's research for his own agricultural work and writing—in other words, Carver's work made Rodale's possible. As environmental sociologist Monica White writes, "Carver's research led him to believe that composting was a key element of agricultural productivity. Many of his studies sought to identify the breakdown rates of various plant-based products that were easily accessible to farmers, thus allowing them to turn waste into nutrient-rich soil." As he did with countless other subjects in his bulletins (written purposefully in a style accessible to field workers and practitioners), not only did Carver offer an ingenious method for stewarding fecund fields, but he did so in a way that was *intentionally accessible* to Black farmers. Monica White, *Freedom Farmers: Agricultural Resistance and the Black Freedom Movement* (Chapel Hill: University of North Carolina Press, 2018), 38–49, esp. 46–47. See also George Washington Carver, "How to Build Up Worn Out Soils," Bulletin No. 6, Experiment Station, Tuskegee Normal and Industrial Institute, 1905.

21. Cf. Donna J. Haraway, *Staying with the Trouble: Making Kin in the Chthulucene* (Durham, NC: Duke University Press, 2016), 4, 55, 97, 134–168; Sebastian Abrahamsson and Filippo Bertoni, "Compost Politics: Experimenting with Togetherness in Vermicomposting," *Environmental Humanities* 4, no. 1 (2014): 125–148; Kim Q. Hall, "Toward a Queer Crip Feminist Politics of Food," *philoSOPHIA* 4, no. 2 (2014):177–196.

22. Humus, after all, derives from the Latin for "earth" or "ground. So, too, do "human" and "humus" share etymological roots.

23. The gendered connotations here are strikingly apparent, perpetuating the long-standing articulation of feminine as passive and masculine as active. For some of the ecological consequences of this harmful binary, see, for example, Vandana Shiva, *Biopiracy: The Plunder of Nature and Knowledge* (Berkeley, CA: North Atlantic Books, 1999), 43–64.

24. Haraway, *Staying with the Trouble*, 4.

25. Haraway, 55.

26. Ultimately, even in gardening settings, one should aim to keep soil organic matter at the levels it would otherwise develop itself at its ecological peak. See, for example, Steve Solomon and Erica Reinheimer, *The Intelligent Gardener: Growing Nutrient-Dense Food* (Gabriola Island, BC: New Society Publishers, 2013), esp. 237–276.

27. "An Analysis of Composting as an Environmental Remediation Technology," *United States Environmental Protection Agency*, EPA530-R-98-008, April 1998, https://www.epa.gov/sites/production/files/2015-09/documents/analpt_all.pdf.

28. Abrahamsson and Bertoni, 126. Vermicomposting refers to the popular practice of using worms to compost vegetation.

29. Abrahamsson and Bertoni, 142.

30. Abrahamsson and Bertoni.

31. Abrahamsson and Bertoni, 133–134.

32. Abrahamsson and Bertoni, 134.

33. See Schmidt et al., esp. 49–52.

34. Schmidt et al., 49.

35. Schmidt et al.; emphasis mine.

36. See Delores Williams, *Sisters in the Wilderness: The Challenge of Womanist God-Talk* (Maryknoll, NY: Orbis Books, 1993), esp. 54–74.

37. Maria Puig de la Bellacasa, "Making Time for Soil. Technoscientific Futurity and the Pace of Care," *Social Studies of Science* 45, no. 5 (2015): 708.

38. Puig de la Bellacasa, "Making Time for Soil, 709.

39. In reference to the third point, Jenny O'Dell's brilliant articulation of "doing nothing" as a mode of resisting the "attention economy" and its endless need for "productivity" merits reference. See Jenny O'Dell, *How to Do Nothing: Resisting the Attention Economy* (Brooklyn, NY: Melville House, 2019).

40. Bruno Latour, *Down to Earth: Politics in the New Climatic Regime*, trans. Catherine Porter (Cambridge, MA: Polity Press, 2018), esp. 29–56.

41. Kathryn Yusoff, *A Billion Black Anthropocenes or None* (Minneapolis: University of Minnesota Press, 2018), xiii; emphasis mine.

42. Latour, *Down to Earth*, 16. This is also a similar argument to the one made by John B. Cobb and Herman E. Daly and their use of Alfred N. Whitehead's "fallacy of misplaced concreteness" to critique capitalism's externalization of the ecological as inessential to its equations. See John B. Cobb Jr. and Herman E. Daly, *For the Common Good: Redirecting the Economy Toward Community, the Environment, and a Sustainable Future* (Boston: Beacon Press, 1994).

43. Cf. Gayatri Chakravorty Spivak, *Death of a Discipline* (New York: Columbia University Press, 2003), 71–102.

44. Cf. Jasbir Puar, *The Right to Maim: Debility, Capacity, Disability* (Durham, NC: Duke University Press, 2017), esp. 141–147.

45. Latour, *Down to Earth*, 70.

46. Cf. Anna Lowenhaupt Tsing, *The Mushroom at the End of the World: On the Possibility of Life in Capitalist Ruins* (Princeton, NJ: Princeton University Press, 2015), 17–25.

47. It's important to note that the question of "Whose land?" does not seem to robustly factor into Latour's argument. This question is especially crucial for those who dwell on stolen and unceded land.

48. Latour, *Down to Earth*, 86; emphasis original.

49. Latour, 92.

50. Latour, 93.

51. Latour.

52. See Bruno Latour, *Politics of Nature: How to Bring the Sciences into Democracy*, trans. Catherine Porter (Cambridge, MA: Harvard University Press, 2004).

53. Latour delves into these matters particularly in his 2017 *Facing Gaia*. See Bruno Latour, *Facing Gaia: Eight Lectures on the New Climatic Regime*, trans. Catherine Porter (Cambridge, MA: Polity Press, 2017), esp. 1–74, 146–183, 220–254.

54. See, for example, William E. Connolly, *Facing the Planetary: Entangled Humanism and the Politics of Swarming* (Durham, NC: Duke University Press, 2017), 32.

55. This expansion even furthers existing notions of soils as a force of their own, in which soil is considered as a "material background of our habits and habitat. . . ." Background is hardly ground; backgrounds are foundations upon which the *anthro-* is permitted to continue to wreak havoc. Cf. Timothy Neale, et al., "An Anthropogenic Table of Elements: An Introduction," *Cultural Anthropology*, 2019, https://culanth.org/fieldsights/an-anthropogenic-table-of-elements-an-introduction.

56. Cf. David Abram, *Becoming Animal: An Earthly Cosmology* (New York: Vintage Books, 2011), esp. 25–80, 201–258. Haraway, *Staying with the Trouble*, 9–29; Tsing, 27–36.

57. Cf. Haraway, *Staying with the Trouble*, 58–98.

58. To ensure clarity, these reflections, when taken to their potential logical extremes, could very well read as drawing equivalencies between, say, microbial life and human flourishing. As a white man, I am wary of this sort of contention, given the ways in which, to caricature here, environmentalists and other ecologically concerned folks who inhabit similar positionalities to my own historically tend(ed) to overlook those who've suffered slavery, colonialism, exile, and beyond while still maintaining the value of some particular endangered species. Should it need to be said, the protection of species and conservation of wildlands is important to me for ethical, epistemological, and even theological reasons. But I wish to hold together and hold in tension the recognition of the webs that enable human life all the while acknowledging how arguments to conserve these webs often come at the expense of so-called others—that is, those who don't fit in the paradigms of white, cis-, straight male exceptionalism.

59. Cf. adrienne maree brown, ed., *Pleasure Activism: The Politics of Feeling Good* (Chico, CA: AK Press, 2019); Stacy Alaimo, *Exposed: Environmental Politics and Pleasures in Posthuman Times* (Minneapolis: University of Minnesota Press, 2016), esp. 17–40, 65–142.

60. See, for example, adrienne maree brown, *Emergent Strategy: Shaping Change, Changing Worlds* (Chico, CA: AK Press, 2017).

61. Catherine Keller, *A Political Theology of the Earth: Our Planetary Emergency and the Struggle for a New Public* (New York: Columbia University Press, 2018), 72; emphasis mine.

62. For a soil-centric illustration of these concerns as practiced in regenerative agriculture, see Anna Krzywoszynska et al., "To Know, To Dwell, To Care: Towards an Actionable, Place-Based Knowledge of Soils," in *Thinking with Soils: Material Politics and Social Theory*, eds. Juan Francisco Salazar et al. (New York: Bloomsbury, 2020), 89–106.

63. For an extension of this form of thinking soil as radical alterity, as "refusal" to be subsumed in the tow of indiscriminate "relationality," as maintaining a degree of otherness, see Manuel Tironi, "Soil Refusal: Thinking Earthy Matters as Radical Alterity," in *Thinking with Soils: Material Politics and Social Theory*, ed. Juan Francisco Salazar et al. (New York: Bloomsbury, 2020), 175–190.

64. Eva Haifa Giraud, *What Comes after Entanglement?: Activism, Anthropocentrism, and an Ethics of Exclusion* (Durham, NC: Duke University Press, 2019), 2; emphasis mine.

65. For an example of Giraud's analysis of various approaches to animal activism using this lens of "exclusion," see Giraud, *What Comes after Entanglement?*, 69–117.

66. Giraud, 4.

67. Giraud.

68. van Dooren, *Flight Ways*, 60–61.

69. van Dooren, 181.

70. Cf. Alfred North Whitehead's notion of "negative prehensions"; Alfred North Whitehead, *Process and Reality: An Essay in Cosmology*, corrected ed., ed. David Ray Griffin and Donald Sherburne (New York: Free Press, 1978), 23–24.

71. Here one might consider the importance of "speculative thinking" and its relation to new ethical possibilities. Donna Haraway, drawing on social anthropologist Marilyn Strathern, writes, "It matters what matters we use to think other matters with; it matters what stories we tell to tell other stories with; it matters what knots knot knots, what thoughts think thoughts, what descriptions describe descriptions, what ties tie ties. It matters what stories make worlds, what worlds make stories" (Haraway, *Staying with the Trouble*, 11). Haraway also refers to Whitehead's *Adventures of Ideas* (1933) and its influence on Isabelle Stengers' *Cosmopolitics* as useful exemplifications of "speculative thinking" and its ethical mattering. See Alfred N. Whitehead, *Adventures of Ideas* (New York: The Free Press, 1933); Isabelle Stengers, *Cosmopolitics*, trans. Robert Bonono, 2 vols. (Minneapolis: University of Minnesota Press, 2010, 2011).

72. Giraud, *What Comes after Entanglement?*, 4.

73. Giraud, 20.

74. For a soil-driven extension of this argument, see Manuel Tironi et al., "Soil Theories: Relational, Decolonial, Inhuman," in *Thinking with Soils: Material Politics and Social Theory*, eds. Juan Francisco Salazar et al. (New York: Bloomsbury, 2020), 24–27.

75. Tironi et al., "Soil Theories, 11. Cf. Donna J. Haraway, *When Species Meet* (Minneapolis: University of Minnesota Press, 2008), 70–73.

76. Giraud, *What Comes after Entanglement?*, 19–20.

77. Giraud, 69.

78. Giraud, 74.

79. On the potential of caucus spaces and other relevant tactics for the work of environmental justice, see Leah Penniman, *Farming While Black: Soul Fire Farm's Practical Guide to Liberation on the Land* (White River Junction, VT: Chelsea Green Publishing, 2018), 263–280, esp. 278.

80. Penniman, *Farming While Black*, 176.

81. Penniman, 172.

82. Penniman.

83. Wendell Berry, *The Art of the Commonplace: The Agrarian Essays of Wendell Berry*, ed. Norman Wirzba (Berkeley, CA: Counterpoint, 2002), 180. While Berry's reflections on "pluralism" in general are complicated and imperfect (especially concerning race and racial justice), this quote here does helpfully capture the present argument for the exclusionary, which is also to say *differential*, characteristics of the proposed social-ecological ground. It may verge on essentializing peoples and places, and it may too leave unquestioned *how* different peoples became connected to or associated with different places. Still, it performs a meaningful illustration of the eco-social implications of exclusion and its role in a more robust pluralism.

84. See, for example, Connolly, *Facing the Planetary*, 121–174.

85. Stefano Harney and Fred Moten, *The Undercommons: Fugitive Planning and Black Study* (New York: Autonomedia, 2013), 10–11.

Conclusion

Epigraph: Catherine Keller, *Cloud of the Impossible: Negative Theology and Planetary Entanglement* (New York: Columbia University Press, 2015), 21.

1. Again, one must call into question instances in which death is figured as somehow necessary and/or sacrificial, given the differential nature in which this sort of argument has been used to justify the marginalization and erasure of numerous communities and cultures. See Chapter Four for more on this.

2. Cf. Alfred N. Whitehead on "concrescence": Alfred N. Whitehead, *Science and the Modern World* (New York: The Free Press, 1925), 21–22, 41–42.

3. Cf. Judith Butler, *Precarious Life: The Powers of Mourning and Violence* (London: Verso, 2004), 22.

Bibliography

"10 Point Program." *The Red Nation.* https://therednation.org/10-point-program/.
Abrahamsson, Sebastian, and Filippo Bertoni. "Compost Politics: Experimenting with Togetherness in Vermicomposting." *Environmental Humanities* 4, no. 1 (2014): 125–148.
Abram, David. *Becoming Animal: An Earthly Cosmology.* New York: Vintage Books, 2011.
Alaimo, Stacy. *Bodily Natures: Science, Environment, and the Material Self.* Bloomington: University of Indiana Press, 2010.
———. *Exposed: Environmental Politics and Pleasures in Posthuman Times.* Minneapolis: University of Minnesota Press, 2016.
Amador, J. A., and J. H. Görres. "Role of the Anecic Earthworm *Lumbricus terrestris L.* in the Distribution of Plant Residue Nitrogen in a Corn (*Zea mays*) - Soil System." *Applied Soil Ecology* 30 (2005): 203–214.
"An Analysis of Composting as an Environmental Remediation Technology." *United States Environmental Protection Agency,* EPA530-R-98-008, April 1998. https://www.epa.gov/sites/production/files/2015-09/documents/analpt_all.pdf
Anzaldúa, Gloria. *Borderlands/La Frontera: The New Mestiza.* San Francisco: Aunt Lute Books, 1987.
Arsenault, Chris. "Only 60 Years of Farming Left if Soil Degradation Continues." *Scientific American,* 5 Dec 2014. Accessed 29 Feb 2020. https://www.scientificamerican.com/article/only-60-years-of-farming-left-if-soil-degradation-continues/.
Baker-Fletcher, Karen. *Sisters of Dust, Sisters of Spirit: Womanist Wordings on God and Creation.* Minneapolis, MN: Augsburg Fortress Press, 1998.
Barad, Karen. *Meeting the Universe Halfway: Quantum Physics and the Entanglement of Matter and Meaning.* Durham, NC: Duke University Press, 2007.

———. "Posthumanist Performativity: Toward an Understanding of How Matter Comes to Matter." In *Material Feminisms*, edited by Stacy Alaimo and Susan Hekman, 120–154. Bloomington: Indiana University Press, 2008.

Baskin, Yvonn. *Under Ground: How Creatures of Mud and Dirt Shape Our World*. Washington, D.C.: Island Press, 2005.

Bennett, Jane. *Vibrant Matter: A Political Ecology of Things*. Durham, NC: Duke University Press, 2010.

Bergson, Henri. *Creative Evolution*. Translated by Arthur Mitchell. New York: Dover, 1998.

———. *The Creative Mind: An Introduction to Metaphysics*. Translated by Mabelle L. Andison. Citadel Press, 1992.

Berlant, Lauren. *Cruel Optimism*. Durham, NC: Duke University Press, 2011.

Berry, Wendell. "The 50-Year Farm Bill." *The Atlantic*, 13 Nov 2012. Accessed 7 March 2020.

———. *The Art of the Commonplace: The Agrarian Essays of Wendell Berry*. Edited by Norman Wirzba. Berkeley, CA: Counterpoint, 2002.

———. *The Unsettling of America: Culture and Agriculture*. Berkeley, CA: Counterpoint, 1977.

Betcher, Sharon. *Spirit and the Politics of Disablement*. Minneapolis, MN: Fortress Press, 2007.

Blouin, M., M. E. Hodson, E. A. Delgado, et al. "A Review of Earthworm Impact on Soil Function and Ecosystem Services." *European Journal of Soil Science* 64 (2013): 161–182

Brady, Nyle C., and Raymond R. Weil. *The Nature and Properties of Soils*. 15th edition. New York: Pearson, 2017.

Brannen, Peter. "When a Killer Climate Catastrophe Struck the World's Oceans." *The Atlantic*, 6 Dec 2018. Accessed 29 Feb 2020. https://www.theatlantic.com/science/archive/2018/12/oxygen-loss-during-mass-extinction/577537/

brown, adrienne maree. *Emergent Strategy: Shaping Change, Changing Worlds*. Chico, CA: AK Press, 2017.

———. *Pleasure Activism: The Politics of Feeling Good*. Chico, CA: AK Press, 2019.

brown, adrienne maree, and Walidah Imarisha, ed. *Octavia's Brood: Science Fiction Stories from Social Justice Movements*. Oakland, CA: AK Press, 2015.

Buchanan, Susan, Erica Burt, and Peter Orris. "Beyond Black Lung: Scientific Evidence of Health Effects from Coal Use in Electricity Generation." *Journal of Public Health* Policy 35, no. 3 (2014): 266–277.

"The Buffalo Creek Flood and Disaster: Official Report from the Governor's Ad Hoc Commission of Inquiry." *West Virginia Archives & History*. 1973. http://www.wvculture.org/history/disasters/buffcreekgovreport.html.

Bullard, Robert D., Paul Mohai, Robin Saha, and Beverly Wright. "Toxic Wastes and Race at Twenty 1987–2007: A Report Prepared for the United Church of Christ Justice & Witness Ministries." *United Church of Christ (UCC)*, March 2007.

Burt, Erica, Peter Orris, and Susan Buchanan. "Scientific Evidence of Health Effects from Coal Use in Energy Generation." *Healthcare Research Collaborative*. University of Illinois at Chicago School of Public Health. April 2013. https://www.groundwork.org.za/archives/2012/ClimateHealthRoundtables/Health%20effects%20from%20coal%20use%204-10-2013.pdf.

Butler, Judith. *Precarious Life: The Powers of Mourning and Violence*. London: Verso, 2004.

Butler, Octavia. *Parable of the Sower*. New York: Grand Central Publishing, 1993.

Campt, Tina M. *Listening to Images*. Durham, NC: Duke University Press, 2017.

Cardenal, Ernesto. *Psalms*. New York: Crossroad, 1981.

Cardon, Zoe G., and Julie Lynn Whitbeck. *The Rhizosphere: An Ecological Perspective*. Cambridge, MA: Elsevier Academic Press, 2007.

Carney, Judith. *Black Rice: The African Origins of Rice Cultivation in the Americas*. Cambridge, MA: Harvard University Press, 2009.

Carter, Chris. "Blood in the Soil: The Racial, Racist, and Religious Dimensions of Environmentalism." In *The Bloomsbury Handbook of Religion and Nature: The Elements*, edited by Laura Hobgood and Whitney Bauman, 45–61. New York: Bloomsbury, 2018.

Carver, George Washington. "How to Build Up Worn Out Soils." Bulletin No. 6, Experiment Station, Tuskegee Normal and Industrial Institute, 1905.

Cat, Linh Anh. "Soil Erosion Washes Away $8 Billion Annually." *Forbes*, 21 May 2019. Accessed 21 April 2020. https://www.forbes.com/sites/linhanhcat/2019/05/21/soil-erosion-washes-away-8-billion/#66c3f4fb5b6c.

Césaire, Aimé. "Poetry and Knowledge." In *Lyric and Dramatic Poetry: 1946–1982*. Charlottesville: University of Virginia Press, 1990.

Chen, Mel Y. *Animacies: Biopolitics, Racial Mattering, and Queer Affect*. Durham, NC: Duke University Press, 2012.

Clay, Elonda. "How Does It Feel to Be an Environmental Problem? Studying Religion and Ecology in the African Diaspora." In *Inherited Land: The Changing Grounds of Religion and Ecology*, edited by Whitney Bauman, Richard Bohannon, and Kevin O'Brien, 148–167. Eugene, OR: Wipf & Stock, 2011.

"Climate Change and Agriculture: A Perfect Storm in Farm Country." *Union of Concerned Scientists*, 20 March 2019. Accessed 21 April 2020. https://ucsusa.org/resources/climate-change-and-agriculture.

Coal River Mountain Watch. "Brushy Fork Impoundment." YouTube video. March 30, 2017. https://www.youtube.com/watch?v=Oej3runt_-A.

———. "Marsh Fork Elementary." YouTube video. March 30, 2017. https://www.youtube.com/watch?v=pCw1BtgnGM4.

Cobb, Jr., John B., and Herman E. Daly. *For the Common Good: Redirecting the Economy Toward Community, the Environment, and a Sustainable Future*. Boston: Beacon Press, 1994.

Cohen, Jeffrey Jerome. *Stone: An Ecology of the Inhuman*. Minneapolis: University of Minnesota Press, 2015.

Cohen, Jeffrey Jerome, and Lowell Duckert. "Eleven Principles of the Elements." In *Elemental Ecocriticisms: Thinking with Earth, Air, Water, and Fire*, edited by Jeffrey Jerome Cohen and Lowell Duckert, 1–26. Minneapolis: University of Minnesota Press, 2015.

Coleman, David C., D. A. Crossley, and Paul F. Hendrix. *Fundamentals of Soil Ecology*. 2nd edition. Cambridge, MA: Elsevier Academic Press, 2004.

Coleman, Monica A. *Making a Way Out of No Way: A Womanist Theology*. Minneapolis, MN: Fortress Press, 2008.

Connolly, William E. *Climate Machines, Fascist Drives, and Truth*. Durham, NC: Duke University Press, 2019.

———. *Facing the Planetary: Entangled Humanism and the Politics of Swarming*. Durham, NC: Duke University Press, 2017.

"Contemplate," *Merriam Webster*, https://www.merriamwebster.com/dictionary/contemplate.

Cronon, William. "The Trouble with Wilderness; or, Getting Back to the Wrong Nature." In *Uncommon Ground: Rethinking the Human Place in Nature*, edited by William Cronon, 69–90. New York: W. W. Norton, 1995.

Cusa, Nicholas of. *De docta ignorantia*. In *Nicholas of Cusa: Selected Spiritual Writings*, translated by H. Lawrence Bond. New York: Paulist, 199.

David, Amanda. "Rootwork Herbals." *Rootwork Herbals*, Accessed 13 May 2020. https://www.rootworkherbals.com/about-the-herbalist-amanda-david

De La Torre, Miguel A. *Embracing Hopelessness*. Minneapolis, MN: Fortress Press, 2017.

Deleuze, Gilles. *Bergsonism*. Translated by Hugh Tomlinson and Barbara Habberjam. New York: Zone Books, 1988.

———. *Difference and Repetition*. Translated by Paul Patton. New York: Columbia University Press, 1994.

———. *The Fold: Leibniz and the Baroque*. Translated by Tom Conley. Minneapolis: University of Minnesota Press, 1993.

Deleuze, Gilles, and Felix Guattari. *A Thousand Plateaus: Capitalism and Schizophrenia*. Translated by Brian Massumi. Minneapolis: University of Minnesota Press, 1987.

———. *What Is Philosophy?* Translated by Hugh Tomlinson and Graham Burchell. New York: Columbia University Press, 1994.

Derrida, Jacques. *Of Grammatology*. Translated by Gayatri Chakravorty Spivak. Baltimore, MD: Johns Hopkins University Press, 1976.

———. *Margins of Philosophy*. Translated by Alan Bass. Chicago: University of Chicago Press, 1982.

———. *On the Name*, ed. Thomas Dutoit. Translated by David Wood, John P. Leavey, and Ian McLeod. Stanford, CA: Stanford University Press, 1995.

———. *Positions*. Translated by Alan Bass. Chicago: University of Chicago Press, 1981.

———. *Rogues: Two Essays on Reason*. Translated by Pascale-Anne Brault and Michael Naas. Stanford, CA: Stanford University Press, 2005.

Edwards, C. A., and N. Q. Arancon. "Interactions Among Organic Matter, Earthworms and Microorganisms in Promoting Plant Growth." In *Soil Organic Matter in Sustainable Agriculture*, edited by F. Magdoff and R. R. Weil, 327–376. Boca Raton, FL: CRC Press, 2004.

Erikson, Kai. *Everything in Its Path: Destruction of Community in the Buffalo Creek Flood*. New York: Simon and Schuster, 1976.

Eshel, Amram, and Tom Beeckman, eds. *Plant Roots: The Hidden Half*. Boca Raton, FL: CRC Press, 2013.

Eswaran, H., R. Lal, and P.F. Reich. "Land Degradation: An Overview." *Natural Resources Conservation Service Soils*. 2001. Accessed 29 Feb 2020. https://www.nrcs.usda.gov/wps/portal/nrcs/detail/soils/use/?cid=nrcs142p2_054028.

Faber, Roland, and Jeremy Fackenthal. "Introduction: The Manifold of Theopoetics." In *Theopoetic Folds: Philosophizing Multifariousness*, edited by Roland Faber and Jeremy Fackenthal, 1–14. New York: Fordham University Press, 2013.

Fazzo, L., F. Minichilli, M. Santoro, et al. "Hazardous Waste and Health Impact: A Systematic Review of the Scientific Literature." *Environmental Health* 16, no. 107 (2017): 1–11.

Fukuoka, Masanobu. *The One-Straw Revolution: An Introduction to Natural Farming*. Translated by Chris Pearce, Tsune Kurosawa, and Larry Korn. Emmaus, PA: Rodale Press, 1978.

Gaard, Greta. "Ecofeminism Revisited: Rejecting Essentialism and Re-Placing Species in a Material Feminist Environmentalism." *Feminist Formations* 23, no. 2 (Summer 2011): 26–53.

Gebara, Ivone. *Longing for Running Water: Ecofeminism and Liberation*. Minneapolis, MN: Fortress Press, 1999.

Geredien, Ross. "Post-Mountaintop Removal Reclamation of Mountain Summits for Economic Development in Appalachia." 7 December 2009. Accessed 7 May 2020. http://ilovemountains.org/reclamation-fail/mining-reclamation-2010/MTR_Economic_Reclamation_Report_for_NRDC_V7.pdf.

Giraud, Eva Haifa. *What Comes after Entanglement? Activism, Anthropocentrism, and an Ethics of Exclusion*. Durham, NC: Duke University Press, 2019.

Glave, Dianne. *Rooted in the Earth: Reclaiming the Relationship of African American Environmental Heritage*. Chicago: Lawrence Hill Books, 2010.

Glissant, Édouard. *Poetics of Relation*. Translated by Betsy Wing. Ann Arbor, MI: University of Michigan Press, 1997.

Glissant, Édouard, and Manthia Diawara. "One World in Relation: Édouard Glissant in Conversation with Manthia Diawara." *Nka Journal of Contemporary Aftrican Art* 28 (2011): 5–19.

Halberstam, J. Jack. *The Queer Art of Failure*. Durham, NC: Duke University Press, 2011.

Hall, Kim Q. "Toward a Queer Crip Feminist Politics of Food." *philoSOPHIA* 4, no. 2 (2014): 177–196.

Haraway, Donna J. *Staying with the Trouble: Making Kin in the Chthulucene*. Durham, NC: Duke University Press, 2016.
———. *When Species Meet*. Minneapolis: University of Minnesota Press, 2008.
Harney, Stefano, and Fred Moten. *The Undercommons: Fugitive Planning and Black Study*. New York: Autonomedia, 2013.
Harris, Melanie L. *Ecowomanism: African American Women and Earth-Honoring Faiths*. Maryknoll, NY: Orbis Books, 2017.
"Haudenosaunee Environmental Task Force." *Haudenosaunee*. http://hetf.org/
"Health Impacts." *Coal River Mountain Watch*. Accessed 5 May 2020. https://www.crmw.net/resources/health-impacts.php.
Hedges, John I., et al. "The Molecularly-Uncharacterized Component of Nonliving Organic Matter in Natural Environments." *Organic Geochemistry* 31 (2000): 945–958.
hooks, bell. *Appalachian Elegy: Poetry and Place*. Lexington: University Press of Kentucky, 2012.
Husserl, Edmund. "Grundlegende Untersuchungen Zum Phänomenologischen Ursprung Der Räumlichkeit Der Natur." In *Philosophical Essays in Memory of Edmund Husserl*, edited by Marvin Farber, 307–325. Cambridge, MA: Harvard University Press, 1940.
"Indigenous Environmental Justice Project." *York University*. https://iejproject.info.yorku.ca/.
"Indigenous Environmental Network." *Indigenous Environmental Network*. www.ienearth.org.
The Invisible Committee. *Now*. Los Angeles: Semiotext(e), 2017.
Irigaray, Luce. *The Forgetting of Air in Martin Heidegger*. Translated by Mary Beth Mader. Austin: University of Texas Press, 1999.
Jantzen, Grace. "Eros and the Abyss: Reading Medieval Mystics in Postmodernity." *Literature and Theology* 17, no. 3 (September 2003): 244–264.
Jarvis, Brooke. "The Insect Apocalypse Is Here: What does It Mean for the Rest of Life on Earth?" *The New York Times Magazine*, 27 November 2018. https://www.nytimes.com/2018/11/27/magazine/insect-apocalypse.html?fbclid=IwAR1giFvMYWLJuhW8A7g LmKToppP_RQVnn7oU6RWoswWctsXJcboF9X5Tmds.
Jennings, Willie James. *The Christian Imagination: Theology and the Origins of Race*. New Haven, CT: Yale University Press, 2011.
Karban, Richard. *Plant Sensing and Communication*. Chicago: University of Chicago Press, 2015.
Katongole, Emmanuel. *Born from Lament: The Theology and Politics of Hope in Africa*. Grand Rapids, MI: Wm. B. Eerdmans, 2017.
Keller, Catherine. *Cloud of the Impossible: Negative Theology and Planetary Entanglement*. New York: Columbia University Press, 2015.
———. *Face of the Deep: A Theology of Becoming*. New York: Routledge, 2003.
———. "Introduction: The Process of Difference, the Difference of Process." In *Process and Difference: Between Cosmological and Poststructuralist Postmodernisms*,

edited by Catherine Keller and Anne Daniell, 1–30. Albany, NY: State University of New York Press, 2002.

———. *Political Theology of the Earth: Our Planetary Emergency and the Struggle for a New Public.* New York: Columbia University Press, 2018.

———. "Talking Dirty: Ground Is Not Foundation." In *Ecospirit: Religions and Philosophies for the Earth*, edited by Laurel Kearns and Catherine Keller, 63–76. New York: Fordham University Press, 2007.

Kimmerer, Robin Wall. *Braiding Sweetgrass: Indigenous Wisdom, Scientific Knowledge, and the Teachings of Plants.* Minneapolis, MN: Milkweed Editions, 2013.

King, Katrina Quisumbing, Spencer D. Wood, Jess Gilbert, and Marilyn Sinkewicz. "Black Agrarianism: The Significance of African American Landownership in the Rural South." *Rural Sociology* 83, no. 3 (2018): 677–699.

Kleber, Markus, and Mark G. Johnson. "Advances in Understanding the Molecular Structure of Soil Organic Matter: Implications for Interactions in the Environment." In *Advances in Agronomy*, 106: 77–142. London: Academic Press, 2010.

Klein, Naomi. *This Changes Everything: Capitalism vs. the Climate.* New York: Simon and Schuster, 2014.

Koenker, Ernest B. "Potentiality in God: Grund and Ungrund in Jacob Boehme." *Philosophy Today* 15, no. 1 (2001): 44–51.

Kofman, Ava. "Bruno Latour, the Post-Truth Philosopher, Mounts a Defense of Science." *The New York Times Magazine*, 25 October 2018. https://www.nytimes.com/2018/10/25/magazine/bruno-latour-post-truth-philosopher-science.html?searchResultPosition=1.

Krzywoszynska, Anna, et al. "To Know, To Dwell, To Care: Towards an Actionable, Place-Based Knowledge of Soils." In *Thinking with Soils: Material Politics and Social Theory*, edited by Juan Francisco Salazar, et al., 89–106. New York: Bloomsbury, 2020.

Latour, Bruno. *Down to Earth: Politics in the New Climatic Regime.* Cambridge, MA: Polity Press, 2018.

———. *Facing Gaia: Eight Lectures on the New Climatic Regime.* Translated by Catherine Porter. Cambridge: Polity Press, 2017.

———. *Politics of Nature: How to Bring the Sciences into Democracy.* Translated by Catherine Porter. Cambridge, MA: Harvard University Press, 2004.

———. *We Have Never Been Modern.* Translated by Catherine Porter. Cambridge, MA: Harvard University Press, 1993.

Lehmann, Johannes, and Markus Kleber. "The Contentious Nature of Soil Organic Matter." *Nature* 528 (2015): 60–68.

Leopold, Aldo. *A Sand County Almanac: And Sketches Here and There.* Oxford: Oxford University Press, 1966.

Logan, William Bryant. *Dirt: The Ecstatic Skin of the Earth.* New York: W. W. Norton, 1995.

Lorde, Audre. *Sister Outsider.* Trumansburg, NY: Crossing Press, 1984.

Lyons, Kristina M. *Vital Decomposition: Soil Practitioners and Life Politics.* Durham, NC: Duke University Press, 2020.

Macauley, David. *Elemental Philosophy: Earth, Air, Fire, and Water as Elemental Ideas.* Albany: State University of New York Press, 2010.

MacKendrick, Karmen. "Remember—When?" In *Sexual Disorientations: Queer Temporalities, Affects, Theologies*, edited by Kent L. Brintnall, Joseph A. Marchal, and Stephen D. Moore, 277–291. New York: Fordham University Press, 2017.

Madden, Kathryn Wood. "Images of the Abyss." *Journal of Religion and Health* 42, no. 2 (Summer 2003): 117–131.

McNear, Jr., D. H. "The Rhizosphere—Roots, Soil and Everything in Between." *Nature Education Knowledge* 4, no. 3 (2013): 1–7.

Merchant, Carolyn. "Reinventing Eden: Western Culture as Recovery Narrative." In *Uncommon Ground: Rethinking the Human Place in Nature*, edited by William Cronon, 132–159. New York: W. W. Norton, 1995.

Mies, Martha, and Vandana Shiva. *Ecofeminism.* London: Zed Books, 2014.

Miller, David L. "Theopoetry or Theopoetics." *Cross Currents* 60, no. 1 (March 2010): 6–23.

Mills, Jon. "Retracing the *Ungrund*." In *The Unconscious Abyss: Hegel's Anticipation of Psychoanalysis*, 21–52. Albany: State University of New York Press, 2002.

Morton, Timothy. *Dark Ecology: For a Logic of Future Coexistence.* New York: Columbia University Press, 2016.

"Mountaintop Removal Reclamation FAIL." ilovemountains.org. Accessed 7 May 2020. http://ilovemountains.org/reclamation-fail/?lat=38.5062&lon=-80.521&zoom=15#map.

Nash, Linda Lorraine. *Inescapable Ecologies: A History of Environment, Disease, and Knowledge.* Berkeley: University of California Press, 2006.

Neale, Timothy, et al. "An Anthropogenic Table of Elements: An Introduction." *Cultural Anthropology.* 2019. https://culanth.org/fieldsights/an-anthropogenic-table-of-elements-an-introduction.

Neruda, Pablo. *Stones of the Sky / Las Piedras del Cielo.* Translated by James Nolan. Port Townsend, WA: Copper Canyon Press, 1987 (1970).

O'Dell, Jenny. *How to Do Nothing: Resisting the Attention Economy.* Brooklyn, NY: Melville House, 2019.

Oele, Marjolein. "E-Co-Affectivity beyond the Anthropocene: On Soil and Soil Pores." In *E-Co-Affectivity: Exploring Pathos at Life's Material Interfaces*, 139–164. Albany: State University of New York Press, 2020.

"Panther Creek Mining, LLC." *Blackhawk Mining.* 2020. https://www.blackhawkmining.com/panther_creek_mining_llc.php.

Penniman, Leah. *Farming While Black: Soul Fire Farm's Practical Guide to Liberation on the Land.* White River Junction, VT: Chelsea Green Publishing, 2018.

Philpott, Tom. *Perilous Bounty: The Looming Collapse of American Farming and How We Can Prevent It.* New York: Bloomsbury, 2020.

Plato. *Theaetetus*. Edited by Bernard Williams and Myles Burnyeat. Translated by M. J. Levett. Indianapolis, IN: Hackett Publishing Company, 1992.

Podesta, John. "The Climate Crisis, Migration, and Refugees." *Brookings*, 25 July 2020. Accessed 22 April 2020. https://www.brookings.edu/research/the-climate-crisis-migration-and-refugees/.

Poppick, Laura. "The Ocean Is Running Out of Breath, Scientists Warn." *Scientific American*, 25 Feb 2019. Accessed 29 Feb 2020. https://www.scientificamerican.com/article/the-ocean-is-running-out-of-breath-scientists-warn/.

Powers, Richard. *The Overstory*. New York: W. W. Norton, 2018.

Pseudo-Dionysius. *Pseudo-Dionysius: The Complete Works*. Translated by Colm Luibheid. New York: Paulist Press, 1987.

Puar, Jasbir. *The Right to Maim: Debility, Capacity, Disability*. Durham, NC: Duke University Press, 2017.

Puig de la Bellacasa, Maria. "Making Time for Soil. Technoscientific Futurity and the Pace of Care." *Social Studies of Science* 45, no. 5 (2015): 691–716.

Rambo, Shelly. "The Posture of Words." *Literature and Theology* 33, no. 3 (September 2019): 255–261.

Rankine, Claudia. *Citizen: An American Lyric*. Minneapolis, MN: Grey Wolf Press, 2014.

"Records Collection: TVA Kingston Fossil Plant Fly Ash." *United States Environmental Protection Agency (EPA)*. Accessed 5 May 2020. https://semspub.epa.gov/src/collection/04/AR61117.

Ribot, Jesse. "Cause and Response: Vulnerability and Climate in the Anthropocene." In *New Directions in Agrarian Political Economy: Global Agrarian Transformations*, vol. 1, edited by Madeleine Fairbairn, et al., 667–705. New York: Routledge, 2016.

Riley, Shamara Shantu. "Ecology Is a Sistah's Issue Too: The Politics of Emergent Afrocentric Ecowomanism." In *This Sacred Earth: Religion, Nature, Environment*, 2nd Edition, edited by Roger S. Gottlieb, 368–371. New York: Routledge, 2004.

Rilke, Rainer Maria. *Letters to a Young Poet*. Translated by Stephen Mitchell. New York: Vintage Books, 1986.

Ripple, William J., and Robert L. Beschta. "Wolves and the Ecology of Fear: Can Predation Risk Structure Ecosystems?" *BioScience* 54, no. 8 (August 2004): 755–766.

Rivera, Mayra. "Poetics Ashore." *Literature and Theology* 33, no. 3 (September 2019): 241–247.

———. *Poetics of the Flesh*. Durham, NC: Duke University Press, 2015.

———. *The Touch of Transcendence: A Postcolonial Theology of God*. Louisville, KY: Westminster John Knox, 2007.

Rubenstein, Mary-Jane. *Strange Wonder: The Closure of Metaphysics and the Opening of Awe*. New York: Columbia University Press, 2008.

Said, Edward W. *Beginnings: Intention and Method*. New York: Basic, 1975.

"The Sankofa Community Farm at Bartram's Garden." *Bartram's Garden*. https://bartramsgarden.org/explore-bartrams/the-farm/.

Schmidt, Michael W., et al. "Persistence of Soil Organic Matter as an Ecosystem Property." *Nature* 478 (2011): 49–56.

Schrijver, Karel, and Iris Schrijver. *Living with the Stars: How the Human Body Is Connected to the Life Cycles of the Earth, the Planets, and the Stars*. Oxford: Oxford University Press, 2015.

Scott, Darieck. *Extravagant Abjection: Blackness, Power, and Sexuality in the African American Literary Imagination*. New York: New York University Press, 2010.

Shiva, Vandana. *Biopiracy: The Plunder of Nature and Knowledge*. Berkeley, CA: North Atlantic Books, 1999.

———. *Who Really Feeds the World?: The Failures of Agribusiness and the Promise of Agroecology*. Berkeley, CA: North Atlantic Books, 2016.

Shotwell, Alexis. *Against Purity: Living Ethically in Compromised Times*. Minneapolis: University of Minnesota Press, 2016.

Smith, Sally, and David Read. *Mycorrhizal Symbiosis*. 3rd edition. Cambridge, MA: Elsevier Academic Press, 2008.

"Soil Texture Calculator." *United States Department of Agriculture: Natural Resources Conservation Service*. Accessed 13 May 2020. https://www.nrcs.usda.gov/wps/portal/nrcs/detail/soils/survey/?cid=nrcs142p2_054167.

Solnit, Rebecca. *Hope in the Dark: Untold Histories, Wild Possibilities*. 3rd edition. Chicago: Haymarket Books, 2016.

Solomon, Steve, and Erica Reinheimer. *The Intelligent Gardener: Growing Nutrient-Dense Food*. Gabriola Island, BC: New Society Publishers, 2013.

"Soul Fire Farm." *Soul Fire Farm*. http://www.soulfirefarm.org/.

Spivak, Gayatri Chakravorty. *Death of a Discipline*. New York: Columbia University Press, 2003.

Stamets, Paul. *Mycelium Running: How Mushrooms Can Help Save the World*. Berkeley, CA: Ten Speed Press, 2005.

Steinbock, Anthony. *Home and Beyond: Generative Phenomenology After Husserl*. Evanston, IL: Northwestern University Press, 1995.

Stengers, Isabelle. *Cosmopolitics*. Translated by Robert Bonono, 2 volumes. Minneapolis: University of Minnesota Press, 2010, 2011.

Stern, Gerald. *The Buffalo Creek Disaster: How the Survivors of One of the Worst Disasters in Coal-Mining History Brought Suit Against the Coal Company—And Won*. New York: Vintage Books, 2008.

Strand, Mark. *Reasons for Moving, Darker and the Sargentville Notebook: Poems*. New York: Knopf, 1992.

Surface Mining Control and Reclamation Act of 1977, 30 U.S.C. 1201 (1977).

Taylor, Owen. "Landscapes of Resistance." *Heirloom Gardener*. Fall 2019.

Taylor, Tess. "Apocalypto for a Small Planet." In *Work & Days*, 49. Pasadena, CA: Red Hen Press, 2016.

Tironi, Manuel. "Soil Refusal: Thinking Earthy Matters as Radical Alterity." In *Thinking with Soils: Material Politics and Social Theory*, edited by Juan Francisco Salazar, et al., 175–190. New York: Bloomsbury, 2020.

Tironi, Manuel, et al. "Soil Theories: Relational, Decolonial, Inhuman." In *Thinking with Soils: Material Politics and Social Theory*, edited by Juan Francisco Salazar, et al., 15–38. New York: Bloomsbury, 2020.

"Toxic Wastes and Race in the United States: A National Report on the Racial and Socio-Economic Characteristics of Communities with Hazardous Waste Sites." United Church of Christ (UCC), 1987.

"Truelove Seeds." *Truelove Seeds*. https://trueloveseeds.com/.

Tsing, Anna Lowenhaupt. *The Mushroom at the End of the World: On the Possibility of Life in Capitalist Ruins*. Princeton, NJ: Princeton University Press, 2015.

Tuana, Nancy. "Viscous Porosity: Witnessing Katrina." In *Material Feminisms*, edited by Stacy Alaimo and Susan Hekman, 188–213. Bloomington: Indiana University Press, 2008.

Van Cauwenberghe, Lisbeth, Ann Vanreusel, Jan Mees, Colin R. Janssen. "Microplastic Pollution in Deep-Sea Sediments." *Environmental Pollution* 182 (2013): 495–499.

van Dooren, Thom. *Flight Ways: Life and Loss at the Edge of Extinction*. New York: Columbia University Press, 2016.

Van Horn, O'neil. "Dark Hope: Notes on Uncertain Futures." *Literature and Theology* 33, no. 3 (September 2019): 278–291.

———. "On the Matter of Hope: Weaving Threads of Jewish Wisdom for the Sake of the Planetary." In *Earthly Things: Immanence, New Materialisms, and Planetary Thinking*, edited by Karen Bray, Heather Eaton, and Whitney Bauman, 111–122. New York: Fordham University Press, 2023.

Waksman, Selman. *Humus: Origin, Chemical Composition and Importance in Nature*. Baltimore, MD: Williams and Wilkins, 1936.

———. "What Is Humus?" *Chemistry* 11 (July 7, 1925): 463–468.

Walcott, Derek. "The Antilles." In *What the Twilight Says: Essays*. New York: Farrar, Straus and Giroux, 1998.

Walker, Alice. "The Only Reason You Want to Go to Heaven Is that You Have Been Driven Out of Your Mind (Off Your Land and Out of Your Lover's Arms)." *On the Issues* VI, no. 2 (Spring 1997): 16–23, 54–59.

Warren, Calvin. *Ontological Terror: Blackness, Nihilism, and Emancipation*. Durham, NC: Duke University Press, 2018.

White, Jr., Lynn. "The Historical Roots of Our Ecologic Crisis." *Science* 155.3767 (March 10, 1967): 1203–1207.

White, Monica M. *Freedom Farmers: Agricultural Resistance and the Black Freedom Movement*. Raleigh: University of North Carolina Press, 2019.

Whitehead, Alfred North. *Adventures of Ideas*. New York: The Free Press, 1933.

———. *Process and Reality: An Essay in Cosmology*. Corrected edition. Edited by David Ray Griffin and Donald Sherburne. New York: The Free Press, 1978.

———. *Science and the Modern World.* New York: The Free Press, 1925.

Williams, Delores. "Sin, Nature, and Black Women's Bodies." In *Ecofeminism and the Sacred,* edited by Carol J. Adams, 24–30. New York: Continuum, 1993.

———. *Sisters in the Wilderness: The Challenge of Womanist God-Talk.* Maryknoll, NY: Orbis Books, 1993.

Winters, Joseph R. *Hope Draped in Black: Race, Melancholy, and the Agony of Progress.* Durham, NC: Duke University Press, 2016.

Yusoff, Kathryn. *A Billion Black Anthropocenes or None.* Minneapolis: University of Minnesota Press, 2018.

Index

Abrahamsson, Sebastian, 108
aesthetics of earth, 48–49. *See also* Glissant, Édouard
agribusiness, 38
Alaimo, Stacy, 29–30, 55, 137n16
anarchism, 84, 86
Anthropocene, 2, 37, 49, 67, 69–72, 76, 105, 112, 125–27; purity and, 78–79, 81; "we" of the, 71, 154n10. *See also* climate change
antifoundationalism, 22, 31–32. *See also* foundationalism
Anzaldúa, Gloria, 146n1
apophasis, 46, 52–55, 92–93, 95, 123; unsaying and, 52, 55–56. *See also* poetics
apophatic folding, 52–53, 92–93, 122, 128
aporias, 37–41, 46, 50, 57–58, 101–2
atomism, 139n34. *See also* Whitehead, Alfred N.

Barad, Karen, 28–29, 140n50
becoming, 26, 31, 125, 139n34; lines of, 28
beginnings, 1–2, 125; origins *versus*, 22–23, 28. *See also* Said, Edward W.
Bergson, Henri, 28, 33
Berlant, Lauren, 86–87
Berry, Wendell, 1, 37–40, 57, 120, 133n15, 142n78, 144n96, 145n107
Bertoni, Filippo, 108
Black agricultural traditions, 12, 162n20
Black environmental perspectives, 11–12, 162n20
Bolden-Newsome, Chris, 99

borderlands, 146n1. *See also* Anzaldúa, Gloria
Brady, Nyle C., 32, 34, 36, 103–4, 106, 143n91–92, 144n106
brown, adrienne maree, 14
Butler, Judith, 56–59, 127, 151n71
Butler, Octavia E., 96–97, 100

Campt, Tina M., 88–90, 94, 96
Carter, Christopher, 11
Césaire, Aimé, 56–57
Christian theology, 12–13; colonization and, 13; creation and, 13; environmental racism and, 12–13; white supremacy and, 12
Clay, Elonda, 11
climate change, 24, 47, 49, 67, 112, 127; disproportionate effects of, 2, 16, 31, 71; white supremacy and, 113
Cohen, Jeffrey Jerome, 135n6
compost, 106–9; vermi-, 108
Connolly, William E., 83–84
contextuality, 40, 54, 76, 101, 107–8, 121
corporeality, 58; trans-, 30–31, 55
creativity, 70; poiesis and, 45–46, 52–54
cruel optimism, 87–90, 92–93. *See also* Berlant, Lauren; dark hope:optimism *versus*

dark hope, 8–9, 67–70, 75–77, 81–82, 89, 91, 93, 95, 100; agency and, 70, 72, 77–78, 87–88, 90; apophatic, 92; dark of, 94; disturbance and, 79, 94; failure and, 77–78; as ground, 75; loss and, 76; nonlinear, 83, 92–94;

dark hope (*continued*)
  novelty and, 78, 95; optimism *versus*, 69–70, 76, 80, 82, 85, 87–88, 91, 156n55; pessimism *versus*, 69–70, 80, 82; presence and, 79–80, 83–86, 88–89; progress *versus*, 68, 72, 76, 84, 86, 91, 93–94, 100; as salvaging, 67, 80–81; temporality and, 83; uncertainty and, 69–70, 90–92, 95; as way-making, 70, 84, 88, 91. *See also* seed-sowing
(de)composition, 100, 102–3, 105–6, 108–12, 115–16, 120–22, 126; as matterphor, 110; progress *versus*, 110–12, 115–16
Deleuze, Gilles, 26–28, 34, 140n44. *See also* ground: as concept
Derrida, Jacques, 20–22, 24–25, 136n11, 137n23
destituent potential, 85–86
différance, 21, 25, 136n11. *See also* Derrida, Jacques
divinity as grounding, 45, 52
Duckert, Lowell, 135n6

earth-ground, 3, 6–7, 9, 19, 31–32, 44, 71, 94, 101, 119, 122–23, 127, 135n1; cultivation and, 121; decolonization and, 135n1; ethics of exclusion and, 117–21; locality of, 38–40; race and relations to, 11–13, 40. *See also* soil
edges of language, 42–43, 50, 52, 55–56. *See also* poetics
environment, 140n55; human inseparability from, 55–57
environmental justice, 43, 55, 127–28, 134n17; environmentalism *versus*, 10; poetics and, 48
environmental racism, 11–12
eschaton, 125

fallacy of misplaced concreteness, 142n80. *See also* Whitehead, Alfred N.
foundationalism, 20–21, 23–24, 109; origin as, 22. *See also* antifoundationalism
fragmentation, 85, 117–20
futurity, 80, 83, 85–89, 92; Black, 89–90

Giraud, Eva Haifa, 117–21
Glissant, Édouard, 44–49, 51–52, 60, 148n28
governance, 72–73; hope and, 72–74; policy *versus* planning and, 72–75
gradualism, 83
grammar of geology, 71. *See also* Yusoff, Kathryn
ground: aporias of, 37–40, 55, 57, 101–2; as beginning, 22, 24; common ground *versus*, 4, 131–32n4; as concept, 2–5, 8–10, 13–14, 19, 24–26, 122, 126; depth of, 25–27, 117; entanglement and, 117, 126; foundation *versus*, 6–7, 18–24, 26, 29, 31, 106–7, 109, 136n12, 137n16, 138n27; human inseparability from, 29–30, 56; matrices of, 7, 11, 14, 25, 27, 31, 37, 41, 75, 116, 122–23, 126; navigating, 54; as process, 26, 81; as soil, 4; as static *versus* changing, 33; as transversal, 24, 59, 126; vulnerability and, 127
groundlessness, 25, 50–51, 79, 117, 138n27
Guattari, Felix, 26–28, 34, 140n44

Halberstam, Jack, 74, 77–78, 122
Haraway, Donna J., 79–80, 94, 107, 156n55, 165n71
Harney, Stefano, 72–75
Heidegger, Martin, 21, 24
horizontality, 8, 37, 40, 44–45, 53, 77, 100, 112–13, 115, 121, 128. *See also* perspective
humankind and cosmology, 56
humus, 33, 103–7, 109
Husserl, Edmund, 135n1

intra-action, 28–31, 36, 49, 54–55, 61, 79, 107, 140n50. *See also* Barad, Karen; rhizomatic relations
Invisible Committee, The, 84–88

Jennings, Willie, 12–13

Keller, Catherine, 19, 23, 27, 42, 59, 67, 116, 125, 132n9, 138n27, 150n51
khora, 25
Kleber, Markus, 105

land: remediation of, 81–82; as territory, 49
Latour, Bruno, 112–15
Lehmann, Johannes, 105
Leopold, Aldo, 34
Logan, William Bryant, 32–33, 105
luminous dark, 47, 52. *See also* dark hope

materiality, 29, 44, 55, 58
matterphor, 107, 110, 135n6
meaning, 21, 23, 47, 59. *See also* luminous dark
metaphysics, 26, 28–29, 109, 136n11
Moten, Fred, 72–75
movement, 33–34, 58
mystery, 38, 45, 49

Nash, Linda, 30
nationalism, 12–13, 114

INDEX   181

negative theology, 132n9. *See also* apophasis
Nicholas of Cusa, 150n52

O'Dell, Jenny, 18
Oele, Marjolein, 29, 154n10
ontotheology, 21, 137n16

Penniman, Leah, 40, 82, 98–99
perspective, 7–8, 42–45, 49, 77, 95, 100, 105, 112–15, 121, 125
planetary politics, 101–3, 105–6, 108–9, 111, 113–16, 122–23, 126–27; terrestrial perspective of, 102, 106, 109, 112–16, 121, 123, 126–27
poetics, 44–54, 58; apophatic, 52–53, 58; environmental justice and, 47; as gathering, 47; as grounding, 47–48; as incarnation, 48, 53; making, 48, 52–53; processes of creation of, 58; of relation, 45–46, 48–49, 52; terrestrial, 46, 49–50. *See also* apophasis; Glissant, Édouard
poiesis, 44, 46, 48, 52–53, 59, 146n2, 150n51; as interactivity, 48
porosity, 29–31, 36, 54–55, 58, 77, 79
postmodernism, 24–25. *See also* groundlessness
poststructuralism, 20
Pseudo-Dionysius, 132n9
Puig de la Bellacasa, Maria, 111

refusal, 74, 76–77, 86, 88–90, 92. *See also* dark hope
relational ontology, 56–57, 140n50, 151n70; individuality *versus*, 59
relational responsibility, 58–59, 80, 116, 118–19, 123, 127
relations, 30, 48–49, 52, 56–59, 61, 79, 84, 87, 116–19, 123, 127, 148n28; loss of, 56, 151n61
rhizomatic relations, 36, 53–54, 84. *See also* intra-action
Rilke, Rainer Maria, 43
Rivera, Mayra, 47
Rubenstein, Mary-Jane, 50–53, 93–94

Said, Edward W., 22–23, 137n16
seed-keeping, 99–100. *See also* Bolden-Newsome, Chris; Taylor, Owen
seed-saving, 98–100
seed-sowing, 93–94, 96–99; narrative and, 94, 98–99. *See also* dark hope

sense, 44–45, 51, 54–55, 57, 60, 65; grasp *versus*, 54, 57, 60
Shiva, Vandana, 99
Shotwell, Alexis, 81
signification, 20–22
soil, 15–17, 32, 102, 145n107, 164n55; compost and, 106–7; contextual nature of, 37–41, 106, 108, 133n15; earthworms and, 35, 143n91; fungi and, 35–36, 143n92; human relations to, 10, 36–37, 39–41; humus and, 33, 103–6; matrices of, 7, 33–34, 36–37, 41, 102, 109, 116; as opposed to substance, 32; organic matter, 103–5; as political metaphor, 106, 108–9; as process, 32–34, 105, 107, 110, 112; rhizomatic webs of, 34–38, 84, 102, 133n15; roots and, 35, 138n31; tending to, 37
Steinbock, Anthony, 135n1
systematization, 54

Taylor, Owen, 99
temporalities, 83, 87, 115; of the Anthropocene, 82; of Earth, 84
theopoetics, 8, 54, 58–61; terrestrial, 46–47, 54, 58–61. *See also* negative theology; poetics
tikkun olam, 8, 68
trace, 21, 136n11. *See also* Derrida, Jacques
transcendence, 21–22, 46; immanence *versus*, 27, 45, 60, 140n44; relational, 60
Tsing, Anna Lowenhaupt, 78–79, 91
Tuana, Nancy, 31

undercommons, 74–75
undoing, 55–57; openness and, 56, 58; poetics of, 55
ungrounding, 55, 117
Ungrund, 25, 138n28

Van Dooren, Thom, 101, 118
vulnerability, 56–58, 127

Walcott, Derek, 47–48
Weil, Raymond R., 32, 34, 36, 103–4, 106, 143n91–92
White, Monica, 12, 99, 162n20
Whitehead, Alfred N., 139n34, 142n80
Winters, Joseph R., 76
wonder, 50–53; as opening, 51; potentiality and, 53. *See also* Rubenstein, Mary-Jane

Yusoff, Kathryn, 22, 70–71, 112–13, 154n8

O'NEIL VAN HORN is Assistant Professor of Theology at Xavier University in Cincinnati, Ohio. He holds a PhD in Philosophical and Theological Studies from Drew University and is a former Louisville Scholar (2021–2023). He has published various works in the fields of theopoetics, constructive ecotheology, and environmental philosophy.

www.ingramcontent.com/pod-product-compliance
Lightning Source LLC
Chambersburg PA
CBHW020412080526
44584CB00014B/1296